POCKET
BIRDS
OF BRITAIN AND EUROPE

JONATHAN ELPHICK
JOHN WOODWARD

DK

LONDON, NEW YORK, MUNICH,
MELBOURNE, AND DELHI

DK LONDON
Senior Art Editor Ina Stradins
Senior Editor Angeles Gavira
DTP Designer Rajen Shah
Illustrator Andrew Mackay
Production Controller Elizabeth Cherry
Managing Art Editor Philip Ormerod
Managing Editor Liz Wheeler
Category Publisher Jonathan Metcalf

DK DELHI
Project Designer Shefali Upadhyay
Project Editor Ranjana Saklani
Designers Elizabeth Thomas,
Sukanto Bhattacharjya
Editor Glenda Fernandes
DTP Designer Sunil Sharma
Managing Art Editor Shuka Jain
Managing Editor Ira Pande
DTP Co-ordinator Pankaj Sharma
Cartographer Suresh Kumar

First published in Great Britain in 2003.
This edition published in 2012 by
Dorling Kindersley Limited
80 Strand, London WC2R 0RL
Penguin Group (UK)

Copyright © 2003, 2009, 2012
Dorling Kindersley Limited
2 4 6 8 10 9 7 5 3 1
001-183681-Jan/2012

A CIP catalogue record for this book
is available from the British Library

ISBN 978-1-4053-9456-7

Reproduced by Media Development Printing,
Great Britain
Printed and bound in China by Hung Hing

Discover more at
www.dk.com

CONTENTS

AUDIO

This url and password give you access to 60 different bird sounds, which are astonishingly varied and can help you tell apart very similar-looking birds.

Type the web address into your internet browser, then enter the password to access the bird sounds.

http://www.dk.com/dkpocketbirds
Password: dkpktbirdsong

 The birds that you can hear online have this symbol next to the heading of their profile in this book.

How this book works

This guide covers the 320 most commonly seen bird species in Europe. These are divided into six easily recognized groups: Passerines, Gamebirds and other non-passerines, Wading birds, Waterfowl, Seabirds, and Owls and Birds of Prey. Within each group, the birds are arranged broadly by family, so that similar looking species appear together for ease of comparison, and generally in ascending order of size, so the smallest birds are at the beginning of a section and the largest at the end.

▽ GROUP INTRODUCTIONS

Each of the six groups opens with an introductory page describing the group's shared characteristics. Photograps of representative species show the diversity in the group.

COMMON NAME

COLOUR BANDS
Bands are colour-coded, with a different colour representing each of the six bird groups.

SCIENTIFIC NAME

DESCRIPTION
Conveys the main features and special characteristics of the species and points out differences between the bird and similar species.

FLIGHT ILLUSTRATION
Shows the bird in flight, from above and/or below. Note that differences of sex, age, or season are not always visible in flight.

OTHER KEY INFORMATION
These boxes provide consistent information on the following points:
VOICE: a description of the bird's calls and songs.
NESTING: the type of nest, its usual location, the number of eggs in a clutch; the number of broods in a year; the breeding season.
FEEDING: how, where, and on what the bird feeds.
SIMILAR SPECIES: lists birds that look similar to the featured bird.

Crossbill
Loxia curvirostra

This large, powerful finch is of spruces, pines, and other crossed bill to prise the cone extract the seeds with its tor acrobatically and often nois treetops, but has to drink fre to moisten its diet of dry see

dark wings

orange-red to strawberry-red plumage

brightest red on rump

dark tail

VOICE Loud, abrupt calls, jup-ju conversational notes while feeding mixes buzzy notes, calls, warbles.
NESTING Small nest of twigs and in conifer; 3–4 eggs; 1 brood; Jar
FEEDING Eats seeds of conifers spruce and pine; also berries, bu
SIMILAR SPECIES Hawfinch.

Parrot Cross
Loxia pytyopsittacus

A stockier, more bull-necked very similar Crossbill, the Pa northern and eastern Europe moves in large numbers to t The bill is almost as deep as deep lower mandible bulges centre, like that of a parrot.

heavy, stocky body

VOICE Abrupt, loud tjup tjup usually deeper than Crossbill's
NESTING Cup nest of leaves and with grass on conifer twigs, bark eggs; 1 brood; Feb–Mar or as late
FEEDING Conifer seeds, mainly p insects in breeding season.
SIMILAR SPECIES Crossbill, Hawfi

Waterfowl

This group contains a large and diverse variety of waterbirds. Ducks, geese, and swans all swim well, have webbed feet, and rather short specialized bills. Mallards are the most widespread and familiar of the ducks, varying from very dark to all-white. They nest practically anywhere near the reach of water – lakes, pools, or estuarine mud. Geese are mostly large, terrestrial birds, with the Greylag Goose having a brown-grey plumage and usually found in lowland areas and marshes. European swans, on the other hand, are all-white birds with long, curved necks, obvious in the Mute Swan. The slate black Coot, superficially duck-like, has broadly-lobed toes and a narrow body that allows it to slip through dense vegetation. It is found on large reservoirs but rarely on sea.

COOT   MUTE SWAN   GREYLAG GOOSE   MALLARD

▷ SINGLE-PAGE ENTRIES

Species that exhibit greater or more complex plumage variations are generally given a full-page.

ADDITIONAL PICTURES

Show you a bird of the same age, sex, and plumage as the main picture, but in a different posture or from a new angle.

TIP BOXES

Describe striking or unique physical features or habits that will help identify a bird.

Puffin
Fratercula arctica

Few seabirds are more instantly recognizable than the Puffin in summer, with its clown-like eye and large, flamboyantly coloured bill. Even at a distance it is usually distinctive, bobbing on the water or whirring through the air like a clockwork toy. In winter, it is less striking, as the colourful eye ornaments and horny plates at the edges of its bill fall away. Its face is also darker, although not as dark as that of a juvenile bird. In summer, Puffins are often sociable, coming to be seen bringing food to their nesting burrows on northern and western coasts, but Puffins in winter plumage are generally rare close inshore.

BREEDS on coastal clifftops, mostly on islands, feeding in nearby waters. Puffins will eat in sea.

grey, white face

black eye ornament

dark grey, white face

black and striped black, orange, yellow, and red bill

Mark apparatus and neck

grey-white face

In breeding Puffin is hard to mistake for any other bird, but in winter Puffin usually seen with white cheeks near water. Winter puffins show duller bill colour as bright plates fall off.

VOICE Loud, croaking growl of reer, aarr, aaharrgar, generally silent outside breeding season
NESTING Digs or occupies ready-made burrow at or near clifftop, often excavated for rabbit or Manx Shearwater, or Rook colonies; 1 egg; 1 brood; May–Jun.
FEEDING Dives into water surface to catch small fish such as sandeels; also takes small squid, crustaceans, and marine worms.
SIMILAR SPECIES Little Auk, Razorbill, Guillemot.

▽ SPECIES ENTRIES

The typical page describes two bird species. Each entry follows the same easy-to-access structure. All have one or more photographs of the species, all taken in the bird's natural setting in the wild; these are supported by artworks showing the bird in flight. Annotations, scale artworks, and a set of simple symbols add key information.

SCALE DRAWINGS

Two small scale drawings are set next to each other in each entry for size comparison. The darker drawing represents the bird being described, while the paler drawing is one of four very familiar birds: Mute Swan, Mallard, Pigeon, and House Sparrow. Sizes below are length from tip of tail to tip of bill.

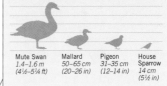

Mute Swan	Mallard	Pigeon	House Sparrow
1.4–1.6 m	50–65 cm	31–35 cm	14 cm
(4½–5¼ ft)	(20–26 in)	(12–14 in)	(5½ in)

GROUP NAME

PASSERINES 53

or eating the seeds ng its hooked, so it can

LIVES IN *extensive woods of spruce, larch, and pine, with easy access to water.*

hooked bill with crossed mandibles ♂

brownish wings

brown wings

green body

pale, streaked ♀

VARIATIONS

These tinted boxes show plumage variations relating to sex, age (juvenile, various immature stages, or adult), and season. The annotation emphasises the main differences from the bird in the main image. This box may also show a subspecies, labelled with its scientific name.

MAPS

Each profile includes a map showing the range of the bird, with colours indicating seasonal movements. Migration ranges are not always mapped because birds often leave one site, turn up in another, and are not seen in between.

■ Summer distribution
■ Resident all year
■ Winter distribution
■ Seen on migration

d version of the l is restricted to e it occasionally ts breeding range.

NESTS *and feeds sparsely in conifer forests, especially of Scots pine, less often Norway spruce and occasionally larch.*

massive bill ♂

♂

more front-heavy than Crossbill

dark wings

often greyer on head ♀

HABITAT PICTURE

Depicts the bird in one of its natural habitats.

HABITAT CAPTION

Describes the various habitats in which you are likely to see the bird.

PHOTOGRAPHS

Illustrate the bird in different views or plumage variations. The characteristic features of the species and differences between it and very similar species are annotated. Unless symbols indicate otherwise, the bird shown is an adult.

SYMBOLS

Symbols indicate sex, age, or season. If an entry has no symbols it means that the species exhibits no significant differences in these.

♀ female   ♂ male

☮ adult   ☯ immature   ☾ juvenile

🌱 spring   ☼ summer   🍂 autumn   ❄ winter

Anatomy

While it is not necessary to know the details of anatomy to identify
a bird, a little more knowledge adds to the interest and enjoyment.
The correct terminology also adds precision to a verbal description:
"a bit of colour on the wing" is vague, while "pale tips to the greater
coverts" is a much more exact description.

It is particularly useful to know how the bird "fits together": how
wing feathers fold over one another as the bird closes its wing, or
where a distinctive mark on the closed wing appears when the wing is
spread. "Primaries" are the wingtip feathers that move out to the end
of the open wing but are often hidden by feathers called tertials when
the bird is perched. Tertials usually
"stay where they are" when the
wing is opened, and may
even be hidden
beneath the
scapulars.

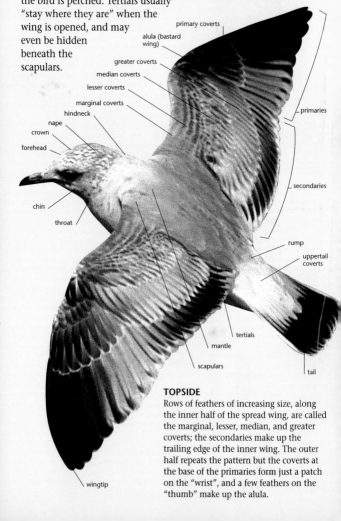

TOPSIDE
Rows of feathers of increasing size, along
the inner half of the spread wing, are called
the marginal, lesser, median, and greater
coverts; the secondaries make up the
trailing edge of the inner wing. The
outer half repeats the pattern but the coverts at
the base of the primaries form just a patch
on the "wrist", and a few feathers on the
"thumb" make up the alula.

UNDERSIDE

The coverts on the underside of a bird's wing form a smaller proportion of the wing area than they do on the upperside, but they are arranged in a similar regular pattern of overlapping rows. At the base of the wing, a triangular patch of feathers in the "wingpit" is formed by a group of feathers called the axillaries. The head, belly, breast, and flanks are covered by shorter, less flexible feathers.

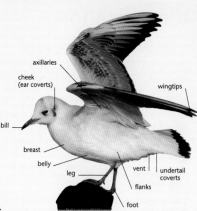

HEAD MARKINGS

A bird's head markings may include a cap, various different kinds of stripes, such as a superciliary stripe over the eye and an eye-stripe through it, and a bib below the bill.

FEATHER TYPES

Soft down feathers form an insulating underlayer. The head and body are covered with body, or contour, feathers. The wings have small, stiff feathers, wider on one side, called coverts, overlying the bases of the large flight feathers, which are also asymmetrical. The tail typically has 10 or 12 feathers.

BODY FEATHER

DOWN FEATHER

PRIMARY COVERT

TAIL FEATHER

PLUMAGE

Feathers not only allow flight and keep a bird warm and dry but also add colour, pattern, and shape, which can be useful for display or camouflage.

tail fanned in display ♂

"beard" of spiky feathers

camouflaging pattern ♀

CAPERCAILLIE

dark plumage prevents mistaken attack by territorial parent

white for long-distance visual contact

GANNET

bold breeding plumage

camouflaged non-breeding plumage

SNOW BUNTING

grey above, pale buff below

browner above, brighter below

EUROPEAN RACE

GREENLAND RACE

WHEATEAR

Identification

Identification of most birds becomes easier with experience: most of us can quickly identify a Robin or a House Sparrow. A familiar bird is like a familiar face in a crowd; an unfamiliar one is just as difficult as trying to find a person you have never seen before in a crowded street, based on a description in a book or from a small photograph. Identifying a bird is usually a process based on a range of information: the place, habitat, time of year, size and shape of the bird, colours, markings, the way it flies and moves, and its general behaviour.

Location

Similar species often live in different habitats, thus exploiting different feeding or nesting opportunities and avoiding competition with each other. Knowing this is helpful in identifying them. For example, Skylarks occur on open ground, rarely even close to a hedgerow, and may perch on a low fence but not on high wires. Woodlarks, by contrast, live along woodland edges and heaths, often close to bushy cover, and will perch high on a tree or wire.

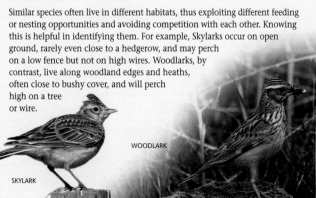

WOODLARK

SKYLARK

Size

Judging size can be difficult but it is a useful clue to identification. If you see an unfamiliar bird, try to estimate its size against a more familiar one. Waders, for instance, range from tiny (Little Stint) or small (Dunlin) to middle-sized (Redshank), large (Bar-tailed Godwit) or very large (Curlew). More subtly, warblers range from tiny (Goldcrest) to small (Garden Warbler) or, for a warbler, large (Great Reed Warbler).

DUNLIN
16–20cm (6½–8in)

REDSHANK
27–29cm (10½–11½in)

LITTLE STINT
12–14cm
(4¾–5½in)

BAR-TAILED GODWIT
33–42cm (13–16½in)

CURLEW
50–60cm
(20–23½in)

Body Shape

Judge a bird's overall shape if you can. Is it long and thin, short and squat, tall or short? The bill and leg lengths affect your judgement but use familiar birds, such as the Blue Tit (dumpy), Blackbird (round but longer-tailed), or Swallow (long-bodied, long-tailed) for comparison. Remember that even small, slim birds can look round and dumpy in cold weather.

small head

thickset body

tiny tail

round body

WREN

WILLOW GROUSE

Bill Shape

Is the bill long or short, thick or thin, straight or curved? Is it pointed, stubby, hooked, narrow, or broad and flattened at the tip? Getting a good idea of its shape will help you to put the bird into a smaller group, narrowing down the possibilities. Bill shape is generally related to the bird's diet, as indicated here.

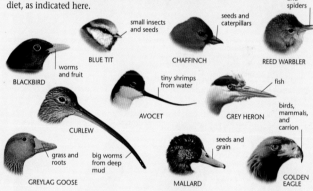

insects and spiders

small insects and seeds

seeds and caterpillars

BLUE TIT

CHAFFINCH

REED WARBLER

worms and fruit

BLACKBIRD

tiny shrimps from water

AVOCET

fish

GREY HERON

birds, mammals, and carrion

CURLEW

grass and roots

big worms from deep mud

GREYLAG GOOSE

seeds and grain

MALLARD

GOLDEN EAGLE

Tail Shape

The tail helps a bird steer and brake in flight, but may also be developed for display. Its shape and proportions are invaluable in pinning down a bird to a family group and can be noted down almost immediately. Look for obvious features, such as a deep notch or fork, long outer or central feathers, or a diamond shape. Be aware, though, that tail shape can change dramatically, for example, a straight, narrow tail can be spread like a fan as the bird soars or lands.

medium length, square-ended

GREAT TIT

very long and narrow

LONG-TAILED TIT

long spike, wide base

PHEASANT

SWALLOW

long, deeply forked

short and rounded

GREY PARTRIDGE

RED KITE

notched, fanned, twisted

Wing Shape

The shape of a bird's wings depends on how it flies: for instance, gliders have longer, narrower wings than smaller, round-winged birds with whirring wing-beats. On most small, fast-moving birds wing shape is of little use because you cannot see much, but on bigger birds slower wing-beats allow a better view.

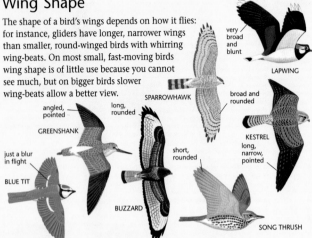

very broad and blunt

LAPWING

SPARROWHAWK

broad and rounded

KESTREL

long, narrow, pointed

angled, pointed

GREENSHANK

long, rounded

just a blur in flight

BLUE TIT

short, rounded

BUZZARD

SONG THRUSH

Colours and Markings

Preciseness is important: does the bird have streaks, bars, or spots? Are they on the wing, back, rump, or head? Head patterns can be very complex (see p. 7). Look for wing and tail patterns, which may be revealed only when the bird opens its wings or spreads its tail. "Bare part" colours, such as those on the legs, around the eyes, or on the bill, can provide useful clues to a bird's identity.

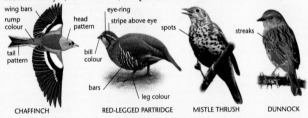

wing bars
rump colour
head pattern
eye-ring
stripe above eye
spots
streaks
tail pattern
bill colour
bars
leg colour

CHAFFINCH   RED-LEGGED PARTRIDGE   MISTLE THRUSH   DUNNOCK

Seasonality

Similar species may be separated by season. For example, the very similar, small, streaky brown Meadow Pipit and Tree Pipit are hard to tell apart, but while both are possible in much of Europe from spring to autumn, in winter Tree Pipits can be discounted, as they have left Europe to winter in Africa.

occurs in Europe in the summer only

resident in western Europe all year or in winter

MEADOW PIPIT   TREE PIPIT

Behaviour

The behaviour of a bird, subtle at first, quickly becomes a valuable aid: the way a Robin flicks its tail and cocks its head, or a Blackbird quickly raises and then slowly lowers its tail on landing are giveaway clues. In addition to such precise details, most birds have a hard-to-define "something" (which birdwatchers call jizz), most easily learned by repeated watching.

ALERT
The Great Tit is bold and active, with bouncy, jerky movements between perches.

HEAD DOWN
The Shelduck upends to reach food under water, taking food that it cannot exploit by dabbling with its bill at the surface.

CHIRPY
House Sparrows are lively, intensely sociable little birds. They spend much time chirruping endlessly and noisily in tight-packed groups.

UNOBTRUSIVE
Quiet and generally inconspicuous but not shy, the Dunnock shuffles mouse-like on the ground, flicking wings and tail. It usually stays close to bushes or other cover.

WADING
The Black-winged Stilt picks food quickly off the surface of the water with its bill, tilting its head one way, then the other.

INELEGANT
Barred Warblers have a distinctive habit of "crashing" heavily and clumsily through bushes, quite unlike the dainty progress of other, smaller warblers.

Flight

Sometimes, the only view you will get of a bird is in flight, when details of plumage and colour are often hard to see. In such cases, the way it flies may be your best clue. Birds have a host of different flight styles: they may fly with long glides on outstretched wings or with constant wing-beats, have shallow or deep beats, flat or arched wings, or hover or dive.

KESTREL HOVERING
Kestrels hunt from the air if there is no perch nearby, hovering as if suspended on a string.

EGYPTIAN VULTURE
The long, broad wings, with widely "fingered" tips, of this juvenile Egyptian Vulture are perfect for prolonged, energy-saving glides.

GOLDFINCH FLOCK
Goldfinches have a particularly light, airy, bouncing flight, with deep, swooping bounds.

Passerines

Passerines are sometimes known as perching birds because they have a unique type of foot that enables them to grip even the most slender branches, although some, like larks, live mainly on the ground. They include over half of the world's bird species, such as swallows and martins, thrushes, warblers, tits, sparrows, and crows. The main subgroup, and the only passerine group to occur in Europe, is that of the songbirds, most of which produce an array of complex sounds. Their lifestyles are varied and they range from aerial hunters of insects (such as the Red-rumped Swallow), to mainly tree-dwelling insect- and seed-eaters (like the Blue Tit), to generalists that are found in many habitats and eat a wide range of food (such as the Carrion Crow).

SONG THRUSH

BLUE TIT

RED-RUMPED
SWALLOW

CARRION CROW

Goldcrest

Regulus regulus

Europe's smallest bird, the agile, busy Goldcrest frequently forages very close to people, apparently oblivious of their presence. This needle-billed, round-bodied bird often gives its high-pitched calls as it searches restlessly for food. It has a plainer face than its close relative, the Firecrest.

FEEDS IN *coniferous and mixed woodland, thickets, and large gardens, throughout the year.*

broad white "V"

olive-green back

blackish wings

yellow inner stripe on black crown

buff below

> **VOICE** *High, sibilant see-see-see call; high, fast song, seedli-ee seedli-ee seedli-ee.*
> **NESTING** *Cup of cobwebs and moss, slung from branch; 7–8 eggs; 2 broods; Apr–Jul.*
> **FEEDING** *Picks tiny insects, spiders, and insect eggs from foliage, often hovering briefly.*
> **SIMILAR SPECIES** *Firecrest, Willow Warbler, Chiffchaff.*

Firecrest

Regulus ignicapilla

Less widespread than the similar Goldcrest, but more common in some parts of Europe, the Firecrest is brighter and more boldly patterned at close range. Its slightly stronger calls and less rhythmic song are useful identification features, especially when the bird is seen in silhouette at the top of a tall conifer tree.

orange crown stripe

white stripe

NESTS IN *conifer trees such as spruce, but also breeds in mixed and deciduous woods. Less tied to conifers than Goldcrest.*

bright green above

dark wings with pale bars

"V" shaped white wingbar

> **VOICE** *High zeet call; song a sharp, quick, accelerating zi zi zi zezezeeee.*
> **NESTING** *Moss and lichen cup beneath branch; 7–11 eggs; 2 broods; Apr–Jul.*
> **FEEDING** *Takes insects and spiders from foliage, often while hovering.*
> **SIMILAR SPECIES** *Goldcrest, Chiffchaff, Pallas's Warbler (rare).*

whitish below

bronze-yellow neck

Wren

Troglodytes troglodytes

A tiny, plump, finely-barred bird with a surprisingly loud voice, the Wren has a habit of raising its very short tail vertically. It also has a distinctive flight: fast and direct, often plunging straight into dense cover. Wren populations decline in cold winters, but usually recover quite quickly.

SINGS FROM *exposed perches, but more often seen foraging in thick cover at low level, in woods and thickets.*

very slightly downcurved, fine bill

pale stripe over eye

dark barring

short, rounded tail

rusty-brown above with barred wings

faint bars

strong legs and feet

VOICE *Hard, rattling chit, chiti, tzerr; song amazingly loud, fast, warbling with low trill.*
NESTING *Small, loose ball of leaves and grass in bank; 5–6 eggs; 2 broods; Apr–Jul.*
FEEDING *Forages for insects and spiders in low, thick cover, under hedges, in ditches, and other dark, damp places.*
SIMILAR SPECIES *Dunnock, Robin.*

Penduline Tit

Remiz pendulinus

This is a very small, neat, boldly patterned bird with a sharp, narrow, conical bill. It often feeds high in the trees near rivers, where it can be hard to spot despite its distinctive calls. In winter, it frequently looks for food further afield, where it may be easier to find.

BREEDS IN *riverside willows and poplars; forages among the trees and reedbeds by rivers and in marshes and damp meadows.*

grey head

broad black mask

plain dark tail

♂

red-brown band

♂

plain head

narrower black mask

plain head

♀

VOICE *Call a high, penetrating, pure whistle, psieeee; song a simple mix of trills and calls.*
NESTING *Hanging nest of plant down and cobwebs with tubular entrance, suspended from twig; 6–8 eggs; 1 brood; May–Jun.*
FEEDING *Seizes small insects and gathers reed seeds in typical acrobatic tit fashion.*
SIMILAR SPECIES *Linnet, Red-backed Shrike.*

Long-tailed Tit

Aegithalos caudatus

The tiny rounded body and slender tail of the Long-tailed Tit give it a ball-and-stick shape that is quite unique among European birds. In summer, family parties move noisily through bushes and undergrowth, but in winter they often travel through woodland in much larger groups, crossing gaps between the trees, one or two at a time.

LIVES IN *deciduous or mixed woods with bushy undergrowth; also scrub. Increasingly visits garden feeders.*

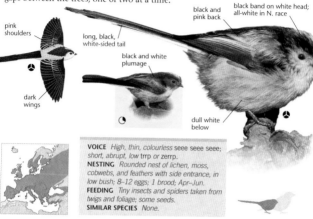

pink shoulders

long, black, white-sided tail

black and pink back

black band on white head; all-white in N. race

black and white plumage

dark wings

dull white below

VOICE *High, thin, colourless seee seee seee; short, abrupt, low trrp or zerrp.*
NESTING *Rounded nest of lichen, moss, cobwebs, and feathers with side entrance, in low bush; 8–12 eggs; 1 brood; Apr–Jun.*
FEEDING *Tiny insects and spiders taken from twigs and foliage; some seeds.*
SIMILAR SPECIES *None.*

Bearded Tit

Panurus biarmicus

The tawny, long-tailed Bearded Tit lives almost exclusively in large reedbeds, although in winter it may briefly occupy tall grasses or reedmace when forced to move on by overcrowding. On windy days it stays out of sight, but in calm weather it can sometimes be located by its loud "pinging" call.

INHABITS *reedbeds, where it breeds and finds most of its food. Sometimes found in nearby tall vegetation.*

big black "moustache"

round wings

bright blue-grey head

tawny, cream, and black above

pale brown head

♀

black back

pale tawny underside

♂

long tail

VOICE *Metallic psching, pink, or ping.*
NESTING *Deep cup of leaves, stems, and reed flowers, low down in reeds standing in water; 5–7 eggs; 2–3 broods; Apr–Aug.*
FEEDING *Caterpillars and reed seeds, taken from among reeds.*
SIMILAR SPECIES *Long-tailed Tit, Reed Warbler.*

Coal Tit

Periparus ater

Although often seen in gardens, the diminutive white-naped Coal Tit is typically a bird of conifer trees, where it makes the most of its minute weight by searching the thinnest twigs for food. Active and fearless, it often joins up with other species of tits in autumn and winter, roaming through woodlands and gardens in large, loose, mixed flocks.

FORAGES AMONG *pines and other conifer trees, but also feeds in low shrubbery and visits garden bird feeders.*

yellower cheek

black head

white nape patch

greyish back

black bib

white cheek

dark wings with two white bars

bright buff underside

VOICE *Call high, sweet* tseu, *thin* tsee, *bright* psuet; *song quick* wi-choo wi-choo wi-choo.
NESTING *Cup of moss and leaves in hole in tree or wall; 7–11 eggs; 1 brood; Apr–Jun.*
FEEDING *Takes tiny insects and spiders from foliage; also seeds and nuts; visits feeders.*
SIMILAR SPECIES *Marsh Tit, Willow Tit, Great Tit.*

Crested Tit

Lophophanes cristatus

The jaunty crest of this species makes it unique among European tits, aiding identification if one has a clear view of its head. But it often feeds high in pine trees, where it is best located by its stuttering call. In the UK it is restricted to northern Scotland, mainly in ancient forests of Scots pine.

FEEDS AND *breeds in mature pine forests, but may occur in mixed or deciduous woods in parts of mainland Europe.*

mottled black and white crest

warm brown back

brown tail

white face with black cheek edge

brown wings

plain wings

black bib

VOICE *Quick, low, stuttering trill,* b'd-rrr-rup; *also thin, high* zit *or* zee *typical of tits.*
NESTING *Cup of moss and hair in decaying tree stump; 5–7 eggs; 1 brood, Apr–Jun.*
FEEDING *Small insects and spiders; seeds in winter, many from stores made in spring.*
SIMILAR SPECIES *Coal Tit, Marsh Tit, Willow Tit.*

Marsh Tit

Poecile palustris

Virtually identical to the Willow Tit in its appearance, the slightly slimmer, neater Marsh Tit is most easily identified by its distinctive *pit-chew* call. Despite its name, it is not found in marshes, but prefers mature broadleaved woodland where it often feeds at low level among thick undergrowth.

FORAGES AMONG *tall deciduous trees in woodland and parks, especially beech and oak; also in gardens.*

glossy black cap and back of neck

black bib, smaller than Willow Tit's

neck slimmer than Willow Tit's

pale grey-buff underside

neat, plain grey-brown upperparts

rounded grey-brown wings

VOICE *Bright pit-chew! and titi-zee-zee-zee; song rippling schip-schip-schip-schip.*
NESTING *Grass and moss cup in pre-existing tree hole; 6–8 eggs, 1 brood; Apr–Jun.*
FEEDING *Mostly insects and spiders in summer; seeds, berries, and nuts in winter.*
SIMILAR SPECIES *Willow Tit, Coal Tit, Blackcap.*

Willow Tit

Poecile montana

More untidy-looking than the very similar Marsh Tit, with a bigger-headed, bull-necked appearance, the Willow Tit lives in a wider variety of habitats with fewer mature trees. It is not particularly attracted to willows, but may feed in damp willow woodland on peat bogs. Its frequent, low, harsh, buzzy calls are quite distinctive, and are the best way of distinguishing it from the Marsh Tit.

LIVES IN *a wide variety of woodland, thickets, and hedgerows. Often visits gardens to raid hanging feeders.*

black bib, slightly larger than Marsh Tit's

big, dull black cap

bull-necked appearance

plain brown rounded wings

pale wing panel

orange-buff flanks

dull grey-buff below

VOICE *Thin zi zi and buzzing airr airr airr; song commonly full, piping tyoo tyoo tyoo.*
NESTING *Digs own hole in rotten tree stump; 6–9 eggs; 1 brood; Apr–Jun.*
FEEDING *Mainly insects and spiders in summer; seeds, berries, and nuts in winter.*
SIMILAR SPECIES *Marsh Tit, Coal Tit, Blackcap.*

Blue Tit

Cyanistes caeruleus

Colourful, tame, and noisy, the Blue Tit is mainly yellow and greenish as well as blue. It is a common visitor to bird feeders where its acrobatic skills make it a favourite garden bird. Its black-and-white face pattern is distinctive. A thin, dark central streak often shows on its yellow underside.

VISITS GARDENS *to feed from nut baskets and other feeders. Lives in woods of all kinds, as well as parks, gardens, and bushy places.*

bright blue cap

white bars on blue wings

blue tail

yellow below

greenish cap

less blue

VOICE *Thin, quick* tsee-tsee-tsee, *scolding* churrrr; *song trilled* tsee-tsee-tsee-tsisisisisisi.
NESTING *Small cup of moss and hair in tree hole/nest box; 7–16 eggs; 1 brood; Apr–May.*
FEEDING *Mainly seeds, nuts, insects, and spiders; often visits garden feeders.*
SIMILAR SPECIES *Coal Tit, Great Tit, Goldcrest.*

Great Tit

Parus major

The bold, even aggressive Great Tit is one of the most familiar garden and woodland birds. Its calls can be confusing, but it is easily identified by the broad black stripe on its yellow breast. Less agile than the smaller tits, it feeds on the ground more often.

BREEDS AND *feeds in wide variety of mixed woodland, as well as parks and gardens. Often uses nest boxes.*

white cheek

green back

pale wingbar

shiny black cap

bright yellow underparts with broad black band

yellow cheeks

band narrower than male

VOICE *Varied calls include ringing* chink *and piping* tui tui tui; *song repeated two-note* tea-cher tea-cher *or* see-too see-too.
NESTING *Cup of moss, leaves, and grass in tree hole; 5–11 eggs; 1 brood; Apr–May.*
FEEDING *Insects, seeds, nuts, especially tree seeds in autumn, winter; often visits feeders.*
SIMILAR SPECIES *Blue Tit, Coal Tit.*

Treecreeper

Certhia familiaris

The slender-billed Treecreeper searches for insect prey by shuffling up the trunks and branches of trees like a mouse, clinging to the bark with its strong toes and propped up on its stiff tail. It usually spirals up one tree, then flies down and lands near the bottom of another to start its next search. This habit makes it easy to identify, even in silhouette.

PROBES BARK *of trees in mixed, deciduous, or coniferous woods. Also occurs in tall hedges, parks, and gardens with mature trees.*

fine, curved bill

white stripe over eye

silky white underside

rounded wings

pale wingbars

mottled brown back

pale feather shafts on notched brown tail

VOICE *Call thin, high* seee *and more vibrant* sreee; *song high, musical series of* tsee *notes ending in falling trill with final flourish.*
NESTING *Untidy nest behind loose bark or ivy; 5–6 eggs; 1 brood; Apr–Jun.*
FEEDING *Takes insects and spiders from bark, probing with bill while shuffling up trees.*
SIMILAR SPECIES *Short-toed Treecreeper.*

Short-toed Treecreeper

Certhia brachydactyla

Almost indistinguishable from the treecreeper by sight, the Short-toed Treecreeper is best identified by its clear calls and less variable, less flowing song. In many parts of Europe the two species do not occur together, which helps. It uses the same foraging technique as the Treecreeper, but occasionally clambers on rocks as well as trees.

SEARCHES FOR *small animals in bark of mature trees, typically in lowland deciduous woods, but also in conifer forest in hills.*

takes insects from crevices

slightly drab above

strong toes

saw-tooth pattern on wings

tail notched and brown

pale wingbars

VOICE *Call strong, short, clear* tsoit; *song well defined* stit-stit-steet, stit-it-steroi-tit.
NESTING *Cup of grass and feathers in crevice; 5–6 eggs; 1 brood; Apr–Jun.*
FEEDING *Insects, spiders, and their eggs, taken by probing and picking at bark during creeping search of trunks and branches.*
SIMILAR SPECIES *Treecreeper.*

Nuthatch

Sitta europaea

Identified by its blue-grey and buff plumage and oddly top-heavy look, the Nuthatch is an agile climber that (unlike other birds) often descends trees head-first, as well as climbing upwards. It wedges nuts and seeds in bark so it can crack them open, with loud blows of its long, grey, chisel-like bill.

FORAGES HIGH *in trees and on the ground in deciduous and mixed woodland, parkland, and large gardens, all year round.*

broad blue-grey wings

buff below, with rusty flanks

acrobatic pose

black stripe

dagger-like grey bill

strong feet for clinging to bark

short tail

VOICE *Loud, liquid whistles, pew pew pew, chwee chwee; fast ringing trills, loud chwit.*
NESTING *Typically plasters mud around old woodpecker hole lined with bark and leaves; 6–9 eggs; 1 brood; Apr–Jul.*
FEEDING *Variety of seeds, berries, and nuts, often wedged in bark for easy cracking.*
SIMILAR SPECIES *Rock Nuthatch (rare).*

Fan-tailed Warbler

Cisticola juncidis

Also known as the Zitting Cisticola, this tiny, streaky bird usually betrays itself by its curious song: a repeated sharp, penetrating *zeet* given with each bound of its deeply undulating song-flight. It is not closely related to any other European species, but despite this it is easy to confuse with other warblers, especially when it is skulking quietly in low vegetation.

NESTS AND *feeds in grassy places such as meadows, marshes, dunes, and the grassy margins of cornfields.*

brown and buff stripes on crown

cream and black stripes on back

pale buff below

very short, rounded wings

tail rounded in flight

short tail, often fanned

thin pink legs

VOICE *Loud chip call; song repeated short zeet... zeet... zeet in bounding song-flight.*
NESTING *Deep, flexible, pear-shaped nest of grass, feathers and cobwebs in tall grass; 4–6 eggs; 2–3 broods; Apr–Jun.*
FEEDING *Insects, spiders, and seeds.*
SIMILAR SPECIES *Sedge Warbler, Whinchat, Grasshopper Warbler.*

Willow Warbler 🔊

Phylloscopus trochilus

The most common and widespread of the leaf warblers, this small, slim bird closely resembles the Chiffchaff. It is most easily recognized by the simple, yet wonderfully evocative song that heralds its arrival in the north in spring. It usually feeds alone, slipping easily through foliage as it searches for insects and other prey.

SINGS WITH *beautiful fluid cadence in light woodland, scrub, and thickets, especially of birch and willow.*

flatter head than Chiffchaff

pale stripe over eye

yellow stripe over eye

grey-green to olive above

greener back

longer wings than Chiffchaff

plain, round wings

buff-white to pale yellow underside

pale yellow-brown legs

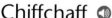
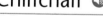

VOICE Sweet, simple, double hoo-eet call; cascading, trilling song, fading with a flourish.
NESTING Domed nest of grass, near ground in thick cover; 6–7 eggs; 1 brood; Apr–May.
FEEDING Picks insects and spiders from foliage; catches some flies in air.
SIMILAR SPECIES Chiffchaff, Wood Warbler, Bonelli's Warbler.

Chiffchaff 🔊

Phylloscopus collybita

By sight the Chiffchaff is very difficult to distinguish from the Willow Warbler, although the slightly plumper Chiffchaff's habit of dipping its tail downward is a useful clue. When it sings, it betrays its identity by repeating its name over and over again – and luckily it sings a lot, particularly in spring. Some Chiffchaffs spend the winter in western Europe, unlike Willow Warblers.

REPEATS ITS *name from perches in woodland, parks, bushy areas, and large gardens; favours taller trees in summer.*

short, round wings

rounder head than Willow Warbler

white crescent under eye

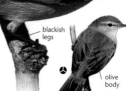

shorter wings than Willow Warbler

blackish legs

olive body

VOICE Call slurred, sweet hweet; song easy, bright chip-chap-chip-chap-chip-chap-chip-chip.
NESTING Domed grass nest, low in bush or undergrowth; 5–6 eggs; 1–2 broods; Apr–Jul.
FEEDING Takes insects and spiders from leaves, slipping easily through foliage.
SIMILAR SPECIES Willow Warbler, Wood Warbler.

Bonelli's Warbler 🔊

Phylloscopus bonelli

FEEDS IN deciduous and coniferous woods, in clumps of oak on bushy slopes, and in small bushy pines.

A southern counterpart of the much brighter Wood Warbler, Bonelli's Warbler is an anonymous-looking, elusive bird. It is usually located by its slightly bubbling trill, but rarely seen more than briefly as it threads its way quietly through the dense foliage of oak or pine trees, searching out its insect prey.

pale yellow rump

faint pale line over eye

round greyish head

pale greenish grey back

green wings with greenish yellow coverts

spike-like bill

dark tail with yellow-green edges to feathers

silky white underside

VOICE Call bright hoo-eet or chew-ee; song loose, bubbly trill, s'r'r'r'r'r'rrrrrrrrrrrrrrrrrr.
NESTING Domed grassy nest under tussock or in bank cavity; 5–6 eggs; 1 brood; May–Jul.
FEEDING Picks insects and small spiders from among foliage.
SIMILAR SPECIES Wood Warbler, Willow Warbler, Chiffchaff.

Wood Warbler 🔊

Phylloscopus sibilatrix

SINGS ecstatically from branches in mature broadleaved woods with open ground beneath the canopy.

One of the biggest of the *Phylloscopus* warblers, the Wood Warbler is also the brightest, with areas of pure lemon-yellow and clear green in its plumage. It feeds quietly, high in the foliage of mature deciduous trees, and can be hard to spot. In early summer, the male is best located by his metallic, trilling song, delivered with such force that the bird's entire body vibrates with the effort.

long, broad yellow stripe over eye

clear green upperside

long wings

pale sulphur-yellow chin and upper breast

silky white underside

VOICE Call loud sweet; song low, sweet sioo sioo sioo, or sharp ticking, accelerating into silvery trill, ti-ti-ti-ti-ti-tik-ik-ik-ikrrrrrrrrrrrr.
NESTING Domed grassy nest in dead leaves on ground; 6–7 eggs; 1 brood; May–Jun.
FEEDING Insects and spiders, from foliage.
SIMILAR SPECIES Willow Warbler, Chiffchaff, Bonelli's Warbler.

Dartford Warbler

Sylvia undata

A skulking, secretive bird of warm heaths and sunny slopes, the Dartford Warbler is often hard to see clearly as it flicks from one bush to another and slips from sight. But in warm, still weather it may perch in full view, when it is easy to recognize. A non-migrant in Europe, it can suffer declines in hard winters.

LIVES ON *heaths with gorse, heather, and small bushes, and on warm, bushy slopes with thorn scrub.*

red eye and eye-ring

duller than male

paler below

brownish grey back

♀

♂

long, slender, dark tail

dark red-brown underside

♂

VOICE *Call distinctive, low, buzzy chrrr; song quick, rattling warble, sometimes given in air.*
NESTING *Grassy cup nest, low in gorse or heather; 3–5 eggs; 2–3 broods; Apr–Jul.*
FEEDING *Searches for insects and many spiders in low vegetation.*
SIMILAR SPECIES *Subalpine Warbler, Whitethroat.*

Subalpine Warbler

Sylvia cantillans

Found in much the same habitats as the similar Dartford Warbler, this species can be very secretive, but a male may suddenly launch himself into a brief, bouncy song-flight. He is easily distinguished from a male Dartford Warbler by his white "moustache"; females and immatures are trickier to identify.

BREEDS ON *bushy slopes, in low, tangled hedges and thorny thickets, and in open evergreen oak woods.*

red eye-ring

blue-grey head and back

bold white stripe

♂

white edge to tail

rusty pink chest

long, slim, grey tail

♂

white eye-ring around red inner ring

pale throat

♀

buff to whitish

VOICE *Call sharp, ticking tet, sometimes repeated; song high, musical warbling.*
NESTING *Small, neat cup nest built in low vegetation; 3–4 eggs; 2 broods; Apr–Jun.*
FEEDING *Insects and spiders, taken from low scrub or leafy trees.*
SIMILAR SPECIES *Dartford Warbler, Whitethroat.*

Lesser Whitethroat 🔊

Sylvia curruca

Smaller and neater than the Whitethroat, with a dark eye-patch and darker legs, the Lesser Whitethroat is a secretive warbler of woodland edges and hedgerows. Although easy to locate by its song, it often moves to a new perch. In autumn, it can be easy to find feeding on shrubs and trees with berries.

LIVES IN *tall, dense thickets at the edges of woods, patches of scrub, and old, thick, overgrown hedgerows.*

slim tail, edged white ♂

plain brown wings

dark eye-patch

grey cap

dull grey-brown back

white eye-ring

head paler in spring ♀

white throat

whitish underside, washed pink

dark grey legs ♂

VOICE *Sharp metallic tak, thin chi; song a rattling, wooden chikachikachikachika.*
NESTING *Cup of twigs or grass built in shrub; 4–6 eggs; 1 brood; May–Jun.*
FEEDING *Picks insects from foliage; also eats many berries in late summer.*
SIMILAR SPECIES *Whitethroat, Blackcap, Subalpine Warbler.*

Whitethroat 🔊

Sylvia communis

Typically a bird of open spaces with low bushes and scrub, the Whitethroat often skulks in low, thick vegetation. It gives itself away by its irritable calls, and often emerges to scold intruders. It sings quite often, sometimes from a low perch or a high wire, but also during a short, bouncing song-flight.

SINGS FROM *perches in bushy, dry, and heathy places with low thorny scrub; also thickets, hedges, dense herbs.*

blue-grey head

broken whitish eye-ring ♂

pale below, washed pink

long dark tail, edged white

pale legs ♂

orange-brown wing panel

very bright wing panel

brown head ♀

VOICE *Harsh tcharr, scolding churr, musical wheet-a-wheet-a-whit; song a chattery warble.*
NESTING *Small, neat cup of stems low in thorny shrub; 4–5 eggs; 2 broods; Apr–Jul.*
FEEDING *Picks insects from foliage; takes many berries and some seeds in autumn.*
SIMILAR SPECIES *Lesser Whitethroat, Subalpine Warbler, Dartford Warbler.*

Blackcap 🔊

Sylvia atricapilla

The Blackcap is a stocky warbler with a typical, hard, unmusical call. Its song, however, is beautiful, rich, and full-throated, less even than the similar song of the Garden Warbler. It may overwinter in northwest Europe, when it visits gardens to take seeds and scraps, often driving other birds away from feeders.

SINGS *brilliantly from perches in woods, parks, and large bushy gardens, with plenty of thick undergrowth.*

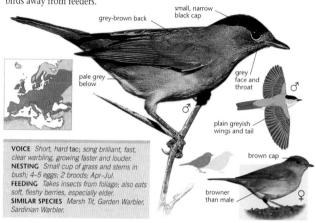

small, narrow black cap

grey-brown back

pale grey below

grey face and throat

plain greyish wings and tail

♂

brown cap

browner than male

♀

VOICE *Short, hard* **tac**; *song brilliant, fast, clear warbling, growing faster and louder.*
NESTING *Small cup of grass and stems in bush; 4–5 eggs; 2 broods; Apr–Jul.*
FEEDING *Takes insects from foliage; also eats soft, fleshy berries, especially elder.*
SIMILAR SPECIES *Marsh Tit, Garden Warbler, Sardinian Warbler.*

Sardinian Warbler 🔊

Sylvia melanocephala

The dark-capped Sardinian Warbler is a bird of stony places with low, scattered bushes and scrub, although it may also frequent taller trees in gardens and orchards. It makes short, bouncy, flights between clumps of cover, and is usually only glimpsed as a small, long-tailed bird disappearing into a bush.

LIVES IN *bushy areas, such as thickets near buildings and walls; also in open woodland with scrub.*

grey head

browner

♀

red eye-ring

large white throat

black cap extending onto cheek

short, round wings

grey back

♂

long tail

dark tail with white sides

whitish underside

♂

VOICE *Hard, short call and fast rattle,* **krr-rr-rr-rr-rr-rr-rr-rr-rr-rr-rr-t**; *song fast, rattling chatter.*
NESTING *Small, neat cup built in low bush; 3–5 eggs; 2 broods; Apr–Jul.*
FEEDING *Takes small insects and spiders, in low vegetation or from ground beneath.*
SIMILAR SPECIES *Male Subalpine Warbler, Blackcap.*

TIP

The red eye-ring is a distinctive feature of the Sardinian Warbler, but is slightly duller on the browner, less boldly marked female.

Moustached Warbler

Acrocephalus melanopogon

A close relative of the Sedge Warbler, and very like it in appearance, the Moustached Warbler is most easily identified by the bold white wedge over its eye and its silky white chin. It is a rare vagrant outside its usual range where, unusually, it is partly resident throughout the year.

LIVES IN *reedbeds and dense waterside rushes or sedges. Very local, and rarely seen outside its breeding range.*

dark crown with few streaks

bold white wedge

black eye-stripe

streaked, rounded tail

white chin

dark streaked, rust-brown back

tawny flanks

VOICE Call throaty or clicking trk-tk-tk-tk; song fast and varied with rising whistles.
NESTING Deep grassy nest lined with plant down, in reeds; 5–6 eggs; 1 brood; Apr–Jun.
FEEDING Takes insects and other small invertebrates from mud and wetland plants.
SIMILAR SPECIES Sedge Warbler, Whinchat.

TIP

Although difficult to distinguish from the Sedge Warbler, it often tilts over and cocks its tail, which the Sedge Warbler does not.

Sedge Warbler 🔊

Acrocephalus schoenobaenus

A small, well-marked, active bird with a loud, fast, varied song, the Sedge Warbler is common in waterside and boggy habitats. It often occurs among reeds, but not always, for it prefers to forage among a variety of vegetation that may include willow and hawthorn scrub, and hedges beside wet ditches.

SINGS FROM *the tops of reeds and bushes in reedbeds and wetlands, also in short song-flights. May also occur in nettles, willowherbs, and thorn bushes.*

silvery white stripe over eye

buff on chest and flanks

tawny back, streaked greyish

whitish below

tawny-buff rump

VOICE Call dry rasping tchrrr, sharper tek; song fast mix of whistles, clicks, and trills.
NESTING Deep nest of grass, moss, and cobwebs; 5–6 eggs; 1–2 broods; Apr–Jul.
FEEDING Insects, spiders, and some seeds, taken from reeds, sedges, nettles, and bushes.
SIMILAR SPECIES Moustached Warbler, Reed Warbler.

Grasshopper Warbler

Locustella naevia

This skulking, secretive warbler spends much of its time in thick undergrowth, creeping like a mouse in search of food. It is rarely seen more than briefly as it darts from a low bush and dives back into cover. But its strange song is unmistakable: a metallic ticking like a fishing reel, usually heard at dusk or on warm, sultry summer days.

finely streaked crown and cheek

CALLS FROM *perches in marshy, grassy areas, low thickets, heaths, and thorn scrub with tangled low growth.*

spotted or streaked olive-brown back

buff below

blunt wings

rounded tail

long, broad tail

VOICE Call loud, piercing psit; song fast, mechanical, reeling sirrrrrrrrrrrrrrrrrrrrrrr.
NESTING Small nest of grass and leaves in low vegetation; 5–6 eggs; 2 broods; May–Jul.
FEEDING Small insects and spiders, taken from very low, thick vegetation.
SIMILAR SPECIES Sedge Warbler, Reed Warbler, Dunnock.

Savi's Warbler

Locustella luscinioides

Unlike other *Locustella* warblers, Savi's Warbler is plain instead of streaked. It resembles a Reed Warbler, but has a more rounded tail and long, thick undertail coverts. Usually restricted to large reedbeds, it is most easily located by its strange song, especially around dawn and dusk.

long, flat head

BREEDS AND *feeds almost exclusively in extensive wet reedbeds; rarely found in grassy habitats on coasts.*

pale throat

brown-buff below, with paler belly

dark under tail

long tail with rounded tip

plain brown above

thick, brown undertail coverts

round wings

rounded tail

VOICE Short, sharp, metallic call; song a slurred, metallic, buzzing zurrrrrrrrrrrrrrrr.
NESTING Large, untidy nest of grass in reeds or sedges; 4 eggs; 2 broods; Apr–Jun.
FEEDING Small insects and spiders, taken from dense vegetation.
SIMILAR SPECIES Grasshopper Warbler, Reed Warbler, Cetti's Warbler.

Melodious Warbler

Hippolais polyglotta

BREEDS IN *open woods, scrub, hedges, and orchards. Spring and autumn migrants stop to feed on coasts.*

The western counterpart of the very similar but more eastern Icterine Warbler, the Melodious Warbler has a slightly rounder head, plainer wings, and weaker, more fluttering flight. More skulking in its habits, it also has a less melodious song, despite its name. Both species appear on west European coasts on migration, where they can be hard to tell apart.

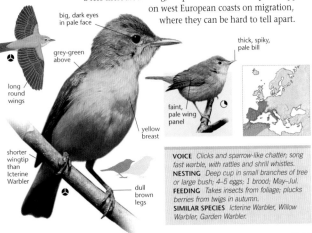

big, dark eyes in pale face

grey-green above

long round wings

shorter wingtip than Icterine Warbler

thick, spiky, pale bill

faint, pale wing panel

yellow breast

dull brown legs

VOICE *Clicks and sparrow-like chatter; song fast warble, with rattles and shrill whistles.*
NESTING *Deep cup in small branches of tree or large bush; 4–5 eggs; 1 brood; May–Jul.*
FEEDING *Takes insects from foliage; plucks berries from twigs in autumn.*
SIMILAR SPECIES *Icterine Warbler, Willow Warbler, Garden Warbler.*

Icterine Warbler

Hippolais icterina

BREEDS IN *deciduous, coniferous, or mixed open woodland. Also coasts on spring and autumn migration.*

Larger than the confusingly similar Melodious Warbler, with which it often occurs during migration, the square-tailed, spike-billed Icterine Warbler has a flatter forehead, slightly peaked crown, longer wingtips, and a more obvious pale wing panel. Less secretive than the Melodious Warbler, it is much more likely to perch in full view.

long, square tail

orange-pink bill with dark ridge

long wingtips

pale wing panel

flat forehead

pale grey-green above

whitish below; pale yellow in spring adult

dull grey legs

VOICE *Call melodious dideroi, hard tik; song prolonged warbling incorporating dideroi call.*
NESTING *Deep cup suspended from forked tree branch; 4–5 eggs; 1 brood; May–Aug.*
FEEDING *Takes insects from foliage; pulls berries from twigs with tug of bill.*
SIMILAR SPECIES *Melodious Warbler, Willow Warbler, Reed Warbler.*

Cetti's Warbler

Cettia cetti

Small, dark, and hard to see at any time, Cetti's Warbler usually stays well out of sight in thick cover. Yet it is often easy to detect because of its frequent, loud, abrupt outbursts of song. It often moves on between phrases, so actually locating the singer is no easy task – it seems to be always one step ahead.

SKULKS IN *dense, damp thickets near rivers, ditches, and reedbeds, and often near extensive marshes.*

thin pale stripe

grey face

pale grey below

rounded tail

short, round, rust-brown wings

dark red-brown above

dark red-brown tail

VOICE Explosive chich or plit; song loud chee! chewee! chewechewechewewe!
NESTING Deep cup of grass and leaves in dense cover; 3–5 eggs; 1–2 broods; Apr–Jun.
FEEDING Takes insects, spiders, snails, and some seeds from near ground in dense cover.
SIMILAR SPECIES Nightingale, Reed Warbler, Sedge Warbler.

Garden Warbler

Sylvia borin

This short-billed, round-faced warbler has no obvious patterning and few distinctive features apart from its song, which is a beautiful outpouring of mellow warbling notes. Normally solitary, it may join other warblers to feed on berries in late summer to fuel its migration. Despite its name, it rarely visits gardens unless they are large and overgrown, or to feed when on migration.

BREEDS AND *feeds in open woods, wooded parkland, tall thickets, shrubs, and trees.*

dull, pale wings

grey neck patch

thin, pale eye-ring

large, dark eyes

pale buff-brown above

pale feather edges, sharper on juvenile

pale buff underside

VOICE Call thick, soft tchak, churrr; song rich, throaty, musical, fast warbling.
NESTING Shallow, skimpy cup of grass and moss in bush; 4–5 eggs; 1 brood; May–Jul.
FEEDING Takes insects and spiders from foliage, berries and seeds in autumn.
SIMILAR SPECIES Blackcap, Reed Warbler, Spotted Flycatcher.

Reed Warbler

Acrocephalus scirpaceus

Although it occasionally nests in willows growing over water, the Reed Warbler is basically a reedbed specialist, adept at grasping vertical stems and shuffling through the dense reeds in search of food. Very like the slightly plumper Marsh Warbler, it is best identified by its repetitive, conversational song.

LIVES IN *extensive, wet reedbeds, reedy ditches, and willows beside lakes and rivers. Migrants can be seen on coasts.*

rump brighter than back

long wing feathers with pale fringes

plain brown above

long tail

pale eye-ring

white throat

dark legs

bright buff underside

VOICE *Call low churr or chk; song rhythmic trrik trrik, chrr chrr, chewe chewe trrt tiri tiri.*
NESTING *Deep grass nest woven around reed stems; 3–5 eggs; 2 broods; May–Jul.*
FEEDING *Insects and spiders taken from mud and thick, wet vegetation; some seeds.*
SIMILAR SPECIES *Marsh Warbler, Sedge Warbler, Savi's Warbler.*

Marsh Warbler

Acrocephalus palustris

Although it has rather duller plumage than the Reed Warbler, and a more rounded form, the Marsh Warbler is very difficult to distinguish until it starts to sing. Then it produces a gloriously musical stream of sweet warbles, whistles, and trills, coupled with fluent mimicry of many European and African birds.

FAVOURS *thick wetland vegetation such as sedges, willowherb, umbellifers, nettles, and shrubs, with or without reeds.*

squarish, dark tail

plain back

yellowish white underside

whitish eye-ring

pale legs

VOICE *Call hard chek; song fluent, fast, with twangy, nasal notes, and much mimicry.*
NESTING *Grass cup suspended in cover by "jug handles"; 4–5 eggs; 1 brood; Jun–Jul.*
FEEDING *Forages in dense cover for insects and spiders; also takes some berries.*
SIMILAR SPECIES *Reed Warbler, Sedge Warbler, Savi's Warbler.*

Barred Warbler

Sylvia nisoria

One of the larger European warblers, the Barred Warbler can resemble the quite unrelated Wryneck, with its heavily barred underside and rather severe expression. It has a clumsy, rather aggressive character, but tends to skulk in thick cover, where it is hard to watch.

BREEDS IN *woodland clearings and bushy places. Rare migrants, mainly in autumn, visit coastal thickets on dunes and low hills.*

dark eyes

bright yellow eyes

dull whitish below

♎1ST ❄

mid-grey above

♂ ☼

white below with close grey bars

long tail with white corners

white wing-bars

♀

> **VOICE** *Loud, dry, hard rattle, trrr-r-r-rt; song long, bright, musical warble.*
> **NESTING** *Substantial nest in thorny bush or scrub; 4–5 eggs; 1 brood; May–Jul.*
> **FEEDING** *Takes insects and spiders from foliage; tugs at berries.*
> **SIMILAR SPECIES** *Wryneck, Garden Warbler, female Blackcap.*

Great Reed Warbler 🔊

Acrocephalus arundinaceus

Massive for a warbler, the almost thrush-sized Great Reed Warbler is hard to miss as it sings from the top of a tall reed stem, producing its distinctive, raucous but slightly hesitant chorus of frog-like croaking phrases. Despite its size, it can be found in remarkably small patches of reeds or tall grass, often along narrow irrigation channels or ditches.

BREEDS AND *feeds in reedbeds and reedy ditches or in strips of reed beside rivers or seasonal floods.*

big, dark-edged bill

white throat

plain warm brown above

pale stripe above eye

dark eye-stripe

bright rump

long wingtips

pale rufous-buff below

broad, dark brown tail

> **VOICE** *Call harsh krrrr or shorter tshak; song repetitive croaking, whistling, warbling grik grik grik, jeek jeek chik grrr grrr girik girik.*
> **NESTING** *Deep nest slung in reed stems above water; 3–6 eggs; 1–2 broods; May–Aug.*
> **FEEDING** *Takes insects, spiders, and other small invertebrates from foliage and reeds.*
> **SIMILAR SPECIES** *Reed Warbler, Song Thrush.*

Pied Flycatcher

Ficedula hypoleuca

PREFERS TO *breed in nest boxes, in mature broadleaved woodland, with clear air beneath canopy for hunting.*

A breeding male Pied Flycatcher is boldly pied and hard to mistake as he dashes out from a forest perch to seize flying insects on the wing. After the autumn moult, males resemble the browner females, but the white wing and tail patches are distinctive in both.

one or two white spots on forehead

black tail with white sides

bold white patch

black wings

black and white plumage

white patch

dull brown and white ♀

VOICE *Sharp* whit *or* whit-ic; *song musical* see, see, see sit, see-sit sitip-seweee.
NESTING *Cup of leaves and moss in tree hole or nest box; 5–9 eggs; 1 brood; Apr–May.*
FEEDING *Catches flies in air, picks insects from foliage and from ground; also eats seeds and berries.*
SIMILAR SPECIES *Spotted Flycatcher.*

Spotted Flycatcher

Muscicapa striata

HUNTS FLYING *insects from perches in open woodland, parkland, and gardens with bushes and trees.*

Sharp-eyed and constantly alert, the Spotted Flycatcher specializes in targeting flying insects from a vantage point on an open perch. Launching itself with a burst of rapid wingbeats, it seizes its quarry in mid-air and usually returns to the same perch: a technique that makes it quite distinctive despite its unremarkable grey-brown plumage.

streaked head

long, narrow wings

cream spots on back

spotted crown

soft brown streaks on breast

silvery white below

long brown tail held downwards

VOICE *Short, scratchy* tzic *or* tzee, tzee-tsuk tsuk; *song short, scratchy, weak warble.*
NESTING *Cup of grass, leaves, moss in vine or cavity; 3–5 eggs; 1–2 broods; Jun–Aug.*
FEEDING *Catches insects in air, sallying from perch and usually returning to same perch.*
SIMILAR SPECIES *Garden Warbler, female Pied Flycatcher.*

Sand Martin

Riparia riparia

The smallest of the European swallows and martins, with the most fluttering flight, the Sand Martin is the first to appear on its northern breeding grounds in spring. At this time it usually hunts over water, where it can rely on a supply of flying insect prey. It feeds on the wing, swooping after flies with fast in-out flicks of its wings. Always gregarious, it roosts in noisy flocks.

BREEDS IN *colonies in earth banks and sand quarries, often near water, excavating rows of nest holes.*

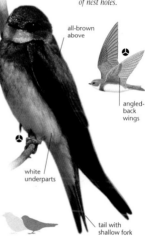

all-brown above

brown breastband

angled-back wings

perches at nest-hole

white underparts

tail with shallow fork

VOICE *Low, dry, rasping or chattering chrrrp; song rambling, chattering, weak twitter.*
NESTING *Bores long hole into earth or soft sandstone; 4–5 eggs; 2 broods; Apr–Jul.*
FEEDING *Catches insects in flight, often over water; sometimes feeds on bare ground.*
SIMILAR SPECIES *Alpine Swift, Swift, House Martin.*

House Martin

Delichon urbicum

Small, stocky, with pied plumage and a bold white rump, the House Martin is a common breeding bird in many towns and villages in northern Europe. It feeds entirely in the air on small flies and similar prey, circling high up over the rooftops or low down over fresh waters. It comes down to the ground only to gather mud, which it uses to build its distinctive nest.

PERCHES IN *flocks on wires before migration. Breeds on house walls, feeding over wetlands and open areas.*

dark wings

white rump

nest on outside wall

blue-black cap

blue-black back

forked tail

white throat

white underside

VOICE *Hard, quick, chirping prrit or chrrit, tchirrup; twittering song of similar notes.*
NESTING *Enclosed mud nest with top entrance, under house eaves or (in south of range) cliff overhang; 4–5 eggs; 2–3 broods; Apr–Sep.*
FEEDING *Catches insects in flight, high up.*
SIMILAR SPECIES *Swallow, Sand Martin, Swift.*

Crag Martin

Ptyonoprogne rupestris

BUILDS MUD *nests on walls in old towns, or on crags, cliffs, and in gorges with broad, stony riverbeds.*

Although similar to the Sand Martin in plumage, the Crag Martin is much bigger, with a far more powerful, elegant flight. It soars and floats on upcurrents near cliffs, sweeping to and fro with fast turns. It hunts in the air, but close views are possible at the puddles where it gathers mud for its nests.

streaked chin

dull grey-brown back and rump

dark wedge

white tail spots

very pale brownish grey below

long wings

VOICE *Short, high clicking call, dry tshirr; fast, twittering song.*
NESTING *Mud nest under overhang of cliff, in cave, or on building, bridge, or tunnel; 4–5 eggs; 1–2 broods; Apr–Jun.*
FEEDING *Catches flying insects in mid-air.*
SIMILAR SPECIES *Sand Martin, Alpine Swift, House Martin.*

TIP

Look for a pair of oblong white spots near the tip of the tail. Although not always obvious, they provide a positive identification.

Red-rumped Swallow

Cecropis daurica

LIVES IN *mountain or coastal areas with cliffs and gorges, and old towns and villages.*

Easily identified by its rufous collar and rump when it is perched, the Red-rumped Swallow is more difficult to pick out from a flock of Swallows in the air. It flies with a stiffer, less fluent action, with shallow flaps and long, circling glides, usually over areas with cliffs and caves suitable for nesting.

dark blue cap

dark blue back

pale throat

black tail

black under tail

pale rufous-cream below with faint streaks

tail looks stuck-on

VOICE *Distinctive, thin queek or tsek, sharper keeer; song chirruping warble, lower-pitched and harsher than Swallow's.*
NESTING *Rounded mud nest with entrance tube, under overhang, in cave or under eaves; 3–5 eggs; 2–3 broods; Apr–Jun.*
FEEDING *Catches flying insects in mid-air.*
SIMILAR SPECIES *Swallow, House Martin.*

rufous collar

orange-buff rump

thick streamers

Swallow

Hirundo rustica

The glossy, fork-tailed Swallow is a common sight around European farmsteads in summer, since it prefers to nest in barns and sheds close to a steady supply of its favourite prey, large flies. It catches these on the wing, often swooping low among grazing cattle with a wonderfully fluent, graceful action, using its long tail to steer as it swerves and rolls from side to side through the air. Its tail streamers and deep red chin are usually conspicuous in flight, making it hard to confuse with any other species except the Red-rumped Swallow, which has a distinctive pale nape and rump patch. It often perches on wires, especially in autumn before migrating to Africa.

GATHERS IN *twittering flocks, perching in long rows on wires before migrating. Feeds over grassy or cultivated river valleys, open grassland, or farmland with hedgerows, and breeds in and around villages and farms.*

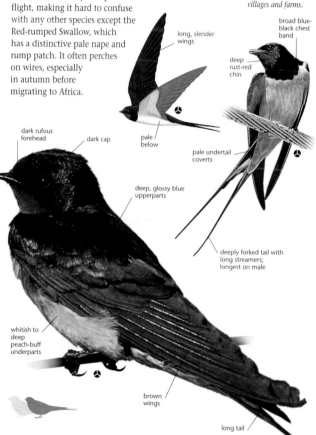

long, slender wings

broad blue-black chest band

deep rust-red chin

pale below

pale undertail coverts

dark rufous forehead

dark cap

deep, glossy blue upperparts

deeply forked tail with long streamers; longest on male

whitish to deep peach-buff underparts

brown wings

long tail

VOICE *Call liquid* swit-swit-swit, *nasal* vit-vit-vit, tsee-tsee; *song quick, chirruping warble.*
NESTING *Open cup of mud and straw; on beam or ledge in outbuilding; 4–6 eggs; 2–3 broods; Apr–Aug.*
FEEDING *Flies low to catch flying insects in its bill, mostly large flies.*
SIMILAR SPECIES *Red-rumped Swallow, House Martin, Swift.*

TIP

Most Swallows nest in barns and similar buildings. They can be watched entering and leaving through open windows or doors as they bring food for their young.

Stonechat

Saxicola torquatus

Small, chunky, and upright, the Stonechat is a bird of open, bushy terrain, such as gorse thickets above coastal cliffs. It likes to perch on the tops of bushes, where its scolding calls and the male's pied head-neck pattern make it conspicuous. It often darts down to snatch prey from the ground, flying back to its perch on whirring wings like a giant bumblebee.

PERCHES prominently in open places with bushes and heather, on heaths, coasts, and moorland.

white wing patch

♂☼

paler head

mottled chest

♀

paler head and throat

black head and throat

white neck patch

short dark tail

rust-red breast

♂☼

VOICE Hard, scolding tsak or tsak-tsak, sharp wheet; song rapid, chattery warble.
NESTING Grassy cup, often in grass with entrance tunnel; 5–6 eggs; 2 broods; May–Jul.
FEEDING Takes insects, spiders, worms and seeds from ground; also catches insects in air.
SIMILAR SPECIES Whinchat, Wheatear, Redstart.

Whinchat

Saxicola rubetra

Although similar to the Stonechat in looks, the Whinchat has a pale stripe over its eye and is a summer visitor to Europe rather than a resident. It favours rough grassland, open heaths, and moors, and is declining in many areas as these habitats are eroded by intensive agriculture and urban development.

BREEDS IN open places with heather, grass, and scattered taller stems of young trees; migrants are seen near coasts.

white triangle on each side of tail

♀ 🦋

white stripe

dark streaked pale back

blackish cheeks

♂ 🦋

streaked cap

♀ 🦋

buff stripe

pale throat

yellow-buff

1ST ☼

♂ 🦋

VOICE Loud, short tictic or wheet-tuc-tuc; song varied, sweet warble with hard notes.
NESTING Grassy nest low in tussock, bush, or on ground; 5–6 eggs; 1–2 broods; May–Jul.
FEEDING Drops to ground from perch for insects and worms; also seeds and berries.
SIMILAR SPECIES Wheatear, Stonechat, Sedge Warbler.

Robin

Erithacus rubecula

The round-bodied, slim-tailed Robin is a shy, skulking woodland bird over most of its range. It is adapted for following animals such as wild boar and taking small animals from the earth they disturb. In the UK, it follows gardeners instead, and has become very tame.

big black eye

orange-red breast

LIVES IN *open forests and woods, on bushy heaths, and in parks and gardens with hedges and shrubs.*

bluish grey on sides of neck and chest

warm brown above

white breast spot

mottled brown body

VOICE *Sharp tik, quick tik-ik-ik-ik, high, thin seep; song rich, sweet, musical, varied warble.*
NESTING *Domed nest of leaves and grass in bank or bush; 4–6 eggs; 2 broods; Apr–Aug.*
FEEDING *Takes spiders, insects, worms, berries, and seeds, mostly from ground.*
SIMILAR SPECIES *Dunnock, Nightingale, Redstart.*

Bluethroat

Luscinia svecica

The shy, secretive Bluethroat is chiefly a bird of wet places such as swampy northern forests and thickets at the edges of reedbeds. In the UK, it is a scarce migrant, usually seen near coasts. Northern birds have a red throat spot; southern birds have a white spot, and eastern birds no spot at all.

rufous panels

♀

bold white stripe

plain wings

BREEDS IN *wet thickets, moist woods, heaths, and bushy tundra; migrants can be seen in coastal thickets and reeds.*

red spot

blue flecks

dark breast band, may have blue spots

♀

dark brown upperparts

red on tail

♂ ☼
RED-SPOTTED RACE

VOICE *Sharp, hard tak, softer wheet; song powerful, bright, musical, accelerating into melodious outburst with much mimicry.*
NESTING *Small grassy cup in low bush; 5–7 eggs; 1 brood; May–Jun.*
FEEDING *Forages on ground close to cover, picking up seeds, insects, and berries.*
SIMILAR SPECIES *Robin, Nightingale.*

Redstart

Phoenicurus phoenicurus

BREEDS IN *open woodland with sparse undergrowth. Migrants seen near coasts or lakes.*

A male Redstart is an extremely handsome bird in spring and summer, best located in its breeding wood by its short, sweet song. The female, less distinctive, shares the male's habit of constantly flicking the rust-red tail up and down. They like old woods with open space beneath the canopy.

white forehead

♂

whitish mottling

♂

♀

pale buff below

rusty rump

orange-rufous below

bluish grey from crown to back

♂

pale rust-red tail with dark centre

VOICE *Clear, rising* wheet, *sharp* tac; *song brief, musical warble, ending with weak trill.*
NESTING *Grassy nest lined with feathers or hair, in hole; 5–7 eggs; 1 brood; May–Jun.*
FEEDING *Forages in foliage or on ground for insects, spiders, small worms; some berries.*
SIMILAR SPECIES *Black Redstart, Robin, Nightingale.*

Black Redstart

Phoenicurus ochruros

LIVES ON *mountains and rocky coasts with cliffs and gorges, in quarries, on derelict industrial sites, and in old towns.*

A bird of rocky slopes with scree and crags, or deep gorges, the Black Redstart also breeds in run-down industrial areas and towns, in old buildings with plenty of holes suitable for nesting. This preference makes it relatively easy to distinguish it from the brighter Redstart, which nearly always lives in woodland.

grey cap

♂

dark rusty tail with darker centre

blackish and sooty grey body

white panel on wings

♂

browner head

pale grey body

red-brown on tail

♀

mousy grey body

VOICE *Call hard rattling, short* tsip, tucc-tucc, tititic; *song warble with crackling trills.*
NESTING *Grassy nest in hole in building, cliff or rocks; 4–6 eggs; 2 broods; May–Jul.*
FEEDING *Leaps and flies after insects; seizes worms on ground; some berries and seeds.*
SIMILAR SPECIES *Redstart, Black Wheatear, Dunnock.*

Nightingale

Luscinia megarhynchos

Famous for the male's rich and varied song, the Nightingale is a secretive bird that can be frustratingly difficult to see. It skulks in thick vegetation, often close to the ground. With its almost anonymous, brown plumage it resembles a large juvenile Robin or a Garden Warbler, but it has a longer rufous-brown tail, conspicuous in flight.

SINGS IN *dense thickets in bushy gullies and heaths, coppiced woodland, and overgrown gardens.*

pale ring around large, dark eyes

grey neck side

rusty rump and tail

warm brown back

tail often raised

grey-buff below

spotted above

rufous tail

plain brown wings

rufous tail

bright rump

♂

VOICE *Calls include low, mechanical, grating* kerrr, *loud, bright* tweet; *song brilliant, varied.*
NESTING *Small cup of leaves, lined with grass and hair, built in low bush; 4–5 eggs; 1 brood; May–Jun.*
FEEDING *Eats worms, beetles, and berries.*
SIMILAR SPECIES *Thrush Nightingale, juvenile Robin, Garden Warbler, Redstart.*

Thrush Nightingale

Luscinia luscinia

This northern and eastern counterpart of the Nightingale is extremely similar in appearance, with very subtle plumage distinctions. The Thrush Nightingale is overall greyer and duller and is less brightly reddish-brown on the rump and tail. It has a faint moustache stripe and a slightly mottled, rather than plain, breast. Its song lacks the dramatic, long, thin rising notes of its more famous relative.

BREEDS IN *dense, shaded woodland thickets, especially in marshes or along riversides, often with alders and birches.*

duller overall than Nightingale

greyish upperparts

faint moustache stripe

faint grey streaks on breast

relatively dull tail and rump

dull rufous tail

VOICE *Sharp whistling* whit *alarm call and creaky notes; song very rich, varied, and loud.*
NESTING *Bulky, loose cup of grass on leaf base, on ground among roots or dead branches, 4–5 eggs; 1 brood; Apr–Jul.*
FEEDING *Insects and some fruit.*
SIMILAR SPECIES *Nightingale, juvenile Robin, Garden Warbler, Redstart.*

Black-eared Wheatear

Oenanthe hispanica

Slimmer, lighter, and less solid than a Wheatear, with a narrower black tail band, the Black-eared Wheatear occurs in two plumage forms – black-throated and pale-throated. A spring male's plumage is a distinctive black and pale buff, but females, juveniles, and males at any other time of year can be difficult to recognize. Common on warm, stony Mediterranean slopes, it readily perches on low bushes and tall stems. It combines the ground-feeding behaviour typical of wheatears with some of the actions of smaller chats such as the Stonechat.

LIVES IN A *variety of warm, open, often barren places with scattered bushes, rocks, and high, stony pastures around the Mediterranean.*

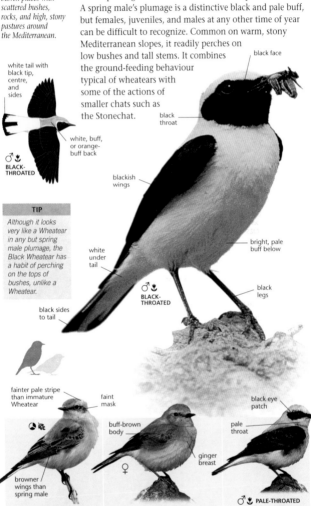

white tail with black tip, centre, and sides

♂ ♟
BLACK-THROATED

white, buff, or orange-buff back

black face

black throat

blackish wings

TIP

Although it looks very like a Wheatear in any but spring male plumage, the Black Wheatear has a habit of perching on the tops of bushes, unlike a Wheatear.

white under tail

bright, pale buff below

black legs

♂ ♟
BLACK-THROATED

black sides to tail

fainter pale stripe than immature Wheatear

faint mask

browner wings than spring male

buff-brown body

♀

ginger breast

black eye patch

pale throat

♂ ♟ **PALE-THROATED**

VOICE *Wheezy tssch, hard tack; song fast, rattling warble, quite bright and explosive, with some mimicry.*
NESTING *Cup of grass and other plant material in hole, under boulders or stones, or at base of bush; 4–5 eggs; 1–2 broods; Apr–Jun.*
FEEDING *Watches from bush top or stone, drops to ground to seize insects and spiders, sometimes chasing after them, then returns to perch; eats some small seeds.*
SIMILAR SPECIES *Wheatear, Stonechat.*

Wheatear

Oenanthe oenanthe

In summer, the Wheatear is a bird of open, rocky habitats, but it often turns up along coasts, on farmland, and even on golf courses while on migration. It has a distinctive habit of flying ahead of people, then perching before moving on again, flashing its white rump every time it moves.

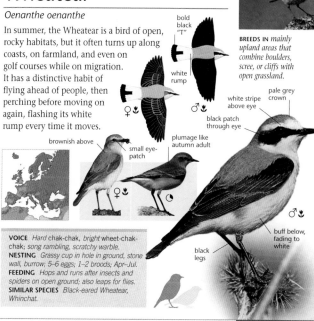

bold black "T"

white rump

♀

♂

BREEDS IN *mainly upland areas that combine boulders, scree, or cliffs with open grassland.*

white stripe above eye

pale grey crown

black patch through eye

brownish above

small eye-patch

plumage like autumn adult

♀

⟳

♂

buff below, fading to white

black legs

VOICE *Hard chak-chak, bright wheet-chak-chak; song rambling, scratchy warble.*
NESTING *Grassy cup in hole in ground, stone wall, burrow; 5–6 eggs; 1–2 broods; Apr–Jul.*
FEEDING *Hops and runs after insects and spiders on open ground; also leaps for flies.*
SIMILAR SPECIES *Black-eared Wheatear, Whinchat.*

Black Wheatear

Oenanthe leucura

Almost all-dark, this large, stout-billed wheatear can be difficult to spot as it forages among the hard shadows cast by the crags and boulders of its rocky Mediterranean habitat. Yet, when it flies off, it betrays its identity by revealing a striking white rump and tail with the typical wheatear "T"-mark. It often flies low and fast, across cliff faces or up and down scree slopes.

RESIDENT ON *rocky, grassy slopes with scree and boulders, often found near the base of cliffs and crags.*

flight-feathers paler in flight

black body

♀

duller, browner than male

black "T" on white tail

♂

white vent

mostly white tail

VOICE *Bright, whistled pewp, hard tet-tet; song low, rich, or lighter, harsh twittering.*
NESTING *Grassy cup in hole in ground or among stones; 5–6 eggs; 1–2 broods; Apr–Jul.*
FEEDING *Forages on ground or swoops from perch for insects and spiders.*
SIMILAR SPECIES *Black-eared Wheatear, Wheatear, Blackbird.*

Tree Sparrow

Passer montanus

Over much of its range the Tree Sparrow is a less suburban bird than the House Sparrow, preferring woods and farmland. The sexes are almost identical, both having the black mask, brown cap, black cheek patch, and white collar. This sparrow often feeds on the ground in company with finches and buntings.

LIVES ON *farmland with scattered trees, in parks, woods, and woodland edges. Also in towns in southern and eastern Europe.*

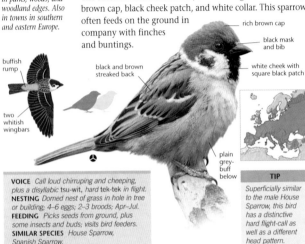

rich brown cap

black mask and bib

white cheek with square black patch

buffish rump

two whitish wingbars

black and brown streaked back

rich brown cap

plain grey-buff below

VOICE Call loud chirruping and cheeping, plus a disyllabic *tsu-wit*, hard *tek-tek* in flight.
NESTING Domed nest of grass in hole in tree or building; 4–6 eggs; 2–3 broods; Apr–Jul.
FEEDING Picks seeds from ground, plus some insects and buds; visits bird feeders.
SIMILAR SPECIES House Sparrow, Spanish Sparrow.

TIP
Superficially similar to the male House Sparrow, this bird has a distinctive hard flight-call as well as a different head pattern.

House Sparrow

Passer domesticus

This common, noisy sparrow is one of the most familiar small birds due to its habit of nesting in buildings. The male has a bold black bib and distinctive grey cap, but the female can be confused with a female finch. Although House Sparrow populations have declined, the birds are still widespread.

LIVES IN *cities, towns, villages, farms, and on farmland; rarely found far from human habitation.*

grey cap

big black bib

whitish wingbar ♂

greyish rump

red-brown above, with dark streaks

unmarked grey below

♂☼

VOICE Lively chirrup, chilp, as loud chorus from flock; song a simple series of chirps.
NESTING Untidy nest of grass and feathers in cavity; 3–7 eggs; 1–4 broods; Apr–Aug.
FEEDING Takes seeds, nuts, and berries, mainly from ground, plus insects for young.
SIMILAR SPECIES Spanish Sparrow, female Chaffinch.

pale stripe

plain plumage

♀

Spanish Sparrow

Passer hispaniolensis

More brightly patterned than the similar House Sparrow, at least in the summer male, the Spanish Sparrow is a highly social species that breeds in colonies and is often found in large flocks. It lives in thickets and on farmland but, in places where House Sparrows are scarce, it may live in towns.

FEEDS IN *farmland, villages, and wet places with willow thickets and tall trees.*

red-brown cap

whitish bar

cream streaks on back

♂ ☼

black bib merges into streaks below

paler bib

♂ ❄

close black streaks on underside

♂ ☼

may have grey streaks

♀

VOICE *Chirruping/chirping calls, slightly higher and more metallic than House Sparrow.*
NESTING *Bulky grass nest in thicket in colony; 3–7 eggs; 1–2 broods; Apr–Jul.*
FEEDING *Eats seeds and berries, mostly taken from ground; feeds insects to chicks.*
SIMILAR SPECIES *House Sparrow, Tree Sparrow.*

Rock Sparrow

Petronia petronia

A rather dull, pale-looking, streaky sparrow of dry, rocky habitats in southern Europe, the Rock Sparrow is often hard to see as it perches on a ledge. It is best located by its loud, twanging call. Its big two-tone pale bill and striped crown are the best identification features; the yellow spot on its breast is far less obvious. The whitish tail spots are distinctive in flight.

LIVES IN *dry, stony, or sandy areas, rocky places, gorges, and mountain regions. Visits pools to drink.*

cream and blackish stripes

big pale bill

yellow breast spot

pale crown

pale wing-bar

pale below with brown-grey stripes

dull brown body with dark streaks

brown tail, tipped with pale spots

VOICE *Distinctive twangy, nasal, repeated tyeoo, tee-vit, or peoo.*
NESTING *Domed grassy nest in cavity, often in building; 5–6 eggs; 2–3 broods; May–Jul.*
FEEDING *Picks seeds and invertebrates from ground, grass, or from among stones.*
SIMILAR SPECIES *Corn Bunting, female House Sparrow, female Cirl Bunting.*

Dunnock

Prunella modularis

FORAGES FOR *food in low, dense scrub and bushes, on heaths and moors, and in forests, woods, parks, and gardens.*

Although it is one of many small, streaky, sparrow-like birds, the Dunnock has a fine bill, grey head and breast, and forages on the ground with a distinctive, jerky, creeping shuffle. If disturbed, it generally flies at ground level into the nearest thick bush.

red-brown eyes

fine, dark bill

grey throat

rich brown with black streaks

row of pale spots on wings

browner head

orange-brown legs

black-streaked brown wings and back

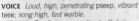

VOICE *Loud, high, penetrating pseep, vibrant teee; song high, fast warble.*
NESTING *Small grassy cup lined with hair, moss, in bush; 4–5 eggs; 2–3 broods; Apr–Jul.*
FEEDING *Picks small insects and seeds from ground, shuffling under and around bushes.*
SIMILAR SPECIES *Robin, Wren, House Sparrow.*

Alpine Accentor

Prunella collaris

BREEDS ON *wide open slopes with short grass and rocks, at high altitude; moves lower in winter.*

Resembling a larger, darker, more streaky Dunnock, the Alpine Accentor is a bird of high mountains with mixed pastures and rock, or almost entirely rocky places. In winter, it moves to lower altitudes, and often turns up around old buildings such as ruined castles on rocky outcrops, where it can be surprisingly tame.

dark wing panel with white spots

grey head

dark streaks on pale back

streaked dull buff or grey below

dark band on closed wings

large red-brown streaks on flanks

TIP

The streaked back, grey head, and rusty flank streaks can be hard to see at a distance, so the best identification clue is the dark mid-wing band.

VOICE *Short, trilling or rolling tru, tschirr, drrp; song erratic, uneven series of trills and squeaky notes, sometimes in flight.*
NESTING *Grassy nest in rock crevice or under rocks; 3–5 eggs; 2 broods; May–Aug.*
FEEDING *Forages on ground for insects, spiders, and seeds.*
SIMILAR SPECIES *Dunnock.*

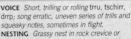

Serin

Serinus serinus

A tiny, bouncy, colourful bird with sharp, spluttering calls, the Serin is one of the most common Mediterranean finches. Males often sing from the tops of spindly conifers, or in a fast, fluttery song-flight. Although Serins are usually easy to identify, they can be confused with escaped Canaries.

LIVES IN *olive groves, orchards, vineyards, open woodland, parks, gardens, and along overgrown roadsides.*

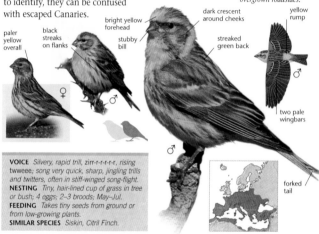

paler yellow overall

black streaks on flanks

♀

stubby bill

bright yellow forehead

dark crescent around cheeks

streaked green back

yellow rump

♂

two pale wingbars

♂

forked tail

VOICE *Silvery, rapid trill, zirr-r-r-r-r-r, rising twweee; song very quick, sharp, jingling trills and twitters, often in stiff-winged song-flight.*
NESTING *Tiny, hair-lined cup of grass in tree or bush; 4 eggs; 2–3 broods; May–Jul.*
FEEDING *Takes tiny seeds from ground or from low-growing plants.*
SIMILAR SPECIES *Siskin, Citril Finch.*

Citril Finch

Carduelis citrinella

The small, neat Citril Finch is a mountain specialist that feeds mainly on the seeds of spruce trees high up in the Alps and Pyrenees. The combination of soft grey, green, and lemon yellow on its body with boldly barred wings is often distinctive, although feeding groups can look very like Siskins or Greenfinches.

BREEDS IN *mountain forests and nearby high rocky pastures up near the tree line, and rarely moves far away.*

grey cap and nape

pale grey neck sides

dull green back

yellow wingbars and rump

♂

dark tail

black and yellow wingbars

♂ ✲

yellow breast

♂ ☼

duller than male

♀

VOICE *Short tek or te-te-te; song quick, varied, rambling warble with wheezy notes and buzzy trills.*
NESTING *Nest of grass and lichens, high in tree; 4–5 eggs; 1–2 broods; May–Jul.*
FEEDING *Takes seeds, both from trees and from the ground beneath.*
SIMILAR SPECIES *Serin, Siskin, Greenfinch.*

Siskin

Carduelis spinus

A specialist at feeding on tree seeds, the neat, slender Siskin is particularly associated with conifers such as pines and spruces. It usually feeds high in the trees, displaying tit-like agility, and in spring the males often sing from treetops. In winter, Siskins forage in flocks, often with Redpolls.

VISITS GARDENS for peanuts, but breeds in spruce and pine forest. More widespread in winter; often in alder and larch along rivers.

black cap and chin

dark streaks on green back

yellow patch each side of black tail

lime-green to yellowish breast

bold yellow wingbars

greyer head than male

like greyer female

♂

♀

VOICE Whistled tsy-zee; hoarse purr; song mixes calls with trills and hard twittering notes.
NESTING Tiny nest of twigs and stems, lined with down, high in tree; 4–5 eggs; 1–2 broods; May–Jul.
FEEDING Eats the seeds of pine, larch, alder, birch, and various other trees.
SIMILAR SPECIES Greenfinch, Redpoll, Serin.

Greenfinch

Carduelis chloris

FEEDS ON sunflower seeds at garden feeders; breeds in open woods, hedges, large gardens.

Males are easy to identify by their green plumage with bright yellow flashes, and a "frowning" look; the duller females and juveniles are also stocky and stout-billed, but trickier to distinguish. In spring, males sing during circling, stiff-winged display flights.

dark patch

bright olive green

yellow stripe

♂☼

browner than adult

streaked all over

greyer above

duller than male

♂✳

♀

yellow patches on tail

♂

flashes of yellow on outer part of grey wings

VOICE Flight call fast, tinny chatter, tit-it-it-it, nasal dzoo-ee, hard jup-jup-jup; song series of rich trills, mixed with buzzy dzweee.
NESTING Bulky nest of grass and twigs in tree; 4–6 eggs; 1–2 broods; Apr–Jul.
FEEDING Takes seeds from trees, herbs, and ground; also berries and nuts.
SIMILAR SPECIES Citril Finch, Serin, Siskin.

Goldfinch

Carduelis carduelis

Flocks of colourful Goldfinches feed on waste ground, farmyards, and field edges, picking soft, milky seeds from thistles, tall daisies, and similar plants with their pointed bills. They are agile feeders, often swinging head-down from seedheads, and have a distinctive dancing flight and tinkling calls.

FORAGES IN *weedy places with tall seed-bearing flowers such as thistles and teasels; also in alder and larch.*

bold black, red, and white head

tawny back

yellow on closed wing

tawny-chestnut patch

black wings

pale underside

big yellow panels

grey head

duller wings

VOICE *Call chattering, lilting skip-i-lip, rough tschair; song mix of call notes and liquid trills.*
NESTING *Neat nest of roots, grass, cobwebs in tree or bush; 5–6 eggs; 2 broods; May–Jul.*
FEEDING *Gathers soft, half-ripe seeds from thistles and similar plants, less often from ground; also eats seeds of alder and larch.*
SIMILAR SPECIES *Siskin, Greenfinch.*

TIP
At a distance the red face can be hard to see, but the yellow wing flashes and bouncy flight action usually make identification easy.

Redpoll

Carduelis flammea

The Redpoll is a very small, active, agile finch that typically feeds in the treetops in noisy, well co-ordinated flocks, often with Siskins. Usually quiet while feeding, it betrays itself by its staccato, chattering flight calls as the flocks move between the trees. It may also gather fallen birch seeds from the ground, and even feed in weedy fields alongside Linnets.

dark red forehead

FEEDS ON *the seeds of birch and larch, in woods and bushy heaths; also in large gardens and scrub.*

tiny bill

small black chin

short, forked tail

pink breast

no pink ♀

♂☼

pale below with long, dark streaks

VOICE *Flight call hard chuchuchuchuchuch, twangy tsooeee; song combines flight call with fast, thin, reeling trill, trreeeeee.*
NESTING *Cup of twigs and grasses in bush or tree; 4–6 eggs; 1–2 broods; May–Jul.*
FEEDING *Mostly tree seeds of birch, plus alder and larch; also takes seeds from ground.*
SIMILAR SPECIES *Twite, Linnet.*

dark tail

streaked back

Linnet 🔊

Carduelis cannabina

Lively and sociable, the Linnet is usually seen in tightly co-ordinated flocks that travel and feed together throughout much of the year. In winter, when the males lose much of their bright colour, the flocks usually feed on the ground. At such times they are easily disturbed, bursting up and dropping into cover at the slightest alarm. They are bolder in the breeding season, when smaller parties can be seen foraging for insects in bushes to feed their nestlings.

FLIES IN *tight, bounding flocks, which feed on heaths, commons, rough grassland, farmland, upland meadows, and coastal marshes. Breeds in gorse scrub, thickets, and hedges.*

pale red forehead, brighter in spring

light grey head

pale cheek spot

dark tail with white side streaks

♂☼

plain orange-brown back

white panel on wings when closed

whitish streaks on dark wings

pink-red chest

♂☼

blackish wings

forked tail

browner head

less pink on chest

brown streaks on body

♂❄

tawny-buff chest

♀

TIP

Although typically shy, Linnets perch conspicuously on low bushes in the breeding season, when the male's plumage is at its most striking.

VOICE *Light, twittering, chattering flight call, tidit tiditit, nasal tseeoo; song quite rich, musical, varied warbling, mixed with chattering notes, often in chorus from flocks.*
NESTING *Small, neat nest of plant stems and roots, lined with hair, in bush near ground; 4–6 eggs; 2–3 broods; Apr–Jul.*
FEEDING *Takes seeds from ground, especially arable weeds, often feeding in groups; feeds young on insects.*
SIMILAR SPECIES *Twite, Redpoll.*

Twite 🔊

Carduelis flavirostris

Like the more colourful Linnet, the Twite is a ground feeder that moves around in flocks, which often rise into the air, circle, and then drop again as one. A good view reveals its pale buff wingbars, rich tawny-buff throat, and the deep pink rump of the breeding male, but from a distance a Twite is an unobtrusive, streaky brown. In winter, when the birds are at their least distinctive, they are best distinguished from Linnets by the nasal *twa-eet* calls that gave the species its name. Unusually, Twites feed their young on small seeds, and the disappearance of flowery meadows from farmland has caused widespread declines.

DRINKS AND *bathes in shallow pools, and feeds on coastal salt marshes in winter. Breeds in weedy fields around upland farms, on mountains and moors, and on rocky ground near coasts.*

narrow buff wingbar

♂ ❁

pink rump

white streaks

yellow bill

rump less pink

♂ ❁

no pink on rump

♀

unmarked, tawny-buff face and throat

grey bill

blackish streaks on tan-brown back

buff below with black streaks

pink rump

dark forked tail (longer than Linnet's), with white streaks

♂ ❁

TIP

A Twite is rather like a Redpoll-Linnet hybrid: its buff wingbars are like the Redpoll's, but the white streaks in its wings and tail recall the Linnet.

VOICE Chattering flight call only slightly harder than Linnet's; distinctive main call twanging, nasal, rising twa-eet; song quick, twittering warble, with buzzing notes, hoarse jangling and chattering trills.
NESTING Deep cup of twigs, grass, and moss, lined with hair, in bush or bank; 4–6 eggs; 1–2 broods; May–Jun.
FEEDING Eats small seeds, particularly those of salt-marsh plants in winter; unlike most finches, feeds young on seeds.
SIMILAR SPECIES Linnet, Redpoll.

Chaffinch

Fringilla coelebs

One of the least specialized of the finches, the Chaffinch is also one of the most successful and abundant. Unusually for finches, pairs breed in separate territories, proclaimed by males singing loudly from prominent perches. At other times they are social and often very tame.

BREEDS IN *coniferous and deciduous forests, woods, hedges, parks, and gardens; some winter in fields.*

two bold white wingbars

greenish rump ♂✿

ochre-brown smudges on head

♂❄

olive head and back

♀

blue-grey head and bill

brownish pink cheeks and throat

brown back

♂✿

pink below, whiter on belly

dark wings

yellowish feather edges

dark tail with white sides

VOICE *Soft* chup, *frequent* pink! *loud* hweet; *song* chip-chip, chirichiri cheep-tcheweeoo.
NESTING *Nest neat cup of grass, leaves, and moss, in tree; 4–5 eggs; 1 brood; Apr–May.*
FEEDING *Eats insects, mostly caterpillars, in summer; otherwise seeds, shoots, and berries.*
SIMILAR SPECIES *Brambling, Bullfinch, female House Sparrow.*

Brambling

Fringilla montifringilla

Very like the Chaffinch, but with a white rump and a darker back, the Brambling is generally less common and very scarce in Europe in summer. In winter, Bramblings may gather in huge feeding flocks, especially in central Europe, but numbers fluctuate from year to year with the supply of beech-mast and other tree seeds.

FEEDS IN *farmland and parks in winter, especially areas with beech, birch, and spruce; breeds in northern forests.*

white rump

big orange-buff upper wingbar ♂✿

"scaly" head

pale throat

bright yellow-orange breast and shoulder

dark back

white belly

dark spots on flanks ♂❄

black head and back ♂✿

duller ♀❄

VOICE *Call hard* chek, *distinctive nasal* tsweek; *song repeated nasal, buzzing* dzeeee.
NESTING *Cup of lichen, bark, and stems, in tree or bush; 5–7 eggs; 1 brood; May–Jun.*
FEEDING *Eats insects in summer, seeds at other times; takes beech-mast from ground.*
SIMILAR SPECIES *Chaffinch, female House Sparrow, Bullfinch (in flight).*

Bullfinch

Pyrrhula pyrrhula

Heavily-built, rather sluggish, and often hard to see as it feeds quietly in dense cover, the Bullfinch is unmistakable when it emerges into the open. The male is a striking sight, with his bold red, grey, and black plumage and bright white rump. Generally shy, its caution may be warranted, because it is often treated as a pest due to its taste for soft buds of fruit trees. It is seriously declining in some regions.

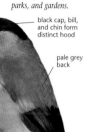

RAIDS FLOWERING *fruit trees in woodland, farmland with hedges, thickets, orchards, parks, and gardens.*

plumage like female

no dark cap

dull brownish back

beige-grey below

grey-white band on dark wing

red-pink below

thick, stubby bill

black cap, bill, and chin form distinct hood

pale grey back

white under tail

black tail

VOICE Call low, clear whistles, peuuw or phiu; song infrequent, warble mixed with calls.
NESTING Cup of twigs, lined with moss and grass, in dense bush or tree; 4–5 eggs, 2 broods, Apr–Jun.
FEEDING Eats soft buds, seeds, berries, and shoots from bushes, shrubs, and fruit trees.
SIMILAR SPECIES Chaffinch, Brambling.

Hawfinch

Coccothraustes coccothraustes

The immensely powerful bill of the Hawfinch is adapted for cracking the toughest seeds, such as cherry stones and olive pits. It usually feeds in the treetops, where it can be elusive and difficult to see well, although its bulky sihouette is distinctive. In winter, it feeds on tree seeds on the ground, where it is more visible, although it flies up if disturbed.

FEEDS AND *breeds in deciduous woodland, orchards, olive groves, and large gardens.*

broad, diagonal, buff and white wingbars

scaly back

barred beneath

very deep, powerful bill

greyer wingbar

tawny cap on big head

grey nape

dark brown back

blue-black wings

broad white tip to short tail

VOICE Call short, sharp, metallic tik or tzik, thin tzree, tikitik; weak scratchy song.
NESTING Nest of twigs, roots, and moss, in old tree; 4–5 eggs; 1 brood; Apr–May.
FEEDING Takes large tree seeds and berries from trees; picks seeds from ground in winter.
SIMILAR SPECIES Chaffinch, Crossbill, Bullfinch.

Common Rosefinch

Carpodacus erythrinus

Although several species of rosefinch occur in Asia, the Scarlet Rosefinch is the only species that breeds in Europe. Nondescript in most plumages, it has a short, thick bill and bold eyes. A breeding male has a bright red head, chest, and rump, but few occur in western Europe, where juveniles are usually seen.

BREEDS IN *deciduous woodland and bushy places, often in wetland areas near lakes and rivers.*

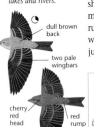

dull brown back

two pale wingbars

cherry red head

red rump

♂☼

pale streaks below

fine streaks on crown and cheeks

♀

hint of narrow wingbars

brown back, wings, and tail

short, rounded bill

white underside

♂☼

VOICE *Call short, hoarse, ascending whistle, vuee or tsoee; soft whistling song.*
NESTING *Small, neat nest of grass, built low in bush; 4–5 eggs; 1–2 broods; May–Jul.*
FEEDING *Eats seeds, buds, shoots, and some insects, from bushes or on the ground.*
SIMILAR SPECIES *Bullfinch, Chaffinch, Crossbill, female or juvenile House Sparrow.*

Pine Grosbeak

Pinicola enucleator

This very large finch combines the bull neck, uncrossed bill, and portly body of a Bullfinch with the plumage pattern of a Crossbill. Males are bright red and grey, females bronze-green or yellow, and grey; both have double white wingbars on black wings. Shy when breeding, this forest bird is tame when it feeds on berries in gardens and streets in winter.

BREEDS IN *coniferous and mixed forests, especially dark, dense, mossy ones with spruce and undergrowth of bilberry.*

♂

yellowish

♀

long tail

thick, round, uncrossed beak

cherry-red and grey plumage

distinctive double white wingbars

black wings

black forked tail

♂

VOICE *Whistling or piping calls, yodelling song.*
NESTING *Untidy, loose cup of twigs low down on branch close to trunk of pine, spruce, birch or juniper; 3–4 eggs; 1 brood; late May–Jul.*
FEEDING *Buds, shoots, seeds; rowan, juniper and other berries; insects during breeding.*
SIMILAR SPECIES *Bullfinch, Parrot Crossbill, Crossbill.*

Crossbill

Loxia curvirostra

This large, powerful finch is specialized for eating the seeds of spruces, pines, and other conifers, using its hooked, crossed bill to prise the cone scales apart so it can extract the seeds with its tongue. It feeds acrobatically and often noisily in the treetops, but has to drink frequently to moisten its diet of dry seeds.

LIVES IN *extensive woods of spruce, larch, and pine, with easy access to water.*

hooked bill with crossed mandibles

dark wings

orange-red to strawberry-red plumage

♂

brightest red on rump

brownish wings

brown wings

♀

green body

dark tail

pale, streaked

VOICE *Loud, abrupt calls, jup-jup-jup, quiet conversational notes while feeding; song mixes buzzy notes, calls, warbles, and trills.*
NESTING *Small nest of twigs and moss high in conifer; 3–4 eggs; 1 brood; Jan–Mar.*
FEEDING *Eats seeds of conifers such as spruce and pine; also berries, buds, insects.*
SIMILAR SPECIES *Hawfinch.*

Parrot Crossbill

Loxia pytyopsittacus

A stockier, more bull-necked, bigger-billed version of the very similar Crossbill, the Parrot Crossbill is restricted to northern and eastern Europe, from where it occasionally moves in large numbers to the south of its breeding range. The bill is almost as deep as it is long; its deep lower mandible bulges in the centre, like that of a parrot.

NESTS *and feeds sparsely in conifer forests, especially of Scots pine, less often Norway spruce and occasionally larch.*

massive bill

♂

heavy, stocky body

more front-heavy than Crossbill

dark wings

often greyer on head

♀

VOICE *Abrupt, loud tjup tjup tjup calls, usually deeper than Crossbill's.*
NESTING *Cup nest of leaves and moss, lined with grass on conifer twigs, bark, or tree; 3–4 eggs; 1 brood; Feb–Mar or as late as Aug.*
FEEDING *Conifer seeds, mainly pine; some insects in breeding season.*
SIMILAR SPECIES *Crossbill, Hawfinch.*

Little Bunting

Emberiza pusilla

Quiet and unobtrusive, and easy to confuse with a small Reed Bunting, the Little Bunting is a rarity in western Europe. It breeds in the mixed birch and conifer forests of the vast taiga zone, from Finland to eastern Siberia, and winters in southern Asia. Only a few stray west to appear on northern coasts in autumn.

BREEDS IN *open spaces in the forests of the far north; migrants seen on coasts and islands, often in damp places.*

black sides to rufous crown

greyish forewing

rufous face, edged black at rear

greyish shoulder

♂ ❄

rufous face

♀

buff, brown and black streaks

white edge to tail

♂ ☼

white with dark streaks below

VOICE *Call short, sharp, ticking zik; song brief warble with clicks, rasps, and whistles.*
NESTING *Nest of grass and moss, on ground under bush; 4–5 eggs; 1 brood; May–Jun.*
FEEDING *Eats insects in summer; picks seeds from ground in autumn.*
SIMILAR SPECIES *Reed Bunting, Lapland Bunting.*

Lapland Bunting

Calcarius lapponicus

Rarely seen in summer, when it breeds in remote, wild places, the Lapland Bunting appears on more southerly coasts in autumn and winter. It keeps a low profile, creeping among the grasses on dunes, salt marshes, and golf courses, and usually stays unnoticed until flushed from underfoot.

FEEDS MAINLY *on salt marshes and short, wet grassland near coasts in winter. Breeds on northern tundra.*

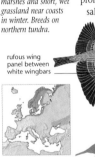

mainly rufous head

dark ear coverts

rufous wing panel between white wingbars

streaked back

dark tail with white sides

black cap, face, and breast

patchy head pattern

♂ ❄

bright rusty nape

♂ ☼

VOICE *Calls staccato rattle and clear whistle, t-r-r-r-r-ik teu; song like Skylark, but shorter.*
NESTING *Nest of moss and grass in tussock or among rocks; 5–6 eggs; 1 brood; May–Jun.*
FEEDING *Gathers seeds on the ground; eats insects in summer.*
SIMILAR SPECIES *Reed Bunting, Snow Bunting.*

Reed Bunting

Emberiza schoeniclus

Easy to find and identify in summer, male Reed Buntings
sing monotonously from low perches among reeds and
other wetland vegetation. In winter, when
the males are far less striking, they are
harder to recognize – especially when
feeding on farmland or even in gardens.

LIVES IN *wet places
with reeds, sedge,
rushes; also willow
thickets and heaths;
gardens in winter.*

hint of pale
collar

♀

cream and black
streaks on back

long,
notched tail

black head

white collar
and moustache

♂☀

rufous
forewing

bold
white
tail sides

duller
head
pattern

♂❄

brown back
with black
streaks

♂☀

streaked,
whitish
underside

pale red-
brown legs

black tail with
broad white sides

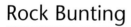

VOICE *Call loud high tseeu, and high, thin,
pure sweee, zi zi; song short, jangly phrase,
srip srip srip sea-sea-sea stitip-itip-itipip.*
NESTING *Bulky nest of grass and sedge, on
ground in cover; 4–5 eggs; 2 broods; Apr–Jun.*
FEEDING *Eats seeds, plus insects in summer.*
SIMILAR SPECIES *Female Chaffinch, female
Lapland Bunting, House Sparrow.*

Rock Bunting

Emberiza cia

Typical of stony ground, where
it often hides in thick bushes
on boulder-strewn slopes, this
slim bunting can be frustratingly
difficult to see. It is more
conspicuous in winter,
when it forages in flocks,
though then the males
are less colourful in their
non-breeding plumage.

pale grey head
with black stripes

rust-brown
streaks

FEEDS IN *grassy places
in rocky areas with dry
bushy slopes, crags,
and boulders, and
often along
road cuttings.*

pale grey
chest

black
tail with
white
edges

bright
rufous-buff
below

♂

rusty
rump

less grey on
chest

♂☀

duller stripes

♀

buffish grey

♂❄

VOICE *Call thin, short, monotonous sip; song
high, clear, erratic warbling.*
NESTING *Nest of grass, roots, and bark, on
ground in cover; 4–6 eggs; 2 broods; Apr–Jun.*
FEEDING *Feeds on insects in summer, takes
seeds from or near ground at other times.*
SIMILAR SPECIES *Cirl Bunting, Ortolan
Bunting.*

Ortolan Bunting

Emberiza hortulana

LIVES IN *a variety of terrain, from warm, bushy, stony slopes to semi-alpine pasture.*

A slim, pale bunting with a sharp, pink bill and an obvious pale eye-ring, the Ortolan Bunting usually feeds in open grassy places such as pastures and dunes. Breeding males have partly green and yellow plumage, and draw attention by singing from bushes and trees on warm, open slopes.

green head

pale eye-ring

yellow moustache and throat

streaked brown above

buff plumage

greyer than juvenile

black tail with white sides

♂ ✿

pale green chest

VOICE *Call thick, metallic* dl-ip; *song fluty, ringing* sia sia sia si sia sru sru sru sru.
NESTING *Hair-lined grass nest, on or near ground; 4–6 eggs; 2–3 broods; Apr–Jul.*
FEEDING *Takes seeds from ground, often from grassy clearings; eats insects in summer.*
SIMILAR SPECIES *Yellowhammer, female Reed Bunting.*

♂ ✿

olive-buff rump

Yellowhammer 🔊

Emberiza citrinella

The repetitive song of the male of this species is a typical sound of warm summer days on farmland and bushy heaths. During colder months, Yellow-hammers form small groups, often with other buntings, to roam the fields in search of seeds.

yellow head with dusky stripes

GATHERS TO *eat seeds in winter; breeds on pastures, heaths, and farmland with hedges.*

less yellow

♀

more streaks

♂ ✿

rufous, buff, and black

black streaks on rufous back

♂ ✿

yellow below with fine dark streaks

black tail with white sides

rufous rump

♂ ✿

VOICE *Call sharp* tsik; *song thin trill, with longer notes at end,* ti-ti-ti-ti-ti-ti-ti-teee-tyew.
NESTING *Nest of grass or straw in bank or below bush; 3–5 eggs; 2–3 broods; Apr–Jul.*
FEEDING *Takes seeds from ground, and also insects in summer.*
SIMILAR SPECIES *Cirl Bunting, female Reed Bunting, Ortolan Bunting.*

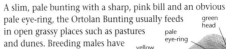

Cirl Bunting

Emberiza cirlus

Throughout much of its range in western and southern Europe, the Cirl Bunting is a common bird of open, bushy slopes, and farmland with plenty of trees, hedges, and thickets. It resembles a Yellowhammer, but is more compact and less yellow. The males have the same habit of singing from bush tops, but they also use inconspicuous perches in trees. Cirl Buntings rely on old grassland with plenty of grasshoppers, so they have suffered serious declines in countries such as the UK, where much of the ancient grassland has been destroyed by intensive farming methods.

LIVES ON *warm, bushy, often stony slopes, around the edges of tall, leafy orchards, and in olive groves. Feeds on weedy or grassy fields in winter, and may visit gardens.*

streaked, dark greenish cap

bright yellow above and below eye

black eye-stripe

black chin

♂☼
olive-buff rump

olive-brown rump
♀

rusty patch on side of breast

pale yellow underside

♂☼

black tail with white sides

striped crown

strongly striped head

♀

fine streaks below

♂❅

dark streaks

TIP

A breeding male is distinguished from a Yellowhammer by its head pattern. Other plumages are more confusing, but the head stripes and olive rump help.

VOICE *Call very simple, short, high, thin sip; song fast, rattling trill on one note, or slower, lighter, more bubbling variant, t-r-r-r-r-r-r-r-r-r-r-r-r or ti-ti-ti-ti-ti-ti-ti-ti-ti-ti-ti-ti-ti-ti.*
NESTING *Rough nest of grass and stalks, built low in shrub or hedge; 3–4 eggs; 2 broods; Apr–Jul.*
FEEDING *Needs to eat grasshoppers and similar insects in summer; otherwise takes seeds from ground.*
SIMILAR SPECIES *Yellowhammer, female Reed Bunting.*

Snow Bunting

Plectrophenax nivalis

The stark black and white of the breeding male Snow Bunting is well suited to its snowy northern breeding habitat, but over much of Europe it is seen only in its subdued winter plumage, when the sexes look very alike. Capable of thriving in the harshest climates, Snow Buntings often spend the winter on barren mountainsides, where they are regularly seen around ski resorts. Elsewhere they gather in flocks on sheltered beaches and gravelly marshes, where they feed on sandhoppers. They have a distinctive low-slung look on the ground, owing to their short legs, and the feeding flocks move forward by repeated leap-frogging flights as the birds at the back fly over those in front.

FEEDS ON *shingle banks and muddy coastal marshes in winter, as well as on exposed mountain slopes. Breeds on northern tundra and mountains.*

small white wing patch

forked black tail with white sides

♂ ❄

long black and white wings

sandy brown back

reddish or orange-brown cap

reddish or orange-brown cheeks

black tail with white sides

♂ ❄

white wing panel

white underside

red-brown on sides of breast

white head

dark grey head and back

stocky body

◑

black back and wingtips

♂ ☀

white below

brown and black streaks

brown cap

♀ ❄

VOICE *Call loud, deep, clear pyiew or tsioo, frequent lighter, trilling, rippling tiri-lil-il-il-il-ip; song short, clear, ringing, fluty phrase, turee-turee-turee-turitui.*
NESTING *Nest of moss, lichen, and grass stems in cavity among rocks; 4–6 eggs; 1–2 broods; May–Jul.*
FEEDING *Takes insects in summer, and mainly seeds and marine invertebrates picked from strandline in winter.*
SIMILAR SPECIES *Reed Bunting, Lapland Bunting.*

Corn Bunting

Miliaria calandra

A big, pale bunting of wide open spaces, the Corn Bunting lives up to its name by favouring farmland with large cereal fields, as well as extensive grasslands. It shares this habitat with the Skylark, but has a quite different song: a unique, jangling rattle given by the male from a prominent exposed perch or in a display flight, with dangling legs. It feeds on insects and seeds on the ground, and the widespread use of weedkillers and insecticides on modern farmland has made it virtually extinct in many intensively farmed regions. Where it is still common, it can often be seen flying overhead in small groups towards dusk, heading for its communal roosts.

PERCHES IN *hedges when disturbed while feeding on meadows, rough grassland, arable fields, and coastal scrub.*

dark stripes on crown

dark lower cheeks

row of dark spots on wing coverts

plain wings

streaked, pale brown back

stocky shape

dark streaks often merge into central smudge on chest

heavy, pale yellowish bill

plain brown tail, with no white at sides

upright posture when singing

pale, streaked breast

TIP

Although it looks like a Skylark and lives in the same places, the Corn Bunting tends to hop rather than walk, and has no white on its tail.

VOICE *Call short, abrupt, clicking* plip *or* quit*; song jangling, dry, fast, rattled phrase resembling rattling keys or broken glass.*
NESTING *Nest of grass and roots, lined with finer material, on ground; 3–5 eggs; 1–2 broods; Apr–Jun.*
FEEDING *Forages on ground, picking up insects and seeds in summer and only seeds in winter.*
SIMILAR SPECIES *Female Reed Bunting, female Yellowhammer, Skylark.*

Wallcreeper

Tichodroma muraria

Thanks to its mainly grey and black plumage, this bird is often hard to see as it creeps and probes for prey among the rocks of its mountain habitat. But it can be quite tame, allowing close views of its stunningly coloured crimson-red wing plumage, as it flits between the rocks like an oversized butterfly.

SEARCHES FOR *food on rocks and cliff faces, in gorges and quarries, typically up near the snow line in summer and lower in winter.*

large white spots on wings

short tail

♀ ☼

small black bib (lost in winter)

♂ ☼

upperwings mainly red

long, curved bill

♂ ☼

black throat (white in winter)

mid-grey body

red patches on black wings

VOICE *Long, rising and falling series of thin, whistled notes.*
NESTING *Untidy nest in cliff hole or deep in crevice between tumbled rocks; 4 eggs; 1 brood; May–Jul.*
FEEDING *Searches rock ledges and, in winter, buildings for insects and spiders.*
SIMILAR SPECIES *None.*

Meadow Pipit

Anthus pratensis

The tinkling song of the Meadow Pipit is one of the evocative sounds of summer in the open hills. Often seen from a distance as it rises in a song flight, or flutters up jerkily with squeaky calls, the bird has a hesitant, nervous manner. A close look is needed to appreciate the subtle distinctions of its plumage.

BREEDS ON *grassland, heaths, dunes, and moors, from coasts to uplands; on farmland and marshes near coasts in winter.*

slim dark bill

pale stripe

soft blackish streaks on brown back

dark tail with white sides

streaked brown back

olive-buff or cream below

evenly streaked flanks and chest

very long hind claw

VOICE *Call sharp, weak* pseeep, *quiet* pip, *in winter flock; song long series of notes and trills in parachuting song flight.*
NESTING *Nest a cup of grass on ground; 4–5 eggs, 2 broods; May–Jul.*
FEEDING *Eats insects and some seeds.*
SIMILAR SPECIES *Tree Pipit, Rock Pipit, Red-throated Pipit, Skylark.*

TIP
Song-flight very like that of Tree Pipit, but it usually begins and ends it on ground, while Tree Pipit flies from perch to perch.

Red-throated Pipit

Anthus cervinus

A visitor to central and eastern Europe from the far north, the Red-throated Pipit has a distinctive call note that instantly marks it out from other, similar-looking streaky birds. It is usually found in damp, grassy places in spring, stopping off on its way south for the winter.

FEEDS ON *open ground, swampy areas, coastal dunes and islands in spring; breeds on northern tundra.*

yellow bill base

pinkish to reddish face and throat

dark brown and cream stripes

short-tailed, stocky shape

even, broad black stripes on white underparts

pale stripe over eye

1ST

duller face

streaked rump

VOICE *Call high, slightly explosive, fading psseeee, hard chup; song rhythmic repetition of sharp ringing notes and buzzy trills.*
NESTING *Grassy cup in vegetation on ground; 4–5 eggs; 1 brood; May–Jun.*
FEEDING *Takes insects and other small invertebrates from ground, plus some seeds.*
SIMILAR SPECIES *Meadow Pipit, Tree Pipit.*

Tree Pipit 🔊

Anthus trivialis

Very like a Meadow Pipit, but with a more confident air, the Tree Pipit is a bird of woodland edges rather than open grasslands. It has a superb song – rich and musical with Canary-like trills – delivered in a song flight that makes summer males relatively easy to identify. Autumn migrants are more confusing, although the call notes help.

BREEDS IN *open woods, woodland glades, edges of plantations, bushy heaths, and moors with scattered trees. Migrants are seen on coasts.*

blackish tail with white sides

strong pale stripe over eye

browner in summer

thin, dark streaks

neat black stripes on pale back

dark spots across wings

buff-yellow below

often pumps tail

pale yellowish, unstreaked flanks

VOICE *Call low teeess, sharp tzit; song loud series of sweet notes and trills, ending in slow sweee-sweee-sweee, from perch or song flight.*
NESTING *Grassy cup in thick grass; 4–6 eggs; 1–2 broods; Apr–Jul.*
FEEDING *Takes small insects from ground.*
SIMILAR SPECIES *Meadow Pipit, Rock Pipit, Skylark.*

Rock Pipit 🔊

Anthus petrosus

For much of the year, the habitat of the Rock Pipit helps to betrays its identity, for it is truly a bird of rocky coasts and islands. Its song-flight and song are similar to those of the Meadow Pipit, but its loud, single call note is distinctive.

BREEDS ON *rocky coasts; on migration and in winter, some visit salt marshes and soft shores, fewer inland by water.*

weak stripe over eye

grey-edged, dark tail

dark back

diffuse streaks on dusky olive back

dull below

blurry dark streaks

dark legs

dull white to yellowish underside

dark legs

VOICE Call slurred *feest* or *pseeep*; song like Meadow's but stronger, in similar song-flight.
NESTING Hair-lined nest on ground, in rock cavity; 4–5 eggs; 1–2 broods; Apr–Jul.
FEEDING Forages mainly on clifftops in summer, on stony/seaweedy shores in winter, for insects, sandhoppers, small molluscs.
SIMILAR SPECIES Water Pipit, Meadow Pipit.

TIP
A Rock Pipit can be distinguished from a Meadow Pipit by its darker, duller, greyer plumage, dark legs, and longer, dark bill.

Water Pipit

Anthus spinoletta

In winter, Water Pipits retreat from their high mountain breeding grounds, mainly to inland marshes and mudflats. They look like migrant Scandinavian Rock Pipits in spring plumage, though Water Pipits are paler, with bolder wingbars.

WINTERS ON *marshes and lagoons with muddy edges; breeds on mountain pastures with scattered rocks.*

bold white stripe over eye

greyish head

warm brown back

pink flush below

white stripe on brown head

dark brown

dark tail with white edges

bold whitish wingbars

white below

dark brown to reddish brown legs

two whitish wingbars

VOICE Call quite strong, thin *fist*; song strong series of trills in high song-flight.
NESTING Grass-lined cup on ground among grass; 4–5 eggs; 2 broods; May–Jul.
FEEDING Takes small insects and spiders, and other invertebrates, from ground.
SIMILAR SPECIES Rock Pipit, Skylark, Wheatear.

TIP
A Water Pipit is easy to confuse with a Rock Pipit, but if the bird is seen away from the coast it is less likely to be a Rock Pipit.

Tawny Pipit

Anthus campestris

The Tawny Pipit is a large, stout-bodied, long-legged, and long-tailed bird with a wagtail-like look. A scarce but annual visitor to the UK, it is widespread in mainland Europe. Breeding birds prefer dry, stony, or sandy areas such as warm Mediterranean slopes with scattered bushes and aromatic shrubs, or sand dunes by the sea. The male's spring song is distinctive, but the singer can be tricky to locate because he usually rises high in a clear sky, dwindling to a mere dot in the blue.

BREEDS ON *bushy, stony slopes, on dry farmland with stony soil, grassland, and dunes; rare migrants can be seen near northern coasts.*

- dark stripe between bill and eye
- long, pale line over eye
- spike-like, pale-based bill
- faint markings on breast
- pale cream-buff underparts
- slender, pinkish or yellowish legs
- sparsely streaked pale back
- pale sandy-brown or grey-brown back
- dark spots on wing coverts
- dark tail with white sides
- plain sandy back
- pale below
- **WORN**
- dark stripe between eye and bill
- scaled and streaked back
- spots form band on breast

TIP

At a distance, the Tawny Pipit looks almost uniform pale buff, with a row of dark spots on the wing coverts, and dark feather centres on the secondaries and primaries.

TIP

Pipits are often difficult to identify by plumage features alone, but the Tawny Pipit typically darts about as it feeds, with its tail moving up and down like a wagtail's.

VOICE *Sparrow-like* schilp, *more grating, emphatic* tsee-i, *short* chup; *song loud repetition of ringing, low-high double note,* tchu-vee tchu-vee, *given in high, undulating flight.*
NESTING *Grass-lined cup made in short vegetation on the ground; 4–5 eggs; 1–2 broods; Apr–Jun.*
FEEDING *Eats mainly small insects of various kinds, which it catches on the ground.*
SIMILAR SPECIES *Water Pipit, juvenile Yellow Wagtail.*

Yellow Wagtail

Motacilla flava

A male Yellow Wagtail in summer is elegant, colourful, and distinctive, but autumn birds, particularly juveniles, are easy to confuse with other species. Unlike other wagtails, it is never seen in Europe in winter, since it migrates to Africa to feed among the grazing herds on the tropical grasslands.

SNATCHES PREY *from beneath feet of farm animals on wet fields; often near water.*

pale line

white lines

buff

pale line

grey-green

♀♣

bright yellow stripe

green crown; some races have bluish, grey, or black crown

green back

two white wingbars

♂♣

bright yellow below

♂♣

white-sided black tail

VOICE Call full, flat or rising tsli, or tsweep; song repetiton of brief chirping phrases.
NESTING Grassy cup in vegetation on ground; 5–6 eggs; 2 broods; May–Jul.
FEEDING Takes insects from ground; skips and leaps after flies in short flycatching sallies.
SIMILAR SPECIES Grey Wagtail, juvenile similar to Tawny Pipit, juvenile Pied Wagtail.

Grey Wagtail

Motacilla cinerea

The extensive yellow in the Grey Wagtail's plumage can lead to confusion with the Yellow Wagtail, but its back is grey instead of green, and the summer male's black bib is distinctive. In winter, it often occurs near puddles, even in cities, when the Yellow Wagtail is far away in Africa.

BREEDS ALONG *clean, often tree-lined rivers or open upland streams; widespread near water in winter, including briefly in urban areas.*

white stripe over eye

grey above

♂☼

white edges

long black tail

♂☼

yellow-green rump

brightest yellow under tail

black bib

broad white bar on dark wings

yellow underparts

pale pinkish legs

grey above

white or dusky throat

buffish below

paler

♀☼

VOICE Sharp, explosive tchik, zi, or zi-zi; song penetrating, metallic trills and warbles.
NESTING Grassy cup in hole in bank, or under bridge; 4–6 eggs; 2 broods; Apr–Aug.
FEEDING Catches flies and other small insects on ground or in air.
SIMILAR SPECIES Yellow Wagtail, Pied Wagtail.

Pied/White Wagtail

Motacilla alba

Common throughout Europe, this boldly patterned wagtail occurs in two forms. The darker Pied Wagtail of Britain and Ireland has a black back, dark flanks, and blackish wings, and the White Wagtail of mainland Europe (which also occurs as a passage migrant in spring and autumn in the British Isles) has a pale grey back and rump, and pale flanks. Both occur in a wide variety of habitats, from farmland to urban areas. They chase insects with agile leaps and runs, constantly nodding their heads and bobbing their long tails.

ROOSTS INCLUDE *trees in town centres; the birds feed in car parks, roadsides, and rooftops; also in farmyards, fields, often by water.*

black cap, chin, and throat; white chin and throat in winter

whitish face

blackish rump

♂☼

white streaks on wings

black breast

black back

sooty flanks

white feather edges

greyer back

white below

♀ PIED

greyer above

buffish below

white belly

♂☼ PIED
M.a.yarrellii

long black tail with white edges

♂ WHITE WAGTAIL
M.a.alba

pale grey back and rump

black tail, same as Pied form

TIP

Outside the breeding season Pied and White Wagtails form communal roosts, often with hundreds of birds. These roosts may occur in natural sites such as small trees or reedbeds, but in some areas wagtail roosts can be found on buildings, or even inside large commercial glasshouses, where the birds perch in long lines on the steel cross-beams below the roof.

VOICE *Call loud, musical chirp, chuwee, chrruwee, grading into harder tissik or chiswik; song mixture of these calls and trills.*
NESTING *Grassy cup in cavity in bank, wall, cliff, or woodpile, in outbuilding or under bridge; 5–6 eggs; 2–3 broods; Apr–Aug.*
FEEDING *Feeds very actively on ground, roofs, or waterside mud or rocks, walking, running, leaping up or sideways, or flying in pursuit of flies; also takes other insects, molluscs, and some seeds.*
SIMILAR SPECIES *Grey Wagtail, juvenile Yellow Wagtail.*

Short-toed Lark

Calandrella brachydactyla

A small, pale lark of dry cultivated areas and grassland in southern Europe, the Short-toed Lark has the palest, least-marked underparts of any of the regular European larks. On the ground, its long wings and tail give it a long, slim, tapered shape, but it is well camouflaged and best located by its calls or warbling song.

BREEDS IN *dry open places, from arable fields and grassland to semi-desert; migrants often seen near coasts.*

dark tail with pale centre

whitish sides

dark panel between two pale wingbars

dark cap

plain cheeks

dark band across wing coverts

pale stripe over eye

dark patch

few streaks at most

pale, plain underparts

VOICE *Call chirrupy, sparrow-like chrrit or trilp; song short, spitting, unmusical bursts or longer, fast warbling mixed with calls.*
NESTING *Shallow nest on ground in grass; 3–5 eggs; 2 broods; May–Jul.*
FEEDING *Searches on the ground for seeds and insects.*
SIMILAR SPECIES *Skylark, Corn Bunting.*

Woodlark

Lullula arborea

One of the smallest and prettiest of the larks, the Woodlark is a bird of open woodland and sandy heaths. It has a distinct undulating flight with a curiously floppy wing action, and in spring, the males perform their beautiful song from trees or in a high, circling song-flight.

BREEDS IN *open woods, on bushy heaths, and in felled woodland, such as large conifer plantations with bare, sandy ground and short grass.*

tan and black striped cap

white-black-white patch on broad wings

very short tail, white at corners

very short crest

black and white wing patch

whitish stripe reaches back of neck

dark-edged rufous cheek

dark streaks

whitish belly

VOICE *Call three-syllable t'loo-i; song rich, slow tlootlootloo, twee twee twee, dyoo dyoo dyoo, dlui dlui dlui in high song-flight.*
NESTING *Hair- and grass-lined nest on ground by bush; 3–4 eggs; 2 broods; Apr–Jun.*
FEEDING *Picks insects and small seeds from the ground, often on bare, sandy patches.*
SIMILAR SPECIES *Skylark, Tree Pipit.*

TIP
Broad, rounded wings and a very short tail give it a unique appearance in flight; lacks white rear edge to wings found in Skylark.

Thekla Lark

Galerida theklae

Typical of rough, open areas of stony grassland or clearings in open woodland, the Thekla Lark has cryptically coloured plumage that often closely matches the local rocks and soil. It is very like the Crested Lark, but has a blunter, more fan-shaped crest, sharper streaks on its chest, and a straighter bill. It is less common in cereal fields, preferring bushier places.

LIVES ON *rocky, grassy hillsides and mountain slopes, both bare and bushy, and in dry, cultivated areas with trees.*

crest flat

fan-shaped crest

straight bill

sharp, dark streaks on whitish breast

closely streaked, grey-brown back

pale grey

rufous

white belly

dark tail with pinkish centre and rusty sides

VOICE *Call full-throated, musical tu-tewi, tew-tewi-too; song liquid warble in flight.*
NESTING *Shallow hollow on ground, in grass or similar; 3–5 eggs; 2 broods; Apr–Jun.*
FEEDING *Picks shoots, seeds, and insects from ground.*
SIMILAR SPECIES *Crested Lark, Skylark, Woodlark.*

Crested Lark

Galerida cristata

Far more widespread and common than the very similar Thekla Lark, the Crested Lark has a sharper crest and a more curved bill. It is usually seen on farmed land or at roadsides, flying up to reveal its broad wings and short tail. Unlike the Thekla Lark, it seldom perches on bushes.

crest sharply pointed when raised

curved bill

BREEDS IN *cultivated areas or semi-natural vegetation with few trees, sometimes on waste ground.*

blurred streaks

pale, dull rump and inner tail

rusty patch on underwing

blackish tail with grey centre

whitish underparts

orange sides to tail

crest flat

streaked, pale brown back

VOICE *Rich, fluty, liquid call, tree-loo-ee or vee-vee-teu; song similar with melancholy, fluty notes, from perch or high, circling flight.*
NESTING *Small hollow in grass lined with finer stems; 3–6 eggs; 2–3 broods; Apr–Jun.*
FEEDING *Forages on ground, often on bare patches, for insects, seeds, and shoots.*
SIMILAR SPECIES *Thekla Lark, Skylark.*

Shore Lark

Eremophila alpestris

A long, sleek lark with a unique head pattern that is boldest in summer, the Shore Lark breeds in the mountains of Scandinavia and southeast Europe. In winter, it appears on beaches and marshy spots around the Baltic and North Seas, where it often feeds on small animals alongside Snow Buntings.

FEEDS ON *sandy beaches near the high-tide mark in winter, and nearby marshes and fields. Breeds on mountains.*

duller yellow and black on face than summer

broad black upper chest-band

mid-brown upperparts

variable brown lower chest-band

white underparts

plain wings

dark tail with pale centre

tiny "horns"

primrose-yellow and black face

VOICE *Call pipit-like, thin tseeeep or louder seep-seep; song prolonged, quiet warbling from perch or in flight.*
NESTING *Hair-lined grass cup, on ground; 4 eggs; 1–2 broods; May–Jul.*
FEEDING *Creeps over ground, taking seeds, insects, crustaceans, and tiny molluscs.*
SIMILAR SPECIES *Skylark, Rock Pipit.*

Calandra Lark

Melanocorypha calandra

A big, thick-billed lark often found in open steppes and huge cornfields, this lark has white trailing edges to its wings and a large black neck patch that becomes obvious when the bird raises its head. Large non-breeding flocks may gather on salty, marshy scrubland.

LIVES IN *open, dry, stony grassland or farmland; also salty areas near sea or inland.*

deep, pale bill with dark ridge

dark cheeks, pale below

black neck patch

boldly marked head

white trailing edge to blackish underwing

closely streaked back

white below

VOICE *Call dry, sizzly or trilling schrreeup; song in high flight like Skylark's, but slower.*
NESTING *Grass cup on ground, in vegetation; 4–7 eggs; 2 broods; Apr–Jun.*
FEEDING *Searches ground for seeds, shoots, and insects.*
SIMILAR SPECIES *Skylark, Short-toed Lark, Corn Bunting.*

Skylark 🔊

Alauda arvensis

The silvery song of the Skylark is a familiar sound over the farmlands and pastures of Europe, although the bird is becoming less common owing to intensive farming. Rising high in the air, it may hang stationary for several minutes as it pours out a stream of liquid warbles and trills. A typical streaky lark on the ground, it has a distinctive appearance in flight, with its angular, straight-edged wings and short, white-edged tail. It flies with erratic bursts of wingbeats alternating with swoops on almost closed wings. In winter, many gather to feed on farmland in large, loose flocks.

SINGS OVER *open fields, especially with cereal crops, moorlands, heaths, and pastures. Feeds on arable land in winter.*

narrow whitish trailing edge to wing

blackish tail with wide white sides

raised crest blunt, streaked

whitish over eye

dark stripes on back

pale-centred cheeks

buff breast

white belly

closely streaked, pale to warm tan-brown above

long hind claw

TIP

During its song-flight the Skylark rises vertically on constantly flickering wings, then hovers, singing all the while, before spiralling or parachuting to the ground with a final steep plunge.

flattened crest

dark under tail

grey underwings

VOICE *Calls chirruping* shrrup, trrup, *higher* seee; *song fast, rich, continuous outpouring from perch or in high, soaring flight, sounding thinner and higher-pitched at distance.*
NESTING *Grassy cup on ground, in crops or grass; 3–5 eggs; 2–3 broods; Apr–Jul.*
FEEDING *Forages on ground in grass or on bare earth, eating seeds, shoots, grain, and insects.*
SIMILAR SPECIES *Crested Lark, Short-toed Lark, Woodlark.*

Waxwing

Bombycilla garrulus

BREEDS IN *northern conifer forests, but flocks move south to feed on berries in rural and urban areas.*

A winter visitor to eastern and northern Europe, the Waxwing appears in flocks when a poor berry crop in its far northern breeding grounds forces it south. Exotic-looking and very tame, it is easily identified by its pinkish plumage and bright wing markings, but in silhouette when flying it resembles the Starling.

yellow tip to black tail

white bars

large crest

♂

pinkish brown body

waxy red spots on wing

yellow stripe and white edges to primary feathers

rusty under tail

blurred lower edge to bib

fewer red spots or white edges

♀

VOICE *Silvery, high, metallic trill on even pitch, trrreee or siirrrr.*
NESTING *Moss-lined twig nest in birch or conifer; 4–6 eggs; 1 brood; May–Jun.*
FEEDING *Eats insects in summer; eats some insects in winter, often caught in flight, but mostly berries such as rowan and hawthorn.*
SIMILAR SPECIES *Starling.*

Dipper

Cinclus cinclus

HUNTS AQUATIC *prey in clean upland streams, moving to lowland rivers and even coasts in hard winters.*

The Dipper is quite unmistakable, thanks to its unique hunting technique. It feeds underwater, often by walking into a fast-flowing stream and foraging along the bottom. Out of the water it has a distinctive springy character, often bobbing and flicking its tail, and flies low and fast along watercourses.

greyer body

deep brown head

blackish back

plump body

stout dark bill

bold white chest

chestnut band; not in N. race

stout black legs

big feet

blackish tail

VOICE *Call sharp dzit or djink; song loud, rich warbling with explosive, grating notes.*
NESTING *Nest of moss and grass in hole or under overhang; 4–6 eggs; 2 broods; Apr–Jul.*
FEEDING *Forages for aquatic insect larvae, small fish, crustaceans, and molluscs by walking into water, swimming and diving.*
SIMILAR SPECIES *Ring Ouzel.*

Red-backed Shrike

Lanius collurio

A small, slim bird with a long tail and a sturdy bill, this Shrike hunts prey by scanning from a perch. Males are striking, with a grey top to the head, a black mask, and chestnut back; females are browner and duller. A casualty of intensive farming, it is now scarcer over much of its range.

HUNTS AND *breeds on farmland and rough grassland with plenty of hedges, thorn bushes, and scrub.*

black mask

grey crown and nape

white throat

dark patch behind eye

duller back

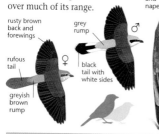

rusty brown back and forewings

grey rump

♂

♀

rufous tail

black tail with white sides

greyish brown rump

pale pink below

♀

slight scaly barring

♂

VOICE *Call harsh hek, hard chek; song low, rambling, with jerky warbling and mimicry.*
NESTING *Untidy nest of grass, feathers, and moss in bush; 5–6 eggs; 1 brood; May–Jun.*
FEEDING *Drops from perch to seize insects and small lizards or rodents on ground.*
SIMILAR SPECIES *Penduline Tit, Nightingale, Linnet.*

Woodchat Shrike

Lanius senator

Strikingly patterned and easy to identify, the Woodchat Shrike often perches prominently on a tree, bush top, or overhead wire as it watches for prey to seize from the ground, or even catch in mid-air. Yet it also skulks quietly in thick cover, where it can be surprisingly inconspicuous.

HUNTS IN *bushy areas, orchards, overgrown gardens, scrubland, and other places with suitable perches.*

dark grey

pale around eye

♀

black tail with white at base

rufous cap

black mask

white rump

♂

grey-brown

crescents

barred grey

☽

white "V" on black back

white below

♂

black tail with white at base

VOICE *Alarm call of short, chattering notes; song quick jumble of squeaks and warbles.*
NESTING *Rough nest of grass and stems in low bush; 5–6 eggs; 1 brood; Apr–Jul.*
FEEDING *Takes big insects from the ground or in air; also small birds, rodents, and lizards.*
SIMILAR SPECIES *Magpie, Red-backed Shrike.*

Lesser Grey Shrike

Lanius minor

Like many other shrikes in its genus, the Lesser Grey Shrike is a striking, neat-looking, handsome bird with mainly black, white, and grey plumage, and a black mask. Pink below, instead of dull white like the Great Grey Shrike, it is the southeastern counterpart of its larger, more northerly relative. Like all shrikes, it specializes in catching prey by pouncing from a perch. It is often obvious as it sits watching for victims, chases them through the air, or drops to the ground in a flurry of white-barred wings. It migrates to Africa in winter, and in parts of Eastern Europe migrants can be seen following long lines of trees beside roads through otherwise open, treeless farmland.

BREEDS AND *hunts in open places with scattered trees, bushes, orchards, and avenues, and at the edges of woodlands, in regions with warm, dry summer climates.*

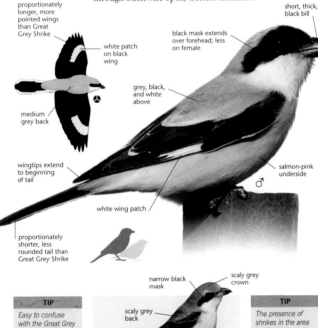

proportionately longer, more pointed wings than Great Grey Shrike

white patch on black wing

medium grey back

wingtips extend to beginning of tail

proportionately shorter, less rounded tail than Great Grey Shrike

short, thick, black bill

black mask extends over forehead; less on female

grey, black, and white above

salmon-pink underside

♂

white wing patch

narrow black mask

scaly grey crown

scaly grey back

TIP

Easy to confuse with the Great Grey Shrike, especially in immature plumage, the Lesser Grey has a stubbier bill and longer wingtips that, when folded, extend to the base of its shorter tail.

TIP

The presence of shrikes in the area is often betrayed by their "larders" – dead insects and other animals impaled on stout thorns, either for butchering or to store them for later.

VOICE *Call short, hard tchek tchek; brief, hard, parrot-like screaming note, tschilip, serves as song, often given in hovering flight.*
NESTING *Untidy nest of grass and twigs, built high in a bush or tree; 5–7 eggs; 1 brood; May–Jun.*
FEEDING *Watches from a high perch such as a branch or overhead wire, and drops onto lizards, large insects such as beetles and crickets, and small birds.*
SIMILAR SPECIES *Great Grey Shrike, juvenile Woodchat Shrike.*

Great Grey Shrike

Lanius excubitor

The largest of the European shrikes, the Great Grey Shrike is a powerful, long-tailed, relatively short-winged bird with a black "bandit" mask. It has a sturdy, sharply hooked bill that it uses to tear apart small animals, from beetles to lizards and small birds. It hunts in the classic shrike manner, watching from a high point and swooping down to seize its victims in its powerful feet. It then carries them back to its perch and may impale them on long thorns or barbed wire for easy dismemberment, a habit that earned it (and its relatives) the old name of "butcher bird". It also chases small birds in flight like a sparrowhawk, using ambush tactics to take them by surprise. During harsh winter weather, birds may form a large proportion of its diet.

PERCHES ON *high vantage points on bushy, heathy, or boggy ground in winter. Breeds in birch woods, wooded bogs, and arid Mediterranean scrub.*

bold white bar on black wings

cold grey above; scaly barring on back and flanks of juvenile

broad black band through eye

long black tail with white sides

black wings with white patch

wingtips do not reach base of tail

dull white underside; faintly barred on juvenile

♂

long tail

slightly duller than male

slight barring on flanks

♀

TIP

Some Great Grey Shrikes that breed in northern Europe migrate west in autumn to spend the winter in the UK. Here they occupy large feeding territories where they are often difficult to find, but can sometimes be seen at great distances as conspicuous white dots on bare bush tops. A closer view reveals the bird's black mask and its long tail, which it often flicks and sways to keep its balance.

VOICE *Call dry trill and various short, hard notes; song composed of short, simple, squeaky notes.*
NESTING *Roughly-built grassy nest in thick bush; 5–7 eggs; 1 brood; May–Jul.*
FEEDING *Swoops onto small rodents, small birds, lizards, and large insects (especially beetles), after watching from vantage point such as a bush top.*
SIMILAR SPECIES *Lesser Grey Shrike, Red-backed Shrike, Magpie.*

Starling

Sturnus vulgaris

A common, active, noisy, sociable, but quarrelsome bird of urban and rural habitats, the Starling is instantly recognizable by its strong-legged walk and waddling run as it pokes and pries in the soil for insect grubs and seeds. Superficially black, its plumage is glossed with iridescent green and purple in summer, and spotted with buff in winter. Outside the breeding season it forms dense flocks that roost in trees, reedbeds, and on buildings, and swirl around the sky in perfectly co-ordinated aerobatic manoeuvres, particularly at dusk. These winter flocks can be so vast that they look like clouds of smoke at a distance, although declines in many areas have made such immense gatherings less common.

GATHERS IN *big winter flocks in forests, city centres, industrial sites, bridges, and piers. Breeds in woods, gardens, and towns.*

short, squarish tail

TIP

Starlings are skilled mimics and can even imitate noises such as telephones. A strange sound coming from an odd place often turns out to be a Starling.

sharp yellow bill

blue-grey bill base; pale pink on female

glossy black body with green and purple sheen

long, strong, red-brown legs

♂

silvery face with dark mask

body feathers tipped buff or whitish

feathers edged bright orange-buff

large spots near tail

dull head last to get adult colours

plain brown body

dark bill

MOULTING

VOICE Loud, slightly grating *cheer*, musical, twangy, whistled *tswee-oo*, variety of clicks, gurgles, squawking notes; song fast mixture of rattles, trills, gurgles, and whistles, often with mimicry of other birds or sounds.
NESTING Loose, bulky nest of grass and stems, in tree hole, cavity in wall or building, or large nest box; 4–7 eggs; 1–2 broods; Apr–Jul.
FEEDING Forages for invertebrates, seeds, and berries on the ground, in small to large flocks; catches flying ants in mid-air.
SIMILAR SPECIES Spotless Starling, Blackbird.

Spotless Starling

Sturnus unicolor

Despite its name, the Spotless Starling does have tiny pale greyish spots in winter, and females may retain spots into spring, but summer birds are intensely dark with a subtle purple sheen. The Iberian equivalent of the Starling, it is common in villages and towns, where noisy groups often line the roofs of ancient buildings. Some still breed in holes in trees and rock faces, but where possible it prefers to nest in roof spaces. In winter, it is joined by Starlings that migrate south over the Pyrenees; mixed feeding flocks of the two species can be quite difficult to separate.

BREEDS IN *towns and villages, often in old buildings with tiled roofs. Feeds on nearby farmland.*

slightly broader wings and bulkier body than Starling

short, squarish tail

flight-feathers dark red-brown against light

yellow bill

bluish bill base; pinkish on female

purple-black body with no spots and dull oily sheen; duller in winter

long, loose, pointed plumes around neck and breast

all-dark wings retained until winter

no orange-buff feather edges like Starling's

♂☼

reddish pink legs

gradually acquires adult colours

plain brown back and wings

☽ MOULTING

TIP

Spotless Starlings often associate with common Starlings in winter flocks, but they can usually be identified by their darker, duller, less spotted plumage, and their browner wings in flight.

VOICE *Calls with Starling-like squawling and quarrelling notes; song has loud, musical, long-drawn py-eeew and parrot-like sounds.*
NESTING *Bulky, untidy nest, usually in roof space or wall cavity; 4–7 eggs, 1 brood; Apr–Jun.*
FEEDING *Forages on the ground for insects, spiders, and other small invertebrates, plus seeds; often feeds around cattle and near human habitations.*
SIMILAR SPECIES *Starling.*

Rock Thrush

Monticola saxatilis

A small, colourful thrush of mountain pastures and rocky fields with stone walls, the Rock Thrush has a habit of perching on boulders, poles, and other prominent places. The male is particularly striking, although his plumage becomes much duller by midsummer.

LIVES ON *high alpine meadows and grassy slopes with boulders and crags; also cliffs and deep gorges. Summer visitor, wintering in Africa.*

pale bars above

dark spots

white on back; dark on female

rusty tail with dark centre

dark brown wings

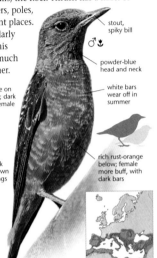

♂ ⚓

stout, spiky bill

powder-blue head and neck

white bars wear off in summer

rich rust-orange below; female more buff, with dark bars

VOICE *Call squeaky* whit *and hard* chak; *song fluty, rich warble, often in song-flight.*
NESTING *Grassy cup in cavity in wall, rocks, or scree; 4–5 eggs; 1 brood; May–Jun.*
FEEDING *Watches for prey from a high perch, dropping onto insects, lizards, and worms; also eats berries and seeds.*
SIMILAR SPECIES *Wheatear, Redstart.*

Blue Rock Thrush

Monticola solitarius

Although it looks dark at a distance and can be hard to pick out from the rocks, the male Blue Rock Thrush is intensely blue at close range, and easy to identify. The brown female is darker than a female Rock Thrush, with a longer bill and tail, the latter lacking any rusty red colour.

BREEDS IN *gorges and mountainous areas with boulders and crags; also around buildings near coasts.*

dark brown

brownish wings

fine brown bars

dark bars

rich, bright blue head

dark tail with no rusty-red

♀

♂

long bill

dark blue body

♂

VOICE *Call deep* chook, *higher squeaky notes; song rich, melancholy warbling.*
NESTING *Grassy cup in hole in wall or cliff, or in rocks; 4–5 eggs; 1–2 broods; May–Jul.*
FEEDING *Picks insects, spiders, worms, lizards, berries, and seeds from ground.*
SIMILAR SPECIES *Blackbird, Spotless Starling, juvenile and female Rock Thrush.*

Redwing

Turdus iliacus

A small, sociable thrush with a bold head pattern and well-defined streaks below, the Redwing is named for its distinctive rusty-red underwings and flanks. It is a winter visitor to much of Europe from the taiga forests of the far north, and typically forages in flocks for berries, often with Fieldfares. In hard winters, it often visits large gardens for food.

FEEDS IN *winter flocks on farmland with hedges, bushy heaths, and gardens. Breeds in northern conifer and birch woods.*

bold pale stripe over eye

dark cap

reddish underwing

dark brown back

pale stripe under dark cheeks

short, square tail

dull rust-red flanks

silvery white below, with dark streaks

TIP
On calm, clear autumn nights, migrant Redwings can often be heard flying overhead, calling to each other to stay in contact.

VOICE *Flight call thin, high seeeh, also chuk, chittuk; song variable repetition of short phrases and chuckling notes.*
NESTING *Cup of grass and twigs, in low bush; 4–6 eggs; 2 broods; Apr–Jul.*
FEEDING *Worms, insects, and seeds taken from ground, berries in winter.*
SIMILAR SPECIES *Song Thrush, Skylark.*

Song Thrush 🔊

Turdus philomelos

Small, pale, and neatly spotted below, the Song Thrush is a familiar bird with a wonderfully vibrant, varied, full-throated song. Well-known for its habit of smashing the shells of snails to extract their soft bodies, it also hauls many earthworms from their burrows. It is declining in many areas, particularly on farmland.

BREEDS AND *feeds in broadleaved woodland, farmland with trees and hedges, parks and gardens with shrubs.*

orange-buff underwings

pale eye-ring

plain olive-brown upperparts

plain wings

"V"-shaped brown spots

dark-spotted white belly

dark-spotted yellowish buff flanks

pale pinkish legs and feet

VOICE *Short, high stip; song exuberant repeated phrases of musical and harsh notes.*
NESTING *Grassy cup lined with mud in bush or tree; 3–5 eggs; 2–3 broods; Mar–Jul.*
FEEDING *Takes earthworms, snails, slugs, insects, berries, and fruit, mainly from ground.*
SIMILAR SPECIES *Mistle Thrush, Redwing, female Blackbird.*

Ring Ouzel

Turdus torquatus

Typical of wild, open country, and declining where such places are invaded by weekend visitors, the Ring Ouzel resembles a slimmer, more upright Blackbird. It is often seen with its head up, tail cocked, and wings drooped, but it is a wary, elusive bird, quick to fly out of sight when disturbed.

BREEDS MAINLY *on high ground, on open moors with rocks, gullies, and eroded peat bogs. On coasts during migration.*

dull breast band

duller

white breast band

♀

brown-black back

wings paler than body

pale wings

♂

sooty black underside ♂

VOICE *Hard, rhythmic* tak-tak-tak; *song loud, wild repetition of short, musical, fluty phrases.*
NESTING *Loose cup of twigs and grass in hole or crevice; 5–6 eggs; 2 broods; Apr–Jun.*
FEEDING *Takes insects, worms, seeds, and fruit; eats many berries on migration.*
SIMILAR SPECIES *Blackbird, Dipper, Blue Rock Thrush.*

Blackbird 🔊

Turdus merula

A smart, plump thrush with a distinctive habit of raising its tail on landing, the Blackbird is a familiar garden bird. The glossy black male is easy to recognize, but the brown female can be confused with other thrushes despite her darker plumage. Males sing superbly, especially from high perches towards dusk.

LIVES IN *woods with leaf litter, also parks and gardens, and farmland with tall hedges.*

yellow bill and eye-ring

paler wingtips

all-black body

dark bill

dark brown legs ♂

gingery body

🌓

dull black

🌓 ♂ 1ST ❄

♀ dark brown

mottled below

VOICE *Low, soft* chook, *frequent* pink-pink-pink, *fast alarm rattle, high* srreee; *song superb, musical, varied, full-throated warbling.*
NESTING *Grass and mud cup in shrub or low in tree; 3–5 eggs; 2–4 broods; Mar–Aug.*
FEEDING *Finds worms, insects, and spiders on ground; fruit and berries in bushes.*
SIMILAR SPECIES *Ring Ouzel, Song Thrush.*

Fieldfare

Turdus pilaris

A large, handsome thrush with a striking combination of
plumage colours, the Fieldfare is usually identifiable by its
blue-grey head and white underwing. It is a winter visitor to
most of Europe, like the smaller Redwing, and the two often
feed together in mixed flocks, stripping berries
from fruiting trees and shrubs.

FEEDS ON *farmland,
bushy heaths, woods,
orchards, and gardens
in winter; breeds
in woodland.*

white
under-
wings

pale
grey rump

black
tail

blue-grey head
with black mask

dark brown
back

black and
yellow bill

orange-buff breast
with heavy black spots

whiter
flanks

dense black
chevrons on
white flanks

VOICE *Loud, chuckling* chak-chak-chak, *low,
nasal* weeip; *song a rather unmusical mixture
of squeaks, warbles, and whistles.*
NESTING *Cup of grass and twigs in bush or
tree; 5–6 eggs; 1–2 broods; May–Jun.*
FEEDING *Mostly eats worms and insects on
the ground; also fruit from trees and bushes.*
SIMILAR SPECIES *Mistle Thrush, Blackbird.*

Mistle Thrush

Turdus viscivorus

Big, bold, and aggressive, the Mistle Thrush is
the largest of the European thrushes. It has
a tall, long-necked look compared to the
Song Thrush, and often flies much
higher when disturbed. Males often
sing from the tops of tall trees in all
weathers, and in winter
single birds defend
berry-laden trees
against Fieldfares,
Redwings, and
other birds.

BREEDS ON *farmland
with tall trees, edges of
moorland near forest,
woodland clearings,
orchards, and parks.*

bold dark
eye

slender
neck

grey-brown
back

pale outer
coverts

pale
rump

white
underwings

bold black spots
on creamy buff
underside

whitish tail
sides

pale head

pale
spots

VOICE *Loud, rattling chatter,* tsairrk-sairr-
sairr-sairk; *song repeated wild, fluty phrases.*
NESTING *Loose cup of twigs and grass high
in tree; 3–5 eggs; 2 broods; Mar–Jun.*
FEEDING *Hops on ground, taking seeds and
invertebrates; also eats berries and fruits.*
SIMILAR SPECIES *Song Thrush, Fieldfare,
female Blackbird.*

Golden Oriole

Oriolus oriolus

black mask
pink-red bill

Despite its stunning colours and loud song, the Golden Oriole can be a difficult bird to see clearly. It stays hidden in dense foliage, offering fleeting views that are sometimes followed by a clear sighting as it flies to the next belt of woodland. It forages among open tree crowns, rarely coming down.

BREEDS IN *places with airy, leafy trees, such as poplar plantations, riverside forest, and well-wooded parks.*

black wings with yellow wingbars

bright yellow body

yellowish green back and forewings

bold yellow rump

rather pointed wingtips

vivid black and yellow plumage

long, slim body

no black mask

greener than male

yellow rump

pale below with dark streaks

VOICE *Call hoarse, Jay-like meeaik, fast gigigi; song loud, penetrating, wee-dl-eyo or weeoo.*
NESTING *Shallow nest below forked branch, high in tree; 3–4 eggs; 1 brood; May–Jun.*
FEEDING *Takes caterpillars and other invertebrates from foliage; also eats berries.*
SIMILAR SPECIES *Mistle Thrush, Green Woodpecker.*

Siberian Jay

Perisoreus infaustus

This is the smallest European member of the crow family, smaller than the Jay and with a longer tail. Mainly dark brownish grey, the rust-orange patches on its wings and tail flash in its deeply undulating flight. It often clings upside down from branches when feeding. Elusive in the breeding season, it is often tame in winter or when food is scarce.

RESTRICTED TO *northern coniferous forests, mainly dense, mature ones, and has decreased as a result of human encroachment.*

very dark face

small bill

bright rust-orange wingbars

rust-orange wing patch

neck feathers often "fluffy"

brownish grey upperparts

fairly long tail

rust-orange tail sides

VOICE *Usually silent, but has many different calls, including harsh screams and mewing.*
NESTING *Deep cup of lichen, lined with feathers and hair, on loose platform of twigs; 3–4 eggs; 1 brood; Apr–Jun.*
FEEDING *Wide range of animal and plant food; hides food stores in trees.*
SIMILAR SPECIES *Appearance unmistakable.*

Nutcracker

Nucifraga caryocatactes

This pale-spotted, Jackdaw-sized crow is a bird of mountain conifer forests, where it often perches conspicuously on the tops of tall conifers. Unmistakable in a good view, it sometimes turns up in improbable places when failures of its food supply drive it away from its normal range in mass "irruptions".

BREEDS IN *eastern forests with spruce, hazel, and pine. May move south and west if seed crops fail.*

dark brown cap

dagger bill

broad, dark blue-black wings

white tail tip

white under tail

bold white spots all over dark brown body

white under short tail

VOICE *Occasional long-drawn-out, hard rattle in spring and summer; otherwise silent.*
NESTING *Grass-lined nest of twigs in tree, usually spruce; 3–4 eggs; 1 brood; May–Jul.*
FEEDING *Eats mainly seeds of hazel, pine, and spruce trees, which it stores in caches to eat in winter; also some large insects.*
SIMILAR SPECIES *Starling.*

TIP
Although a much bigger bird, the Nutcracker can resemble a Starling. Look for the striking white vent and white tail tip.

Jay

Garrulus glandarius

Noisy but shy, the Jay often keeps to thick cover and beats a swift retreat if disturbed, flying off with a flash of its bold white rump. It has a curious habit of allowing ants to run over its plumage, probably to employ the ants' chemical defences against parasites.

BREEDS IN *woodland and parks, especially with oak trees, and visits gardens.*

moustache thick and black

pinkish grey body

barred blue wing panel

"anting" posture

raised crest

white patch on black wings

white rump

white under tail

black tail

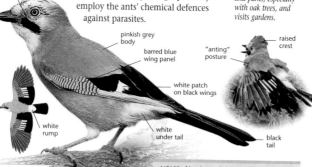

VOICE *Nasal, mewing pee-oo, short bark; loud, harsh, cloth-tearing skairk!*
NESTING *Bulky stick nest, low in dense bush; 4–5 eggs; 1 brood; Apr–Jun.*
FEEDING *Eats mainly insects in summer, with some eggs and nestlings; stores acorns in autumn for use in winter.*
SIMILAR SPECIES *Hoopoe.*

Magpie

Pica pica

A handsome crow with boldly pied plumage and a long, tapered tail, the Magpie is unmistakable. In sunlight it has an iridescent sheen of blue, purple, and green. It has a reputation for wiping out songbirds, but research shows that its fondness for eating eggs and chicks has little overall effect on populations.

BREEDS ON farmland with hedges, woodland edges, and urban parks. Visits gardens to find food.

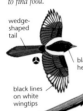

wedge-shaped tail

black head

black lines on white wingtips

black wings, glossed green-blue

long black tail, glossed green and bronze-purple

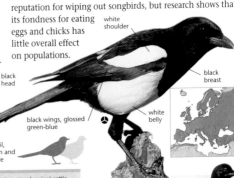

white shoulder

black breast

white belly

black head

tail shorter than adult's

rather duller than adult

VOICE *Hard, chattering, mechanical rattle, tcha-tcha-tcha-tcha or chak-ak-ak-ak.*
NESTING *Big domed nest of sticks and mud, high in tree; 5–8 eggs; 1 brood; Apr–Jun.*
FEEDING *Mostly takes insects, grain, and scraps from a wide range of places; eats eggs and chicks in summer.*
SIMILAR SPECIES *None.*

Jackdaw

Corvus monedula

A small, short-billed crow with a black cap and a pale grey nape, the Jackdaw is a very sociable bird that often flies in flocks, performing spectacular aerobatics with much calling. It also feeds in mixed flocks with Rooks, when its compact shape becomes obvious.

LIVES AROUND cliffs, quarries, old buildings, woods, farmland with mature trees, or towns and villages where there are old houses with chimneys.

rounded wings

grey-black body

grey nape

pale eyes

black cap

short, thick bill

dark grey under-wings

TIP
Although similar to other black crows such as the Rook, the Jackdaw is distinctly smaller, with shorter legs and a shorter bill.

VOICE *Noisy kyak or tjak! with squeaky, bright quality; some longer calls like chee-ar.*
NESTING *Pile of sticks lined with mud, moss, and hair, in hole in tree, cliff, or building, or in chimney; 4–6 eggs; 1 brood; Apr–Jul.*
FEEDING *Takes worms, seeds, and scraps from ground; also caterpillars and berries.*
SIMILAR SPECIES *Rook, Chough.*

Alpine Chough 🔊

Pyrrhocorax graculus

The Alpine Chough is a high-altitude specialist that forages on the highest alpine grassland and nests on cliffs and crags. It has slightly rounder wings and a longer tail than the Chough – more visible at long range than its shorter, yellow bill. The two species often feed together on pastures at lower altitudes, and on coastal clifftops in winter, when the mountains are icebound.

BREEDS IN *mountains, on cliffs, and alpine pasture; often feeds near coasts in winter.*

short, slightly curved, pale yellow bill

glossy black body

rounder wings with shorter "fingers" than Chough

long tail, beyond wingtips

red legs

VOICE *Rippling or sizzling zirrrr or hissy chirrish, penetrating zee-up.*
NESTING *Bulky nest of stems in cliff cavity; 3–5 eggs; 1 brood; May–Jul.*
FEEDING *Forages on grassland for insects, spiders and other invertebrates, berries, seeds, and scraps from around ski lifts.*
SIMILAR SPECIES *Chough, Rook.*

Chough 🔊

Pyrrhocorax pyrrhocorax

Sociable, noisy, exuberant, and spectacularly agile in the air, the Chough is a bird of wild rocky places with ancient grassland, where it gets most of its food by probing in the turf. Family parties and larger flocks soar and dive around cliffs, with total mastery of the turbulent air currents, their ringing calls echoing off the rocks.

longish red bill

square-ended wings with long "fingers"

LIVES ON *rocky coasts, high-altitude pastures, gorges, crags, and quarries; also feeds on beaches in winter.*

glossy black body

short tail, not beyond wingtips

paler, orange-red bill

red legs

VOICE *Explosive, ringing, pee-yaa or chia, also shorter chuk and kwarr calls.*
NESTING *Nest of sticks and hair in cavity in rock or ruin; 3–5 eggs; 1 brood; May–Jul.*
FEEDING *Eats ants on old pastures, insects dug from soil, and lichen prised from rocks.*
SIMILAR SPECIES *Alpine Chough, Rook, Carrion Crow.*

Rook

Corvus frugilegus

Well known for its loud cawing calls, the Rook is a big, black, intensely social crow. It is slightly smaller than the similar Carrion Crow, and the adult is distinguished by the bare, parchment-white face that gives it a very long-billed look. The Rook – even the black-faced juvenile – has a peaked, rather than flat-topped crown. Ragged thigh feathers give it a "baggy trouser" effect. Rooks generally forage in groups, often with Jackdaws, probing the ground for insect grubs and other morsels which they store in a pouch beneath the bill to transport back to the nest. Flocks gather in noisy mass flights around the colony, often with soaring, diving, and swooping aerobatics.

BREEDS IN *treetop colonies, typically in farmland, parks, and villages or small towns with scattered tall trees for nesting.*

wings more pointed than Carrion Crow's

narrow, rounded tail

black plumage with purple-blue or bronze gloss

peaked crown

bare white skin around base of long, pointed bill

body deeper, more angular, less sleek than Carrion Crow's

loose, ragged thigh feathers

rounded tail

bill thinner than Crow's

black bill base

looser feathers and slighter body than Crow

TIP

Rooks are far more sociable than Carrion Crows. They normally nest in colonies, while Crows typically nest in pairs, but the distinction is not completely reliable. Occasionally a pair of Rooks will nest in isolation, and Crows (and Ravens) may sometimes associate in loose flocks. So while a gathering of big black birds is likely to consist of Rooks, it is worth checking.

VOICE *Loud, raucous, but relaxed cawing,* caaar, grah-gra-gra, *plus variety of higher, strangled or metallic notes, especially around colony.*
NESTING *Big nest of sticks lined with grass, moss, and leaves, in treetop colony; 3–6 eggs; 1 brood; Mar–Jun.*
FEEDING *Eats worms, beetle larvae, seeds, grain, and roots from ground, especially ploughed fields or stubble, usually in flocks; also forages along roadsides for large insects and roadkill.*
SIMILAR SPECIES *Carrion Crow, Jackdaw, Raven.*

Carrion Crow

Corvus corone

The all-black Carrion Crow is easy to confuse with other crows, particularly a juvenile Rook, but its head has a distinctly flatter crown and its body plumage is much tighter and neater-looking, with no "baggy trouser" effect. It is usually seen alone or in pairs, but may gather to feed and roost in flocks in autumn and winter, and often feeds alongside other crows.

LIVES IN *all kinds of open areas, from farmland and upland moors to city centres; also feeds on coasts and estuaries.*

- flat-topped head
- thick, arched bill
- intensely black plumage
- neat, tight body feathering
- squarer wingtips than Rook
- square tail

VOICE Loud, harsh, grating caw, krra krra krra, metallic konk, korr, and similar calls.
NESTING Big stick nest, in tree, bush, on cliff or building; 4–6 eggs; 1 brood; Mar–Jul.
FEEDING Feeds on ground, taking all kinds of invertebrates, eggs, grain, and various scraps; usually in pairs but sometimes flocks.
SIMILAR SPECIES Rook, Raven, Jackdaw.

Hooded Crow

Corvus cornix

A close relative of the all-black Carrion Crow, and sometimes considered a subspecies of it, the Hooded Crow is a much more distinctive bird with a different range. Where the two meet, they interbreed to produce a range of hybrids, with varying amounts of grey plumage.

FOUND IN *a wide range of open habitats; appears to prefer poorer land to Carrion Crow in breeding season.*

- black hood
- black wings and tail
- grey body
- black wings
- pale body

- black wings and tail

VOICE Very like Carrion Crow's; often a more hard, rolling croak repeated 3–4 times.
NESTING Large stick nest, in tree or bush, some on cliffs, 4–6 eggs; 1 brood; Mar–Jul.
FEEDING Wide range of animal food, including carrion, grain, and food scraps.
SIMILAR SPECIES Jackdaw (smaller in size, with a paler area only at the back of its head).

Raven

Corvus corax

LIVES IN *large forests, mountain regions, open moorland, and hills with crags and isolated trees.*

The world's largest perching bird, bigger than a Buzzard, the Raven is a much heavier, more powerful bird than the Carrion Crow, which often shares its habitats and its taste for carrion. It has longer wings, a longer tail, and a big head with a much heavier bill. It often increases the apparent size of its head by bristling up its throat feathers, giving it a bearded appearance that is unmistakable. At a distance it is best identified by its shape and bold, strong flight, which often includes dramatic rolling and tumbling aerobatics, especially early in the breeding season. But the first clue to the presence of a Raven is usually its loud, deep, croaking call, which echoes from the surrounding peaks and crags. Usually seen alone, in pairs, or in family parties, it sometimes gathers in flocks at carcasses and communal roosts.

wedge-shaped tail

long, fingered wings

protruding head

loose throat feathers may be expanded as a "beard"

all-black plumage; metallic green and purplish gloss in strong light

tail diamond-shaped when spread

very large, deep, arched bill

long tail

VOICE Loud, abrupt, echoing crronk crronk crronk or prruk prruk, metallic tonk; various clicking, rattling or quiet musical notes, sometimes in rambling subsong audible only at close range.
NESTING Huge nest of sticks, wool, grass, and heather, used for many years, on cliff or in tall tree; 4–6 eggs; 1 brood; Feb–May.
FEEDING Catches small mammals and birds; eats carrion from dead sheep and roadkills; forages for scraps on shore; eats insects and grain.
SIMILAR SPECIES Carrion Crow, Rook.

TIP

Ravens are usually to be seen flying over the wildest, craggiest country, and even on high, barren peaks, where they often call from prominent rock perches. But they also frequent softer, wooded landscapes and farmland, and they may even be seen flying over towns.

Gamebirds & other Non-passerines

Gamebirds are a mixed group of ground birds with short, slightly hooked bills, short legs, and strong feet for running or scratching for food. They include quails, partridges, pheasants and grouse, and range in size from the little Quail to the large Capercaillie. If disturbed, they suddenly rocket up into the air with noisy, whirring beats of their short, rounded wings, alternating with glides on bowed wings. The other groups covered in this section are very varied and are gathered here for convenience rather than on the basis of strong similarity. They range from the brightly coloured Kingfisher, Bee-eater, Hoopoe, and Roller to the more familiar Cuckoo, the pigeons and doves, the intensely aerial swifts, the tree-climbing woodpeckers, and the large and imposing bustards and Crane.

KINGFISHER   PHEASANT   SWIFT   GREAT SPOTTED WOODPECKER

Kingfisher

Alcedo atthis

HUNTS ALONG *rivers and canals, on marshes, and flooded pits; also on coasts, especially in winter.*

Usually glimpsed as a streak of electric blue as it flies over water, the Kingfisher can be surprisingly hard to see when perched in the dappled shade watching for prey. Its shape is unique: dumpy, almost tailless, with a long, heavy spike of a bill. It is often best located by its shrill whistled calls.

red on base of bill

vivid blue streak

white neck patch

barred blue cap

♂

♀

electric blue

dagger-like black bill

white throat patch

♂

rusty orange below

VOICE *Quite loud, sharp, high kit-cheeee or cheee; high, fast trill in spring.*
NESTING *Deep tubular tunnel, lined with fish bones, in earth bank over water; 5–7 eggs; 2 broods; May–Jul.*
FEEDING *Catches fish, frogs, and aquatic insects, in dive from perch or mid-air hover.*
SIMILAR SPECIES *None.*

Pallid Swift

Apus pallidus

FEEDS OVER ALL *kinds of open countryside, old towns, and villages; breeds in old buildings and roof spaces.*

Very like a common Swift, the Pallid Swift gets its name from its paler, browner plumage. In a good view this is obvious, but the bird is usually seen moving fast against the sky, when its broader-winged, shorter-tailed, broader-headed silhouette is a better guide. Both species occur in many towns in southern Europe, so they can often be compared.

darker brown wingtip

pale band on upper wing

mottled, with pale feather edges

tail often fanned in flight

pale mud-brown underwing

pale chin and throat

VOICE *Scream like common Swift's, but often of lower, falling pitch and more disyllabic.*
NESTING *Unlined cavity in roof space or wall; 2–3 eggs; 1 brood; May–Jun.*
FEEDING *Catches flying insects and drifting spiders in the air.*
SIMILAR SPECIES *Swift, Alpine Swift, Sand Martin.*

Swift 🔊

Apus apus

The only swift to occur over most of Europe, the common Swift is usually instantly identifiable by its scythe-like wings and loud, screaming calls. It spends most of its life in the air, only landing at the nest, and never perches like a swallow. In bad weather, it flies very low, giving good views.

BREEDS IN *holes in old buildings; rarely in cliffs nowadays; hunts over open country, villages, towns, and some large cities.*

whitish edges

all-dark body; browner in late summer

whiter chin and forehead

hindwing slightly paler

pale throat, hard to see

scythe-shaped wings

looks all-black against sky

long, curved wings

forked tail

VOICE *Loud, screeching, shrill screams from flocks, shhreeee, sirrr.*
NESTING *Feather-lined cavity in building, rarely in cliff; 2–3 eggs; 1 brood; May–Jun.*
FEEDING *Entirely aerial, taking flying insects and airborne spiders in its bill.*
SIMILAR SPECIES *Pallid Swift, Alpine Swift, Swallow.*

Alpine Swift 🔊

Apus melba

A very large, powerful swift, bigger than the common Swift, this white-bellied species favours rugged country with cliffs and ravines, often mixing with other swifts, Crag Martins, and choughs. Unlike the common Swift, it often breeds in cliff holes. Its shape and slow wing-beats can make it look like a Hobby or other small falcon at long range.

HUNTS OVER *all kinds of open country, but especially cliffs, gorges, and hill towns in mountainous regions.*

white chin and throat

bold white belly

dark breast band

short, dark, forked tail

dark under tail

white chin and throat, hard to see in shadow

wings swept back in fast glide

VOICE *Loud chorus of Greenfinch-like trills, rising and falling and changing in speed, titititititi-ti-ti-ti-ti-ti ti.*
NESTING *Shallow cup of grass in hole in cliff or building; 2–3 eggs; 1 brood; Apr–Jun.*
FEEDING *Exclusively aerial, catching insects in its open mouth like other swifts.*
SIMILAR SPECIES *Swift, Hobby, Crag Martin.*

Lesser Spotted Woodpecker 🔊

Dendrocopos minor

LIVES IN *woodland, copses, orchards, and tall hedges with old or diseased trees.*

The size of a sparrow, this is the smallest of European woodpeckers and one of the most secretive. It forages high in the slender branches of trees, creeping over the bark and searching for insects with rapid pecks of its small, sharp bill. Its territorial drumming has a rattling quality.

less red than male

barred back

black cap ♀

red cap

black cheek patch

closely barred back ♂

barred wings; no big white shoulder patches ♂

variable streaks below

VOICE *Sharp, weak tchik; nasal, peevish pee-pee-pee-pee-pee-pee; weak drum.*
NESTING *Bores nest hole in tree; 4–6 eggs; 1 brood; May–Jun.*
FEEDING *Takes insects from under bark and also some from woody stems of ground plants.*
SIMILAR SPECIES *Great and Middle Spotted Woodpeckers; Wryneck and Kestrel (call).*

Wryneck 🔊

Jynx torquilla

BREEDS IN *farmed countryside with trees, copses, and more extensive pine or mixed forest; migrants often seen near coasts and on islands.*

Looking more like a big warbler or a small, slim thrush, the Wryneck is a specialized woodpecker that feeds mainly on ants, either taking them from the ground or from bark crevices. It is elusive and hard to see, not least because of its beautiful and subtle camouflaging plumage, but its calls are distinctive. It is named for its habit of twisting its head round when alarmed, giving it a "wry-necked" look.

barred tail

barred wings

long, dark eye-stripe

pale grey crown

large blackish back stripe

fine bars on buff throat

grey, brown, and blackish above

pale spots on wings

VOICE *Quick, nasal kwee-kee-kee-kee-kee, lower in pitch than similar calls of Lesser Spotted Woodpecker and Kestrel.*
NESTING *Existing hole in tree or wall; 7–10 eggs; 1–2 broods; May–Jun.*
FEEDING *Often on ground, taking ants, other insects, spiders, woodlice, and some berries.*
SIMILAR SPECIES *Barred Warbler.*

Middle Spotted Woodpecker

Dendrocopos medius

A quiet, retiring woodpecker that feeds high in the trees and never drums on dead wood to proclaim its territory, this quite boldly coloured bird often escapes notice. Its need for old timber has made it scarce in regions where dead trees are routinely removed by forestry workers.

bright red cap on white, rounded head

short bill

NESTS IN *old woodland with some dead and dying trees; cannot usually survive in over-managed woods.*

black neck patch extends onto chest

streaked yellow-buff below

white shoulder patch

white barring

duller cap

♂

pinkish under tail

♀

> **VOICE** Quite slow, repeated kvek-kvek-kvek, weak kik, rhythmic kuk-uk kuk-uk kuk-uk.
> **NESTING** Bores nest hole in rotten branch; 4–7 eggs; 1 brood; May–Jun.
> **FEEDING** Takes insects, larvae, and sap in high branches, often from dead wood.
> **SIMILAR SPECIES** Great Spotted Woodpecker, Lesser Spotted Woodpecker.

Great Spotted Woodpecker 🔊

Dendrocopos major

The rapid "drum roll" of this bird is a common sound of spring wood-land. The woodpecker itself is often easy to locate, propped on its tail as it hammers at bark or timber. Although similar to the Middle Spotted, it has less red on its head, and more beneath its tail.

red patch on back of head

FEEDS IN *gardens and scrub as well as mature woodland; breeds in both deciduous and conifer woods.*

bold black and white above

bright buff below

♂

all-red crown; less on female

♂

big white shoulder patch

no red

vivid red under tail

♀

> **VOICE** Explosive tchik! fast rattle of alarm; loud, fast, very short drumming.
> **NESTING** Bores nest hole in tree trunk or branch; 4–7 eggs; 1 brood; Apr–Jun.
> **FEEDING** Digs insects and grubs from bark with strong bill; also eats seeds and berries.
> **SIMILAR SPECIES** Middle Spotted Woodpecker, Lesser Spotted Woodpecker.

Green Woodpecker 🔊

Picus viridis

LIVES IN *and around broadleaved and mixed woodland, and heathy places with bushes and trees. Feeds on grassy areas with ants.*

Easily detected, especially in spring, by its loud laughing calls, this big, pale woodpecker forages mainly on the ground. A wary feeder, it is often spotted as it flies up and into cover. Adults are mainly bright green with crimson crowns; young birds are mottled.

bright greenish yellow rump

dark wingtips with pale bars

blackish spots and streaks

red and black moustache; no red in female

black around whitish eye ♂

vivid red cap (in both sexes)

apple-green upperside

greenish yellow rump

VOICE *Loud, shrill, bouncing keu-keu-keuk; song a descending kleu-kleu-kleu-keu-keu.*
NESTING *Bores nest hole in tree; 5–7 eggs; 1 brood; May–Jul.*
FEEDING *Eats ants, ants' eggs, and larvae, mainly on ground, using long, sticky tongue to probe nests.*
SIMILAR SPECIES *Golden Oriole.*

Black Woodpecker 🔊

Dryocopus martius

LIVES IN *mature forest with big trees, or in patchy forest with clumps of large trees. Wanders more widely in winter.*

red cap

pale, dark-tipped bill ♂

Although easily the largest of the European woodpeckers, the Black Woodpecker is often hard to see because of its dark plumage and shy nature. In spring it announces its presence with loud, penetrating calls, and protracted bursts of "machine-gun" drumming, but it rarely allows a close approach.

rounded wings with "fingered" tips

pale, dagger-like bill ♂

glossy black plumage

red only on back of head

wedge-shaped tail

♀

tail used as prop (like other woodpeckers)

VOICE *High, plaintive pyuuu; rolling krri-krri-krri-krri; loud laughing; long, loud drumming.*
NESTING *Makes large nest hole in big tree; 4–6 eggs; 1 brood; Apr–Jun.*
FEEDING *Digs insect larvae from standing and fallen timber; eats ants on the ground.*
SIMILAR SPECIES *Jackdaw, Rook, Carrion Crow, Raven. Green Woodpecker in silhouette.*

Hoopoe

Upupa epops

Surprisingly unobtrusive as it feeds in the dappled shade beneath a tree, the Hoopoe explodes into a dazzling vision of black, white, and pink as it takes flight. It is quite unlike any other European bird, especially when it raises its flamboyant fan-shaped crest.

BREEDS IN *open woods, parks and gardens, orchards, old villages, and old farmsteads.*

black-tipped crest, laid flat

pinkish head and body

slim, slightly curved bill

black and white pattern on wing and tail

erect crest

black and white bars

broad white tail-band

VOICE *Soft, low, hollow poop-poop-poop, often repeated; hoarse scheer.*
NESTING *Hole in tree or wall; 5–8 eggs; 1 brood; Apr–Jul.*
FEEDING *Walks on ground, probing and picking with bill for insects, grubs, and worms.*
SIMILAR SPECIES *Jay, Great Spotted Woodpecker.*

Cuckoo

Cuculus canorus

The Cuckoo's call is well known, but few people are familiar with the bird itself: a quite large, long-winged, long-tailed bird that resembles a small-headed hawk or falcon with barred under-parts. It often perches on trees or on overhead wires, its wings drooped and tail fanned.

pale band

PARASITIZES *nests of small birds in woods, reedbeds, on wooded farmland, bushy moorland, and heaths.*

yellow bill base and eyes

pale spot on nape

medium grey upperparts

wedge shape

grey bars on white underside

dark tail with white spots

yellow legs and feet

dark wingtips

barred above

VOICE *Familiar bright cuc-coo, sometimes cuc-cuc-oo; females has odd bubbling call.*
NESTING *Lays eggs in other birds' nests; 1–25 (usually 9) eggs, 1 per nest; May–Jun.*
FEEDING *Drops to ground to take large, hairy caterpillars; also eats small insects.*
SIMILAR SPECIES *Sparrowhawk, Kestrel, Stock Dove.*

Nightjar 🔊

Caprimulgus europaeus

HUNTS OVER *heaths and open ground with low undergrowth, or in forest clearings. Spends winter in Africa.*

The strange, nocturnal Nightjar is best known for its song: a protracted mechanical trill that sounds wooden and rattling at close range. Invisible by day, thanks to its superb camouflage, it can be seen hawking for flying insects at twilight, in wonderfully light, buoyant, agile flight.

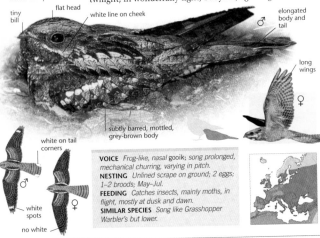

tiny bill

flat head

white line on cheek

elongated body and tail

♂

long wings

♀

subtly barred, mottled, grey-brown body

white on tail corners

♂

white spots

♀

no white

VOICE *Frog-like, nasal gooik; song prolonged, mechanical churring, varying in pitch.*
NESTING *Unlined scrape on ground; 2 eggs; 1–2 broods; May–Jul.*
FEEDING *Catches insects, mainly moths, in flight, mostly at dusk and dawn.*
SIMILAR SPECIES *Song like Grasshopper Warbler's but lower.*

Roller

Coracias garrulus

BRREDS IN *various kinds of open country-side with orchards, woods, bushes, and rough grassland.*

The vivid blue plumage of the Jackdaw-sized Roller is unique in Europe: it cannot be mistaken for any other bird. It often perches on wires and poles, watching for prey, which it pounces upon like a shrike. Its name refers to its spectacular rolling, tumbling display flight.

brilliant turquoise by late spring

paler and much duller than adult

thick dark bill

pale red-brown back

flight feathers blackish above, deep violet below

faintly streaked chest

square tail

violet rump

blackish, turquoise, and violet-blue wings

VOICE *Hard, crow-like rak, rak-aaak, or rak-ak-ak.*
NESTING *Uses hole in tree, wall, or building, or old crow's nest in tree; 4–7 eggs; 1 brood; May–Jun.*
FEEDING *Eats mainly large insects, also rodents and lizards, caught on ground.*
SIMILAR SPECIES *Unique in Europe.*

Bee-eater 🔊

Merops apiaster

The exotic-looking Bee-eater is unmistakable when seen in a good light, for no other European bird has its combination of bright colours. Its shape and actions are even distinctive in silhouette – as it hunts flying insects it rises with rapid beats of its stiff, pointed wings, stalls, and then swoops down in long, curving glides. Its name is appropriate because it really does eat bees, as well as wasps, and seems to have some immunity to their stings. Very sociable, Bee-eaters live in flocks throughout the year and frequently perch in tight groups, almost shoulder to shoulder; they are often easy to see from roads.

PERCHES ON *wires and trees in warm, often sandy, bushy areas with open grassland and low earth cliffs.*

bronze wing patch

tail with central spike

dark cap; greener in juvenile

long, pointed, black bill

dark eye-stripe

yellow throat

blue-green underside

reddish brown back

golden yellow on shoulders

may lose tail spike

translucent wings with black trailing edge

long tail; juvenile has no tail spike

TIP

Bee-eaters often perch on the bare branches of dead trees along rivers, where the abundant insect life ensures them plenty of prey. The riverbanks also make ideal nesting sites, and they often form large breeding colonies that are hives of activity in the summer.

VOICE *Distinctive, far-carrying, soft, deep, rolling, quite liquid notes, prroop prroop, given in chorus from passing flocks.*
NESTING *Digs burrow in sandy bank or flatter ground, nesting in colonies; 4–7 eggs; 1 brood; May–Jun.*
FEEDING *Catches insects in flight, including bees, wasps, butterflies, and dragonflies, in prolonged, fast swoops and slow, gliding flights, as well as in sallies from a perch like a flycatcher.*
SIMILAR SPECIES *Starling (in silhouette).*

Turtle Dove

Streptopelia turtur

The purring song of the Turtle Dove used to be a common feature of high summer, but it is becoming less familiar as its woodland and hedgerow habitats are eliminated by intensive agriculture. Similar to the Collared Dove, it has a darker back, neatly chequered brown-black, and a striped bluish-white and black neck patch.

LIVES IN *wooded farmland, broadleaved woods with sunny clearings, and tall, dense, old hedgerows.*

barred black- and-whitish neck patch

pink breast

blue-grey midwing

dark spots on orange-brown above

white belly

white tip to tail

no neck patch

duller body

VOICE *Deep, purring, pleasant, crooning roooorrr roooorrr.*
NESTING *Small, flimsy platform of thin twigs in hedge or low branches of tree; 2 eggs; 2–3 broods; May–Jul.*
FEEDING *Takes seeds and shoots of arable weeds on ground.*
SIMILAR SPECIES *Collared Dove, Kestrel.*

Collared Dove

Streptopelia decaocto

Identifiable by its pale, grey-brown body, its thin, black half-collar, and monotonous triple coo, the Collared Dove is common on farms and in suburbs. It prefers to nest and roost in tall conifers. The male has a dramatic display flight, rising steeply and gliding down in wide arcs on flat wings, with harsh nasal calls.

LIVES IN *woodlands, parks, gardens, around farm buildings, and in villages and towns.*

grey area on upperwings

dark wingtips

white-tipped tail

black half-collar

pale, grey-brown body

pinkish head and breast

no collar

VOICE *Loud, repeated triple cu-cooo-cuk; also a nasal gwurrrr call in flight.*
NESTING *Small platform of twigs, rubbish; 2 eggs; 2–3 broods (or more); all year.*
FEEDING *Picks grain, seeds, and shoots from ground; often takes seeds from bird tables.*
SIMILAR SPECIES *Turtle Dove, Rock Dove, Kestrel.*

sandy-buff

Stock Dove 🔊

Columba oenas

A compact pigeon of farmland, parks, and uplands, the Stock Dove resembles a small Woodpigeon but has a shorter tail, more bluish plumage, and no white markings. The two dark bars on its folded wing are a lot smaller than those of the similar Rock Dove. Its head is smaller and rounder than a Rock Dove's.

FEEDS IN *a wide variety of places, from flooded fields and farmland with trees to rocky upland moors.*

glossy green neck patch

deep wine-pink breast

black trailing edge and wingtips

pale midwings

dark tail band

grey underwings

two short dark bars on wings

blue-grey body

VOICE *Rhythmic, booming coo, repeated with increased emphasis, ooo-woo ooo-woo.*
NESTING *Tree hole, ledge or cavity in cliff or building; 2 eggs; 2–3 broods; all year.*
FEEDING *Takes seeds, buds, shoots, roots, as well as berries from ground, but not in gardens.*
SIMILAR SPECIES *Rock Dove; Woodpigeon.*

Rock Dove

Columba livia

The wild ancestor of the town or feral pigeon, the Rock Dove is a bird of rocky coasts and crags. It is paler, with an ash-grey back, a green and purple gloss on its neck, two broad black wingbars, and a white rump. Feral pigeons have very varied plumage patterns, and interbreeding between the two forms has made the genuine wild Rock Dove a rarity.

BREEDS ON *coastal cliffs and mountains. Feral birds widespread from coasts to cities, and on farmland.*

tiny white patch

pale grey back

larger white patch

glossy purple and green on neck

dark below

white rump

FERAL PIGEON

white underwing

two long, broad, black bars on wings

VOICE *Deep, rolling, moaning coo, oo-ooh-oorr, oo-roo-coo.*
NESTING *Loose, untidy, sparse nest on ledge or in cavity; 2 eggs; 3 broods; all year.*
FEEDING *Forages for seeds, buds, berries, and small invertebrates on ground.*
SIMILAR SPECIES *Woodpigeon, Stock Dove, Peregrine or other birds of prey in flight.*

Woodpigeon 🔊

Columba palumbus

FEEDS MAINLY on farmland; breeds in a variety of woodland and farmland with trees, also town parks and big gardens.

A large, common, boldly marked pigeon, often found in large flocks, the Woodpigeon is usually identifiable by its white neck patch, pink breast, white wingbar, and plump, small-headed look. Although tame in city parks, it is shy in rural areas where it is persecuted as a pest.

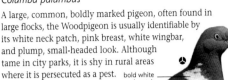

bold white neck patch

rump paler than back

dark tail band

large white midwing patch

grey back

pink breast

dull red legs

white on wings

no white on neck

duller

broad dark band at end of tail

VOICE Husky, muffled, repeated cooing, coo-coo-cu, cu-coo, cook; loud wing clatter in sudden take-off; wing claps in display flight.
NESTING Thin platform of twigs in tree or bush; 2 eggs; 1–2 broods; Apr–Sep.
FEEDING Eats, buds, leaves, berries, and fruit in trees and on ground; visits bird tables.
SIMILAR SPECIES Stock Dove, Rock Dove.

Spotted Crake

Porzana porzana

BREEDS IN extensive flood-meadows; migrants feed in wet marshes, in reedy places, and at the edges of muddy pools.

Although not exactly shy, the Spotted Crake is an elusive bird that typically feeds in dense vegetation, only rarely appearing in the open. It resembles a Water Rail, except that its bill is short and yellow instead of long and red. Its basically brown plumage is beautifully patterned when seen at close range.

grey-buff neck with white spots

browner on head and neck

yellowish bill, red at base

white bars on flanks

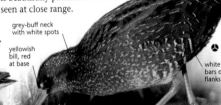

VOICE Repeated, rhythmic, whiplash sound or dripping hwit, hwit, hwit, at dusk or night.
NESTING Small saucer of leaves and stems, in upright stalks above water or in wet marsh; 8–12 eggs; 1 brood; May–Jul.
FEEDING Picks small insects and aquatic invertebrates from mud, water, and foliage.
SIMILAR SPECIES Moorhen, Water Rail.

striped below

buff under tail

Water Rail

Rallus aquaticus

This is a skulking, secretive bird of dense reeds and waterside vegetation, often hard to see but readily identified by its long red bill. When venturing into the open, it soon slips out of sight between plant stems. It can often be detected at dawn or dusk by its squealing calls.

FEEDS AND *breeds in wet reedbeds, swampy willow thickets, and overgrown riversides.*

dark streaked above

red eyes

red, slightly curved bill with black tip

grey chest and face

barred flanks

pink legs

dull legs

untidy bars below

slate-grey below

VOICE *Hard, repetitive, kipkipkipkipkip, extra-ordinary, loud, pig-like squealing, grunting.*
NESTING *Shallow nest of broad leaves and grasses in vegetation raised a little above water level; 6–11 eggs; 2 broods; May–Aug.*
FEEDING *Eats mainly insects and molluscs; also seeds, berries, voles, birds, and carrion.*
SIMILAR SPECIES *Spotted Crake, Moorhen.*

Corncrake

Crex crex

The far-carrying, rasping song of the male Corncrake used to be familiar in meadows throughout Europe, but it is now heard only where the grass is cut late enough to avoid its nests and chicks being destroyed. A slim, streaked bird, it is usually seen only fleetingly as it raises its head to check for danger.

BREEDS IN *wet grass and late-harvested hayfields with dense cover in spring.*

soft grey and buff face

grey throat and breast

short, stout, pink bill

pink legs

narrow, rounded rufous wings

less grey

tawny back with black streaks

♂

♀

VOICE *Loud, repeated double note; at distance light, scratched crik crik, at close range hard, rattling, vibrating crrek crrek.*
NESTING *Small hollow on ground, concealed with grass; 8–12 eggs; 1–2 broods; May–Aug.*
FEEDING *Picks insects, seeds, leaves, and shoots from foliage and ground.*
SIMILAR SPECIES *Spotted Crake, Quail.*

Quail

Coturnix coturnix

A tiny, rounded, sharp-winged, secretive bird of long grass and dense crops, the Quail is often heard but rarely seen unless it ventures briefly into the open. Occasionally, it flies off on surprisingly long wings in a fast, low, short, arc before dropping back into thick cover.

BREEDS AND *feeds in extensive tracts of long grass or cereal fields, mainly in warm, dry areas. Migrants may rest in fields with sparse crops, or other open ground.*

striped crown

cream stripes on brown back

short, dark, pointed tail ♂

dark throat

long dark wings

♂

dark stripes on flanks

pale throat ♀

small, striped head

VOICE *Song unique loud, far-carrying, full, liquid quick-we-wik, also quiet mewing notes.*
NESTING *Slight hollow, well hidden in grass or crops, lined with vegetation; up to 12 eggs; 1 brood; May–Jun.*
FEEDING *Takes seeds, shoots, and small insects from ground or foliage.*
SIMILAR SPECIES *Grey Partridge, Corncrake.*

Grey Partridge

Perdix perdix

This neat gamebird is typical of old-fashioned farmland with hedges. It feeds secretively in long grass, in tight flocks, pausing to raise its head and look around. If disturbed, it rockets off with whirring wings, alternating with short glides on bowed wings.

LIVES MAINLY *on farmland, especially grassy meadows with rich insect life; also on heaths, low moorland, and dunes.*

dull brown bill

orange-brown face

orange tail sides

pale brown wings

streaked back

finely barred grey breast

bold red-brown bars on flanks

dull brown legs

broad, brown belly patch

♂

VOICE *Distinctive low, rhythmic, mechanical, creaky kieeer-ik or ki-yik.*
NESTING *Well-hidden, shallow scrape on ground; 10–20 eggs; 1 brood, Apr–Jun.*
FEEDING *Takes seeds, leaves, and shoots from ground; feeds insects to chicks.*
SIMILAR SPECIES *Red-legged Partridge, juvenile Pheasant. Juvenile similar to Quail.*

Red-legged Partridge

Alectoris rufa

An elegant, attractive gamebird with a bright red bill, the Red-legged Partridge is surprisingly well camouflaged and often hard to spot. It favours warm, open, stony slopes, or farmland with sandy soils. Its plumage looks unmistakable, but in many parts of its range it is easy to confuse with hybrids resulting from crosses with the introduced Chukar Partridge.

BREEDS ON *open slopes with bare ground and dry, sandy arable land; also on grassy heaths and coastal dunes.*

plain pale brown above

white stripe

dark red-brown tail

black-streaked "necklace"

black, grey, and brown bars on flanks

straight, stiff wings

red legs

rufous tail

VOICE *Deep, gobbling and hissing or chuckling mechanical calls, chuk-uk-ar, k'chuk-ar, k'chuk-ar.*
NESTING *Grass-lined scrape beneath low vegetation; 7–20 eggs; 1 brood; Apr–Jun.*
FEEDING *Takes leaves, shoots, berries, nuts, and seeds from ground; chicks eat insects.*
SIMILAR SPECIES *Grey Partridge.*

Pheasant

Phasianus colchicus

The male pheasant is a conspicuous, noisy bird, although very variable, with or without a white neck ring but always with a bold red wattle around the eye. The female is more anonymous-looking and secretive, but the long, pointed tail is very distinctive.

LIVES MAINLY *in woodland edge, arable land, reedbeds, heaths, and moorland edge.*

bare red skin

black markings

♀

long neck

white neck ring

tail longer than female's

♀

often has pale rump

long pointed tail

white markings
PALE FORM

♂

♂
DARK FORM

orange-copper flanks

VOICE *Loud, explosive corr-kok! with sudden whirr of wings; loud clucking in flight.*
NESTING *Hollow on ground, beneath cover; 8–15 eggs; 1 brood; Apr–Jul.*
FEEDING *Takes a variety of food from ground – from seeds and berries to insects and lizards.*
SIMILAR SPECIES *Female like female Grey Partridge, Black Grouse.*

Ptarmigan

Lagopus muta

A smaller version of the Willow Grouse, the Ptarmigan looks more delicate, but is in reality one of the hardiest of all game-birds. It lives on the northern tundra, or the highest, most barren peaks of Scotland, the Alps, and the Pyrenees, where the ground lies under deep snow throughout the winter. It can be hard to see at any time of year, owing to its superb camouflage that changes with the seasons, and its habit of "freezing" on the spot when alarmed. In its white winter plumage it is very like a white Willow Grouse, while summer females look like female British and Irish Red Grouse.

BREEDS ON *tundra, boulder fields, and rocky shores in far north; on high stony peaks in south.*

bright red comb above eye

delicate bill

"salt and pepper" barring on grey upperparts

grey head and body ♂☼

white head and body ♂✻

tail stays black

white wings

white belly

feathered legs ♂☼

red comb

black line between bill and eye

white plumage ♂❄

yellow speckling on brown body

white wings ♀☼

no red comb or black line

white plumage ♀❄

TIP

A Ptarmigan is slightly smaller than a Willow Grouse, and has a smaller bill. Its croaking call is also quite unlike the g'back of the Willow Grouse.

VOICE *A variety of low, dry, croaking notes, especially a four-syllable arr-kar-ka-karrrr; also a cackling "belch".*
NESTING *Nests in a scrape on the ground, lightly lined with grass; 5–9 eggs; 1 brood; May–Jul.*
FEEDING *Gathers food on the ground, taking shoots, leaves, buds, seeds, and berries of a variety of low-growing shrubs; also takes insects, which are an important food for chicks.*
SIMILAR SPECIES *Willow Grouse.*

Willow Grouse

Lagopus lagopus

A thickset gamebird of moors and heaths, the Willow Grouse is very like the tundra-breeding Ptarmigan, and almost indistinguishable in white winter plumage. In the more rugged parts of its range, the two species overlap and can be hard to tell apart. The British and Irish race *L. l. scoticus* is known as the Red Grouse, because of the dark red-brown plumage of the male; it has no white plumage except on the underwing, and does not turn white in winter.

LIVES ON *moors, heaths, and forest clearings in N Europe; Red Grouse found mainly on managed heather moor-land in British Isles.*

thick black bill

red comb

no black on face

brown body ♂☀

white wings

white head and body ♂❄

white wings

tail stays black

rich red-brown body; female yellow-brown, more marbled

dark scaly bars

white belly

white-feathered legs ♂☀

TIP

A Willow Grouse has no black on its face, unlike the male Ptarmigan, and in summer its plumage is a redder brown. White females in winter are virtually identical: the only good identification clue is the Willow Grouse's thicker bill.

thick bill

no black line between bill and eye

white plumage ♀❄

yellow-brown

RED GROUSE *L.i.scoticus* ♀

red-brown, with darker wings

RED GROUSE *L.i.scoticus* ♂

VOICE *Remarkable, deep, staccato calls that echo across the moors, kau-kau-kau-ka-ka-karrr-rrr-g'back, g'back, bak.*
NESTING *Sparsely lined scrape on ground in heather; 6–9 eggs; 1 brood; Apr–May.*
FEEDING *Plucks shoots and seeds from heather while standing or walking slowly over the ground; also takes a variety of berries and seeds; chicks feed on insects.*
SIMILAR SPECIES *Ptarmigan, Grey Partridge.*

Black Grouse

Tetrao tetrix

DISPLAYS AND *lives on moorland edges, forest clearings, heaths, birch scrub, rough pastures, and young conifer plantations.*

The glossy blue-black plumage, long, curved outer tail, and bright red comb of the male Black Grouse are unmistakable, particularly in display when the bird raises its tail to reveal a fan of white feathers. The smaller female is much less distinctive, although her notched tail is a useful clue. In spring, the males gather on communal display grounds (called leks) to compete for females with mock fights, spreading their feathers and calling with repetitive bubbling, cooing notes. They are easily disturbed at such times, and usually fly off and land far away if approached.

TIP

Black Grouse of both sexes have a large white area on their underwings. They also have an elongated look in flight, compared to Willow Grouse, and generally fly higher when flushed.

big red comb

blue sheen on neck

♂

small white shoulder spot

white undertail feathers raised in display

curved, broad-tipped outer tail feathers

glossy black plumage

big, heavy, cockerel-like body

slightly notched tail

pale bar on mid-brown wings

♀

elongated shape

♂

dark-barred, yellow-brown or grey

♀

unique lyre-shaped tail

bold white wingbar

VOICE *Female has gruff bark; displaying male produces far-carrying, dove-like, rolling coo with regular rhythm, and explosive "sneeze".*
NESTING *Hollow on ground beneath heather or bracken, with little or no lining; 6–10 eggs; 1 brood; Apr–Jul.*
FEEDING *Wide variety of seeds, berries, buds, shoots, leaves, and flowers of many shrubs, sedges, and trees such as birch and hazel, changing with seasons; chicks eat insects.*
SIMILAR SPECIES *Capercaillie, female Red Grouse.*

Capercaillie

Tetrao urogallus

The magnificent Capercaillie is by far the largest of the grouse. The male in particular is a massive, dark, turkey-like, aggressive bird; the female is much smaller, but still big in comparison with other grouse, with an orange breast and a broad tail. Males display competitively in spring, attracting females with their remarkable voices and wing-flapping leaps. Generally shy and secretive, the Capercaillie is sensitive to disturbance and is now seriously threatened in many parts of its range, including Scotland.

LIVES IN *ancient pine forests and boggy forest clearings with bilberry, juniper, and heather; less often in mature pine plantations.*

short, stout, pale, hooked bill

red comb

♀

dark bars on orange tail

♂

big, rounded tail

brown wings

black tail, speckled with white

broad, round tail when fanned in display

"beard" of spiky feathers

bold white shoulder spot

huge, blackish body

brown wings

♂

dark bars on rufous-ginger body

cream with black and rufous bars

orange breast

♀

TIP

Despite its size, the Capercaillie roosts in the trees, and often feeds up in the branches in winter. In summer, it is more likely to be found at ground level. It rarely allows a close approach, but sometimes sits tight until it is forced to burst up from underfoot in a cacophony of flapping wings.

VOICE *Pheasant-like crowing; male in spring utters bizarre "song" of clicks and belches, ending with cork-popping and wheezy gurgling.*
NESTING *Hollow on ground, often at base of tree, lined with grass, pine needles, and twigs; 5–8 eggs; 1 brood; Mar–Jul.*
FEEDING *Eats shoots, leaves, and buds of several shrubs and trees, berries of various herbs and shrubs, especially bilberry, and pine needles taken from treetops in winter.*
SIMILAR SPECIES *Female Black Grouse.*

Hazel Grouse

Bonasa bonasia

brown back and wings

♂

pale rump contrasts with black tail band

This very secretive gamebird is hard to spot, spending much of its time among the undergrowth of dense coniferous forests in deep shade. It is more often seen at long range, flying off with loud wingbeats, when you may glimpse its pale grey rump contrasting with the black band at the end of its longish tail and its brown back and wings.

short crest

black throat

TIP

The best way to find this shy forest resident is to listen for the distinctive sounds it makes; it may be high in a tree rather than on the ground.

spotted chest and underside

♂

grey rump

VOICE Liquid trills; male's song is a rhythmic sequence of very high-pitched notes.
NESTING Cup of grass, twigs, and leaves on ground, hidden among undergrowth; 7–11 eggs; 1 brood; late Mar–July.
FEEDING Buds, leaves, shoots, flowers, berries, and seeds; also some insects.
SIMILAR SPECIES Female Black Grouse.

Crane

Grus grus

The Crane is one of Europe's most elegant and charismatic birds. Long-legged and long-necked, it strides over the ground with an upright posture, the secondary feathers of its folded wings forming a bushy "tail". In spring and summer, large groups gather for dancing displays, performing elegant leaps and bows, accompanied by loud calls.

BREEDS IN remote reedy marshes or bogs within forests; winters in rolling uplands, open cork oak woodland, and by boggy lakes.

brownish body

dull brown head

dark wingtips

fingered tips

straight, flat wings

long black neck

long trailing legs

grey body, often rusty brown on back

red crown

white on back of head and neck

thick, pale lower neck and chest

very long, thick, dark legs

VOICE Loud, deep, clanging krro; bugling notes as pairs display to each other in spring.
NESTING Big, rough mound of stalks and leaves on ground; 2 eggs; 1 brood; May–Jul.
FEEDING Digs up roots, seeds, grain, and the larvae of insects; also takes voles, frogs, and some young birds; eats acorns in winter.
SIMILAR SPECIES Grey Heron.

Little Bustard

Tetrax tetrax

Although clearly related to the Great Bustard, the Little Bustard is much smaller and more agile. It usually keeps to cover on the ground, and can be difficult to see until it takes to the air, when it often flies low and fast like a partridge, the male's wings whistling in flight.

DISPLAYS AND *breeds on open, rolling plains with grass or cereal crops, and often in dry, stony places.*

pheasant-like head and neck

barred back ♀

black neck feathers inflated in display

white collar

fingered black wingtips

♂

white patches

mottled sandy upperparts

white below

long legs

VOICE Male has short, gruff note repeated every 10 seconds or so, in spring; female has low chuckling note.
NESTING Scrape on ground in thick cover; 3–5 eggs; 1 brood; Apr–Jun.
FEEDING Picks seeds, grain, shoots, buds, roots, and insects from ground.
SIMILAR SPECIES Pheasant, Great Bustard.

Great Bustard

Otis tarda

Massive, thick-legged, and strong-billed, the male Great Bustard is one of the world's heaviest flying birds, and one of the most spectacular in display. The female is a lot smaller. Easily disturbed, they fly off with deep, slow wingbeats, revealing black-tipped, white underwings.

black trailing edge

♂

LIVES ON *open plains with dry grass or cereals, in undisturbed areas with open, extensive views.*

grey head and neck

heavily barred rufous upperparts ♂

slim head and neck

black and rufous bars above

♀

rufous breast

short, broad tail

VOICE Mostly silent.
NESTING Unlined scrape in soil: 2–3 eggs; 1 brood; Apr–Jun.
FEEDING Forages on the ground, taking a variety of small rodents, reptiles, amphibians, and insects.
SIMILAR SPECIES Little Bustard (although much smaller).

Wading Birds

This chapter includes a group of birds that are called waders in Europe and shorebirds in North America. Most species have long legs that enable them to wade in shallow water, while their bills range from short to very long, and may be straight, upcurved, or downcurved. There are a number of distinct types in this group, including the Oystercatcher, Avocet, plovers, sandpipers, "shanks", snipes, godwits, and curlews. While many breed far from the sea by lakes and rivers, and on marshes, wetlands, and tundra, most are found along coasts outside the breeding season. Also included in this chapter are a number of other long-legged birds that wade in shallow water: these include herons, egrets and bitterns, storks, the Spoonbill, and the unmistakable Greater Flamingo.

GOLDEN PLOVER   BLACK-WINGED STILT   GREY HERON   CURLEW

Little Ringed Plover 🔊

Charadrius dubius

The neat-looking Little Ringed Plover is a bird of fresh-water shores and open ground, where it feeds using the run-tilt-run technique typical of plovers. It resembles the more coastal Ringed Plover, but has a white line above a black forehead, no white wingbar, and less brightly coloured legs and bill.

BREEDS ON *shingly and sandy lake shores, dry shingly riverbeds, and also on waste ground, including mine or quarry waste.*

white over eyes and forehead

plain wings

blurred pale area over eyes

black forehead

bold yellow eye-ring

sandy brown above

broken breast band

stubby black bill

long, tapered wingtips

dull legs

narrow black breast band

clean white underside

dull pink legs

VOICE *Short, abrupt, whistled piw or p'ew; song harsh cree-cree-cree-cree in flight.*
NESTING *Hollow on bare ground, usually hard to spot; 4 eggs; 1 brood; Apr–Jun.*
FEEDING *Picks small invertebrates from ground, using run, stop, tilt-forward action.*
SIMILAR SPECIES *Ringed Plover, Common Sandpiper.*

Ringed Plover 🔊

Charadrius hiaticula

A small, pale plover with a striking head and breast pattern and bright orange legs, the Ringed Plover is typically found feeding on sandy beaches in summer, or in tight flocks with other waders at high tide. Migrants may move inland, especially in spring and autumn.

BREEDS ON *sandy and shingly beaches. Also locally but increasingly inland, on river banks or gravel pits.*

black and orange bill

white wingbars

dull head

white over eyes

dull bill

weak band

broad black breast band

dull legs

orange legs

VOICE *Characteristic fluty whistle, a bright, mellow too-lit, also a sharp queep; repeated too-wee-a too-wee-a in song-flight.*
NESTING *Shallow scrape lined with pebbles or grass; 4 eggs; 2–3 broods; Apr–Aug.*
FEEDING *Picks small insects and worms from ground, using run-tilt action.*
SIMILAR SPECIES *Little Ringed Plover.*

Kentish Plover

Charadrius alexandrinus

This small plover is distinguishable from adult Ringed Plovers by its incomplete breast band and dark legs. Spring males are almost all-white below. It is most common in the south; rare migrants occur in Ringed Plover flocks further north.

LIVES MAINLY *in sandy areas near seashores, and beside freshwater lagoons and flooded waste ground inland. Migrants seen on estuaries or inland.*

ginger cap

earth-brown above

black bar

white forehead

paler plumage

black bill

brown chest patch

clean white underparts

black on sides of breast; duller in winter

white wingbar

♂☼

♀

dark legs

VOICE *Short, sharp, whistled* whip, *whistled* bew-ip; *rolled trilling notes.*
NESTING *Shallow hollow in sand, lined with pebbles or shell; 3–4 eggs; 2 broods; Mar–Jul.*
FEEDING *Takes small invertebrates from ground in typical run-tilt plover action.*
SIMILAR SPECIES *Juvenile Ringed Plover, juvenile Little Ringed Plover.*

Dotterel

Charadrius morinellus

The Dotterel is one of the few European birds with reversed sexual roles: the female takes the lead in courtship, is bigger than the male, and brighter in summer. Small flocks of spring and autumn migrants stop off at regular sites in the lowlands, where they are often unusually tame.

BREEDS ON *tundra or on high, rolling or flat mountain-tops with lichens and other sparse cover, often with areas of bare rock and scree.*

broad white stripe over eye

black cap

sharper face pattern

plain wings

pale "V"

rich rust-red with black belly

♀☼

♂☼

duller than female

black belly (white in winter)

VOICE *Soft* pip pip *or sweet* wit-ee-wee; *migrants can give trilled piping on taking wing.*
NESTING *Shallow scraped hollow on ground, usually under cover of low vegetation; 3 eggs; 1 brood; May–Aug.*
FEEDING *Takes flies, beetles, earthworms, and similar invertebrates from ground.*
SIMILAR SPECIES *Golden Plover.*

Golden Plover 🔊

Pluvialis apricaria

In winter, large flocks of Golden Plovers feed on lowland fields, often with Lapwings. Their winter plumage is very like that of the Grey Plover, but lacks black "wingpits", and they have slimmer bills. In summer, birds from the far north have bolder markings and black faces.

FEEDS ON *low-lying arable fields, pastures, and salt marshes in winter; breeds on high moorland and tundra.*

mottled face

weak white wingbars

dark rump

white belly

golden yellow, white, and black spangled

brownish black back

pale yellow breast

buff-yellow spots

white on underwings

white-sided black belly

SOUTHERN RACE

VOICE *Plaintive, whistled tleee, higher tlee, treeoleee; song phee-oo, pheee-oo in flight.*
NESTING *Shallow scrape, lined with lichen and heather, on ground in heather or grass, often where burned; 4 eggs; 1 brood; Apr–Jul.*
FEEDING *Takes insects in summer, mainly earthworms in winter.*
SIMILAR SPECIES *Grey Plover.*

Grey Plover 🔊

Pluvialis squatarola

Like a silver version of the Golden Plover in breeding plumage, but bigger and with a larger bill, the Grey Plover is a more coastal bird that typically feeds on mudflats, and roosts in rather static flocks on nearby fields at high tide. It is easily identified in flight by its black "wingpits".

FEEDS ON *large muddy estuaries and other shores from autumn to spring; breeds on northern tundra.*

bold white wingbars

white rump

spangled silver and black

black wingpits

bold white band from forehead to side of chest

patchy plumage

black underside

🌙 **LATE** ☀ **MOULTING**

mottled grey

pale below

VOICE *High, plaintive 3-syllabled twee-oo-wee! and loud, melancholic, fluted song.*
NESTING *Scrape on ground in short vegetation; 4 eggs; 1 brood; May–Jul.*
FEEDING *Pulls worms, molluscs, and crustaceans from mud in winter; eats mainly insects in summer on Arctic tundra.*
SIMILAR SPECIES *Golden Plover, Knot.*

Lapwing

Vanellus vanellus

Distinguished by its unique wispy crest, the Lapwing is Europe's largest and most familiar plover. At a distance it looks black and white but a close view reveals glossy greenish upperparts. Very sociable, it breeds in loose colonies on undisturbed ground, males performing spectacular tumbling aerial displays while calling loudly. Outside the breeding season it forms large flocks on fields and pastures, often with Golden Plovers and Black-headed Gulls. It gets its name from its flappy, instantly recognizable flight style, and has broad, rounded wings.

BREEDS ON *wet moors, riverside pastures, upland fields and farmland. Winters on arable fields, meadows, and salt marsh.*

white under-wing

broad, rounded wings

♂ ❄

short crest

buff fringes to feathers

shorter crest than summer

black cap extends into wispy crest

purple and copper gloss on dark green back

green back with buffish feather edges

shorter crest than male

mottled throat

white underparts

♀ ❄

cinnamon patch under tail

dull pinkish legs

♂ ❄

TIP

If a Lapwing dives at you in summer with a shrill **weew-ee** *call it is trying to protect its eggs or young, so watch where you walk in case you step on them.*

VOICE *Nasal, strained* weet *or* ee-wit; *wheezy variations on this theme; passionate song in spring,* whee-er-ee, *a* wheep-wheep! *accompanied by loud throbbing from wings.*
NESTING *Shallow hollow on open ground, lined with grass; 3–4 eggs; 1 brood; Apr–Jun.*
FEEDING *Tilts forward to pick insects and spiders from ground, or pull earthworms from soil; often taps foot on ground to attract or reveal prey.*
SIMILAR SPECIES *Unmistakable.*

Little Stint

Calidris minuta

The smallest of the common waders, with a neat, rounded head and a fine, black bill, the Little Stint breeds in the far north but moves south in autumn. Most birds that turn up in western Europe are juveniles that forage frenetically in small parties on muddy shores, often with Dunlins.

BREEDS ON *tundra, but appears beside muddy pools and lagoons while on migration.*

cream lines on back

striking cream "V" on back

streaked cap

dull grey

mottled rufous, black, and cream

short, spiky black bill

breast streaked at sides

VOICE *Hard, dry, sharp* tip *or* trip, *or sometimes* ti-ti-trip.
NESTING *Small, shallow scrape on ground, close to water; 4 eggs; 1 brood; May–Jul.*
FEEDING *Scampers about at water's edge, jabbing bill to catch tiny invertebrates and other animal matter; does not wade in deeply.*
SIMILAR SPECIES *Sanderling, juvenile Dunlin.*

Temminck's Stint

Calidris temminckii

Similar to the Little Stint, but longer, plainer, with no pale "V" on its back, Temminck's Stint is also an Arctic breeder that occurs as a passage migrant in spring and autumn. Much less common than its relative, at least in northwest Europe, it usually feeds quietly and alone in overgrown, swampy places rather than on open shores.

FEEDS ON *muddy or weedy shores by fresh water or estuaries on migration. Breeds on Arctic tundra.*

long rear body

dark spots above

white outer tail

white belly

short, pale legs

dark breast band with paler centre

grey-buff; dark blotches

dull grey-brown above

VOICE *Flight call ringing* tirrr, *often extended into quick, spluttering, dry trill,* tirr-r-r tirr-r-r.
NESTING *Shallow, unlined hollow in vegetation; 4 eggs; 1 brood; May–Jun.*
FEEDING *Picks tiny invertebrates from short vegetation and sticky, wet mud.*
SIMILAR SPECIES *Little Stint, Common Sandpiper.*

Dunlin

Calidris alpina

WINTERS ON *large estuaries, inland marshes, and lake shores. Breeds on damp moorlands and tundra.*

Widespread and common on nearly all European shores in winter, the Dunlin often occurs in huge flocks that feed and roost together on mudflats and marshes, and perform spectacular, perfectly co-ordinated aerobatic flights. Its winter plumage is quite drab, but its thin white wingbar and white-sided, dark rump are useful clues. Breeding birds in summer are far more distinctive: rich chestnut and black above, with a unique squarish black patch on the belly. In silhouette, it has a rather hunched, round-shouldered look. There are three races, with *C. a. alpina* of northern Scandinavia having the brightest breeding plumage and longest, most curved bill. The Greenland race *arctica* is duller, with a short bill; the British and south Scandinavian *schinzii* is intermediate between the two.

dark rump with white sides

thin white wingbars

hunched posture

blurred pale streak over eye

grey-brown above

very slightly downcurved, black bill

dull grey-streaked breast

white belly in winter

short dark legs

cream and black stripes on rufous back

black streaks below

chestnut and black back

black belly patch

dark-streaked, whitish breast

TIP

In winter, the Dunlin is an anonymous-looking wader, with few really distinctive features. It does, however, occur in large flocks and this in itself is a useful clue to identification. In flight, the flocks move with tight precision, like starlings, dashing this way and that, and often sweeping way out over the sea and back again.

VOICE Thin, reedy shrree or rasping treerrr; song-flight develops this into longer, trilled/pulsating "pea whistle"; soft twitter from feeding flocks.
NESTING Small, grass-lined, shallow scoop on ground or in grassy tussock; 4 eggs; 1 brood; May–Jul.
FEEDING Feeds in flocks on muddy or drier shores, sometimes wading quite deeply, probing and picking up worms, insects, molluscs, and other invertebrates.
SIMILAR SPECIES Knot, Sanderling.

Curlew Sandpiper

Calidris ferruginea

The Curlew Sandpiper follows the same migration pattern as the Little Stint, appearing with it in Europe as a passage migrant in spring and late summer. The superbly colourful spring adults are usually seen in southeastern Europe, while the birds that feed in western Europe later in the year are moulting adults or juveniles. They often feed with Dunlins but, being longer-legged and longer-billed, they can wade farther into the water and dig deeper. The more elongated shape of a Curlew Sandpiper gives it a more elegant appearance than a Dunlin, making it stand out in a mixed group. In flight, it shows a distinctive bold white rump.

FEEDS IN *shallow fresh water and marshes, and on coastal mudflats, in spring and autumn. Breeds on high Arctic tundra.*

pale stripe over eyes

dark back with even, pale buff scales

long, slim, slightly down-curved bill

pale peachy-buff breast

white belly

long black legs

bold white wingbars

white rump

TIP

Apart from a few very much rarer sandpipers, the Curlew Sandpiper is the only bird of its group that sports a white rump. Obvious in flight, this can sometimes be spotted when the bird is feeding on the shore or in the water among other waders such as Dunlins, allowing it to be identified with near total certainty.

dark cap

long wings

no streaks

copper-red plumage

pale eye-ring and chin

VOICE Flight call is a distinctive soft, trilling, rolled chirr-up, quite unlike Dunlin's wheezy flight call but rather like feeding calls from Dunlin flocks.
NESTING Simple shallow scrape on ground on tundra; 4 eggs; 1 brood; May–Jul.
FEEDING Uses its longer legs to wade into deeper water than the Dunlin, and probes softer mud with its longer bill to extract small worms, molluscs, and other invertebrates.
SIMILAR SPECIES Knot, juvenile Dunlin.

Sanderling

Calidris alba

black spangled grey

marbled chestnut

In winter, the Sanderling is by far the whitest of small waders. It has a unique feeding style: very quick and nimble, it darts back and forth along the edge of waves as they move in and out to snatch food carried by the surf. In spring and autumn, its back and breast are marbled chestnut, but its belly stays pure white.

FEEDS IN *flocks on broad sandy beaches and estuaries; scarce on other shores and inland. Breeds on northern tundra.*

blackish patch on shoulder

pale back

bright white underparts

black bill

black legs

broad white wingbar

VOICE *Sharp, hard, short* plit *or* twik twik.
NESTING *Scrape on ground, lined with dead willow leaves; 4 eggs; 1 brood; May–Jul.*
FEEDING *Snatches marine worms, molluscs, crustaceans such as sandhoppers, insects, as well as other small animals from the edge of waves.*
SIMILAR SPECIES *Dunlin, Little Stint.*

Red-necked Phalarope

Phalaropus lobatus

The tiny, delicate Red-necked Phalarope spends much of its time at sea, swimming with its head up, and tail and wings upswept. A common breeder in the far north, in most of western Europe it is an occasional autumn migrant, usually in juvenile plumage. It is very like the Grey Phalarope in winter, but its dark eye patch curves down at the rear.

BREEDS ON *pools and wet marshes in extreme north. Winters at sea; rare migrants occur on coastal lagoons.*

bold white stripe on blackish wings

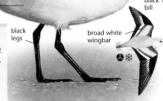

black cap and mask

dark face

needle-like black bill

buff-striped blackish back

bright red neck; male less red

buff stripes on dark grey back

black patch grey

VOICE *Sharp* twik *and variety of quick, twittering notes.*
NESTING *Small hollow in grass tussock in wet marsh; 4 eggs; 1 brood; Apr–Jul.*
FEEDING *Feeds at water's edge on insects and crustaceans, or picks them from water surface, often spinning like a top.*
SIMILAR SPECIES *Grey Phalarope.*

Grey Phalarope

Phalaropus fulicarius

Like the Red-necked Phalarope, the females of this species have brighter plumage than the males. These birds appear erratically on European coasts, usually in grey and white winter plumage, and look like tiny gulls when swimming on the sea.

bold white wingbars

LIVES ON THE *open sea outside the breeding season; occasionally blown onshore by autumn gales.*

♀ ☼

white cheek on black face

black above, striped buff

♀ ☼

black tip to thickish yellow bill

rust-red neck and underparts

yellow bill base

black patch

duller pattern than female

grey back

♂ ☼

VOICE *High* prip *or* whit.
NESTING *Small grassy hollow in northern tundra; 4 eggs; 1 brood; Jun–Jul.*
FEEDING *Picks invertebrates such as small crustaceans and snails from mud and water surface, often while spinning round on water.*
SIMILAR SPECIES *Red-necked Phalarope, Sanderling (in winter).*

Purple Sandpiper

Calidris maritima

Few waders are as tightly restricted to one habitat as this one. It spends most of its time at the very edge of the surf, searching through wave-washed, weed-covered rocks for its food. It is hard to see against the dark seaweed, particularly in its darker winter plumage, but its yellow-based, rather downcurved bill and yellow legs are useful clues to its identity.

FEEDS ON *rocky shores in winter; also around piers and groynes. Breeds on northern tundra and mountains.*

rufous on head

slightly curved bill

♥ ☼

scaly wing pattern

very dark

dark breast streaks

♥ ☼

whitish and rufous edges to feathers

dull yellow

♥ ☼ scaly dark back

dark streaks

VOICE *Simple, low, liquid* weet *or* weet-wit.
NESTING *Slight scrape on ground, lined with leaves, on wide open tundra; 4 eggs; 1 brood; May–Jul.*
FEEDING *Takes a variety of insects, spiders, and other invertebrates in summer; chiefly periwinkles and similar molluscs in winter.*
SIMILAR SPECIES *Dunlin.*

Common Sandpiper 🔊

Actitis hypoleucos

A small, slim, long-tailed wader, the Common Sandpiper can be recognized by the strong "hook" of white on its flank, and the way it bobs its head and swings its tail end up and down. It usually feeds in small, loose groups; when disturbed they fly off at low level with rapid, flickering wing-beats and stiff-winged glides, piping noisily.

BREEDS ON *rocky streams and lakesides with shingle and grass banks. Migrants live in all waterside habitats, including estuaries.*

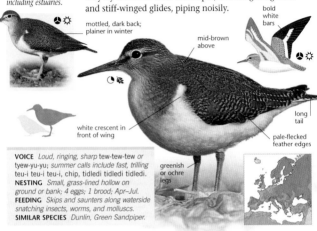

mottled, dark back; plainer in winter

mid-brown above

bold white bars

white crescent in front of wing

long tail

pale-flecked feather edges

greenish or ochre legs

VOICE Loud, ringing, sharp tew-tew-tew or tyew-yu-yu; summer calls include fast, trilling teu-i teu-i teu-i, chip, tidledi tidledi tidledi.
NESTING Small, grass-lined hollow on ground or bank; 4 eggs; 1 brood; Apr–Jul.
FEEDING Skips and saunters along waterside snatching insects, worms, and molluscs.
SIMILAR SPECIES Dunlin, Green Sandpiper.

Wood Sandpiper 🔊

Tringa glareola

Taller, slimmer, and more elegant than Common and Green Sandpipers, the Wood Sandpiper can be identified by its white rump, finely-barred tail, the pale stripe over its eye, and lack of white on its upperwings. It is basically a fresh-water bird, often seen in weedy pools or paddling about on floating vegetation, and not on open seashores.

FEEDS ON *muddy pools, weedy fringes of shallow lagoons, and salt pans, often near coast but not on estuarine mud.*

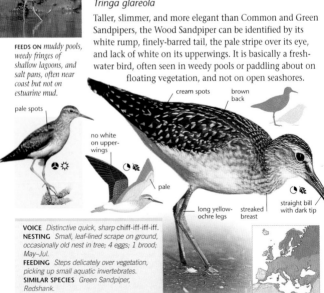

pale spots

cream spots

brown back

no white on upper-wings

pale

long yellow-ochre legs

streaked breast

straight bill with dark tip

VOICE Distinctive quick, sharp chiff-iff-iff-iff.
NESTING Small, leaf-lined scrape on ground, occasionally old nest in tree; 4 eggs; 1 brood; May–Jul.
FEEDING Steps delicately over vegetation, picking up small aquatic invertebrates.
SIMILAR SPECIES Green Sandpiper, Redshank.

Green Sandpiper 🔊

Tringa ochropus

A larger and stockier bird than the Wood Sandpiper, often seen feeding in twos and threes on muddy shores, the Green Sandpiper usually looks very dark above and white below. It bobs like the Common Sandpiper, but not so continuously, and is quick to alarm and take to the air, flying off with loud calls and shooting around the sky.

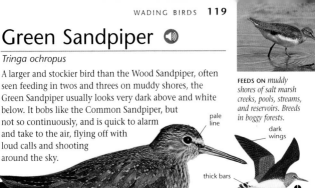

FEEDS ON *muddy shores of salt marsh creeks, pools, streams, and reservoirs. Breeds in boggy forests.*

pale line

dark wings

thick bars

streaked breast

diffuse buff spots

white-speckled, dark grey-brown upperparts

bright white below

greenish legs

VOICE *Loud, full-throated, liquid, almost yodelling tllu-eet, weet-weet!*
NESTING *Old nest of thrush or similar, in tree near forest bog; 4 eggs; 1 brood; May–Jul.*
FEEDING *Picks insects, crustaceans, and worms from water, often wading up to belly.*
SIMILAR SPECIES *Common Sandpiper, Wood Sandpiper.*

Turnstone

Arenaria interpres

Most waders like to feed on soft mud or sand, but the stocky, short-billed Turnstone favours areas of stones, weed, or other debris that it can flick through in search of small animal food. Noisy, active, and often tame, it is colourful in summer but very dark above in winter, with a piebald look in flight.

bold black and white pattern on head

FEEDS ON *sea coasts of all kinds, especially rocky shores and gravelly tidelines. Breeds on rocky northern coasts.*

white wing patch

black, white, and chestnut above

white wingbars

bold black breast band

dull brown and black above

white below

short, vivid orange legs

VOICE *Fast, hard, abrupt, staccato calls, tukatukatuk, teuk, tchik.*
NESTING *Scantily lined scrape on ground close to shore on islands and rocky coasts; 4 eggs; 1 brood; May–Jul.*
FEEDING *Stirs up and turns seaweed, shells, and stones on beach to find invertebrates.*
SIMILAR SPECIES *Purple Sandpiper, Dunlin.*

Collared Pratincole

Glareola pratincola

An unusual, specialized wader, the Collared Pratincole has a swallow-like form related to its aerial feeding habits. It is basically a Mediterranean bird that sometimes strays farther north. Despite its elegance, it can look dumpy when it has its feathers fluffed up on the ground. It often feeds in small groups.

LIVES ON *extensive areas of flat, dry mud, damp pasture, drained marshes, salt pans, and bare ground.*

faint pale spots

no black around bib

earth-brown above

forked tail

pale belly

red-based small bill

pale bib with black edge

white rump

copper-red underwing coverts

VOICE *Sharp, far-carrying, tern-like ki, kitik, rhythmic kirri-tik-kit-ik.*
NESTING *Nests in loose colonies, making shallow scrape in dry mud on the ground; 2–3 eggs; 1 brood; Apr–Jul.*
FEEDING *Catches airborne insects in its bill while flying.*
SIMILAR SPECIES *Green Sandpiper (in flight).*

Jack Snipe

Lymnocryptes minimus

The handsome little Jack Snipe is a secretive bird of dense vegetation, usually seen only when it explodes from almost underfoot and drops back into cover, often a short distance away. Much smaller than a Snipe, it has brighter cream stripes on its back, and its crown has a dark central stripe.

FEEDS IN *deep cover in very wet grass, rushy places with standing water, reedbed edges, and upper edges of weedy salt marshes.*

TIP

When a Jack Snipe is disturbed, it flies straight and low, landing quickly, unlike the larger Snipe which zigzags high into the air.

cream-striped back with green gloss

broad, bright cream stripes

pale edge

black stripe on centre of crown

shorter bill than Snipe

streaked flanks

short greenish legs

VOICE *Usually quiet, but muffled "galloping" in display flight.*
NESTING *Hollow in dry hummock of grass or moss in bog; 4 eggs; 1 brood; May–Jul.*
FEEDING *Walks forward with bouncy, springy action, probing the ground for insect larvae, worms, and seeds.*
SIMILAR SPECIES *Snipe, Dunlin.*

Snipe

Gallinago gallinago

A heavily streaked wader with an extremely long bill, the Snipe can feed only in areas where soft, oozy mud allows it to probe deeply for prey. Less elusive than the Jack Snipe, it rises from cover with harsh, dry calls. In spring, males dive through the air with stiff outer tail feathers fanned to produce a strange bleating hum.

LIVES IN *boggy heaths and wet freshwater marshes with soft mud, moving to coasts in freezing conditions.*

dark brown back with cream stripes

white tail tip

striped head with cream central stripe

very long bill

streaked breast

white belly

barred flanks

probes deep for food

rufous-centred tail

VOICE *Short, rasping scaap; in spring bright, musical chip-per, chip-per, chip-per from perch; also throbbing, wavering "bleat" from tail feathers during switchback display flight.*
NESTING *Grass-lined scrape in dense vegetation; 4 eggs; 1–2 broods; Apr–Jul.*
FEEDING *Probes soft mud for worms.*
SIMILAR SPECIES *Jack Snipe, Woodcock.*

Knot

Calidris canutus

Marbled black, buff, and chestnut with coppery underparts, the Knot is among the most colourful of waders in spring and summer. In winter, it is a dull pale grey, yet it is still spectacular for it forms vast flocks of many thousands that often take to the air, swooping through the sky in dramatic aerial manoeuvres.

ROOSTS IN *dense flocks on muddy estuaries, and feeds on a wide variety of shores. Breeds on tundra.*

pale grey rump and tail

pale stripe

pale grey plumage

straight black bill

chestnut and copper

short grey legs

apricot-tinged below

VOICE *Rather quiet; dull, short nut, plus occasional bright, whistled note.*
NESTING *Shallow hollow on ground near water, on tundra; 3–4 eggs; 1 brood; May–Jul.*
FEEDING *Eats insects and plant matter in summer, molluscs, crustaceans, and marine worms in winter.*
SIMILAR SPECIES *Grey Plover, Dunlin.*

Marsh Sandpiper

Tringa stagnatilis

This is a particularly delicate, elegant wader. It resembles the Greenshank but is smaller, with a finer bill and longer, slimmer legs that project farther beyond the tail in flight. It is rare in western Europe, but migrants pass through the eastern Mediterranean, and turn up regularly at some sites.

BREEDS IN *boggy forest clearings; feeds daintily around the edges of muddy freshwater pools, lagoons, and marshes.*

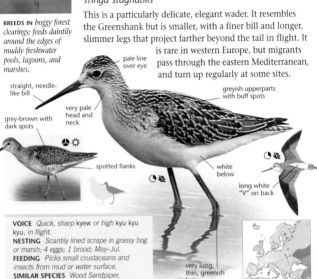

pale line over eye

straight, needle-like bill

very pale head and neck

grey-brown with dark spots

greyish upperparts with buff spots

spotted flanks

white below

long white "V" on back

very long, thin, greenish legs

VOICE *Quick, sharp* kyew *or high* kyu kyu kyu, *in flight.*
NESTING *Scantily lined scrape in grassy bog or marsh; 4 eggs; 1 brood; May–Jul.*
FEEDING *Picks small crustaceans and insects from mud or water surface.*
SIMILAR SPECIES *Wood Sandpiper, Greenshank.*

Redshank 🔊

Tringa totanus

Very conspicuous, thanks to its loud voice and bold white upperwing bands, the Redshank is common on many coasts but scarcer inland in areas where drainage has destroyed wet grassland. A wary bird, it flies off with noisy calls, alerting other birds to danger.

FEEDS ON *estuaries, salt marshes, freshwater marshes, and muddy lake shores. Breeds on salt marshes, wet pastures, and moors.*

broad white band

barred tail

straight, red-based bill

brown with dark spots above

buff feather edges

whitish belly with black spots

bright red legs

orange legs

plain brown

no spots

VOICE *Loud, ringing calls, "bouncing"* tyew-yu-yu, teu, teu-hu, *sharp annoyed* tewk, tewk; *song* tu-yoo, tu-yoo, tu-yoo.
NESTING *Hollow on ground, often with canopy of grass; 4 eggs; 1 brood; Apr–Jul.*
FEEDING *Probes and picks at mud, taking insects, worms, crustaceans, and molluscs.*
SIMILAR SPECIES *Knot, Bar-tailed Godwit.*

Spotted Redshank 🔊

Tringa erythropus

The Spotted Redshank draws attention by its lively feeding actions – small groups are often seen leaping, running, upending, and diving for tiny fish in shallow water. Scarce in winter, they are typically seen on migration in late summer and autumn.

FEEDS IN *lagoons, on salt marshes, and lake shores. Breeds on tundra and forest bogs.*

bold white stripe

pale grey head

plain upperwings

mid-grey upperparts

white back

long, fine, red-based black bill

dark body

heavily barred flanks

plain, pale grey breast

bright white belly

vivid red legs

pale spots

blackish below

VOICE Usual flight call is a distinctive, loud, sharp, clearly enunciated *chew-it!*
NESTING Simple hollow on open ground; 4 eggs; 1 brood; May–Jul.
FEEDING Often hunts in the water, dashing after prey rather than probing; takes fish fry, worms, and molluscs.
SIMILAR SPECIES Redshank, Greenshank.

Greenshank 🔊

Tringa nebularia

An elegant, delicate-looking wader, the Greenshank is a very active, dynamic feeder that often runs through the water, jinking and swerving in pursuit of prey. Rather larger than the Redshank, it looks heavier in flight; it has more white on its back but no white patches on its upperwings.

BREEDS NEAR *moorland pools; feeds on lake shores, wetlands, and estuaries; winters mainly on sheltered salt-marsh creeks.*

pale, scaly feather edges

pale head and neck

slightly upturned bill

clear white below

blackish spots

grey above

streaks on breast

white wedge on back

plain upperwings

long grey-green legs

VOICE Loud, ringing, even-pitched *tew-tew-tew*; lacks "bounce"/hysteria of Redshank call.
NESTING Scrape on ground, in grass or heather; 4 eggs; 1 brood; May–Jul.
FEEDING Probes for worms, insects, and crustaceans in shallow water; chases fish.
SIMILAR SPECIES Marsh Sandpiper, Redshank, Spotted Redshank.

Ruff

Philomachus pugnax

BREEDS IN *lowland wet meadows; migrants and wintering birds live by lakes, marshes, and coastal lagoons.*

In spring, male Ruffs grow a huge ruff of feathers around the neck and curly crown-tufts, very varied in colour and pattern. These help them attract the much smaller females at communal mating grounds (leks). Winter adults are variable; the small head and drooping bill are distinctive features.

ruff of feathers
♂

head often white
♂

blotched back
♀
orange legs

short, barely curved bill
bright ochre-buff head and breast
bright buff feather edges
pale ochre to greenish legs

white rump sides

VOICE *Usually silent; occasionally utters a low, gruff* wek *call.*
NESTING *Grass-lined scrape, well hidden among deep vegetation; 4 eggs; 1 brood; Apr–Jul.*
FEEDING *Probes into soft mud for worms, insects and their larvae; also eats some seeds.*
SIMILAR SPECIES *Redshank, Wood Sandpiper.*

Woodcock

Scolopax rusticola

BREEDS IN *woodland of all types with soft, damp earth, ditches, and bogs nearby for feeding; in similar habitat in winter.*

Its superbly camouflaged plumage ensures that the Woodcock is one of the hardest birds to spot on the ground. The best chance of seeing one is in spring and early summer when the male performs his "roding" display flight at dusk and dawn, as he patrols at just above treetop height, uttering strange croaking and sneezing calls.

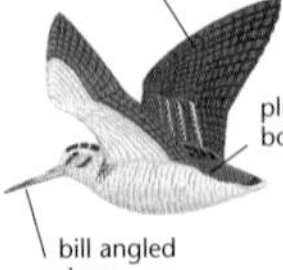
broad wings and flickering wing-action
plump body
bill angled down

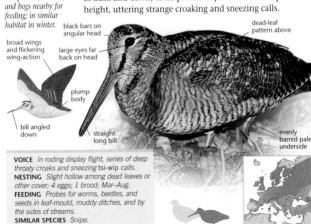

black bars on angular head
large eyes far back on head
dead-leaf pattern above
straight long bill
evenly barred pale underside

VOICE *In roding display flight, series of deep throaty croaks and sneezing* tsi-wip *calls.*
NESTING *Slight hollow among dead leaves or other cover; 4 eggs; 1 brood; Mar–Aug.*
FEEDING *Probes for worms, beetles, and seeds in leaf-mould, muddy ditches, and by the sides of streams.*
SIMILAR SPECIES *Snipe.*

Bar-tailed Godwit

Limosa lapponica

Although they breed only on the Arctic tundra, Bar-tailed Godwits are far more widespread on coasts of Europe in winter than the larger Black-tailed Godwits. Flocks disperse to probe for food in the mud; these often have a habit of rolling and twisting as they fly in to roost at high tide.

WINTERS ON *broad estuaries and sheltered muddy and sandy beaches, rarely inland.*

streaked grey-brown and buff

long, slightly upcurved bill

plain upperwings with dark tips

pale buff breast

🔾1ST❄

quite short, dark legs

coppery red below

♂☀

barred tail

streaked bright buff

🔾

VOICE *Rapid, yelping* kirruk kirruk *flight call.*
NESTING *Shallow scrape on ground, on drier ridge or mound in mainly swampy tundra; 4 eggs; 1 brood; May–Jul.*
FEEDING *Probes in mud and sand for large marine worms and molluscs.*
SIMILAR SPECIES *Black-tailed Godwit, Curlew, Whimbrel.*

Black-tailed Godwit

Limosa limosa

This large, handsome wader is more localized than the Bar-tailed Godwit at all times of year. Its longer legs and longer, straighter bill help distinguish it in all plumages from its smaller relative. It is unmistakable in flight, when it reveals its boldly pied wing and tail pattern.

coppery-red head to breast

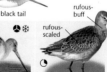

🔾☀

WINTER FLOCKS *prefer narrow, sheltered estuaries with long strips of rich mud; breeds in wet meadows and flooded pastures.*

white wingbars

white rump

🔾❄

black tail

rufous-buff

black bars on flanks

greyer

🔾❄

rufous-scaled

very long legs

🔾

VOICE *Frequent nasal* weeka-weeka-weeka *calls when breeding; rapid* vi-vi-vi *flight calls.*
NESTING *Shallow scrape among dense vegetation; 3–4 eggs; 1 brood; May–Jul.*
FEEDING *Probes deeply for worms, molluscs, and seeds, often wading up to belly in water.*
SIMILAR SPECIES *Bar-tailed Godwit, Oystercatcher.*

Black-winged Stilt

Himantopus himantopus

This beautiful, elegant, jet-black and dazzling white wader has the longest legs relative to body length of any of the world's birds. This enables it to wade into deep water after food. Its centre of distribution is the Mediterranean region, where it breeds by shallow fresh, brackish, or salt waters. Like its relative the Avocet, it is unique in Europe.

ROOSTS IN *flocks on migration; nests on salt pans, coastal lagoons, reedy pools, and flooded fields.*

trailing legs, often crossed

long white "V"

pointed all-black wings

black above

black or grey markings

pale feather edges

all-white head

black above

gleaming white below

extremely long, dark pink legs

VOICE Noisy in summer, giving rasping, strident kyik kyik or kreeek kreeek calls.
NESTING Shallow hollow in mud or sand, often on islets in shallows, lined with grass or leaves; 3–4 eggs; 1 brood; Apr–Jun.
FEEDING Picks insects from water surface, wet mud, or plant stems.
SIMILAR SPECIES Avocet.

Avocet

Recurvirostra avosetta

The Avocet is a distinctive wader, handsome and graceful, with a strongly upturned bill. Conservation and habitat management have helped provide it with its special needs: shallow, brackish water and oozy mud for feeding, and drier islands for nesting. As a result, it has thrived and spread.

WINTERS IN *close flocks that fly and feed on muddy estuaries. Breeds on shallow, saline coastal lagoons and by muddy pools.*

black cap

fine, black, upcurved bill

black bars on wings and back

brown tips to feathers

curved black band on each side of back

rather blunt black wingtips

tilts forward when feeding

long blue-grey legs

VOICE Loud, fluty klute or kloop.
NESTING Scrape on low islet or dry mud, bare or lined with shell fragments and grass; 3–4 eggs; 1 brood; Apr–Jul.
FEEDING Sweeps upcurved bill sideways through water to detect and snap up tiny shrimps and worms.
SIMILAR SPECIES Black-winged Stilt.

Oystercatcher

Haematopus ostralegus

With its dazzling black and white plumage and stout, carrot-coloured, blade-like bill, the Oystercatcher is one of Europe's most unmistakable, and common, waders. A noisy bird, its loud, piercing calls are equally distinctive. The powerful bill is adapted for prising or hammering open cockles, mussels, and other bivalve molluscs.

ROOSTS IN *often huge flocks. Breeds on sandy, muddy, and rocky shores; some inland on grass or river shingle.*

red eyes with orange eye-ring

big, bright orange-red bill

portly, black and white body

dark tip to bill

white "V"

broad white wingbar

browner back

white collar

bill with dark tip

short, sturdy, pale pink legs; duller in juvenile

VOICE *Loud, strident klip, kleep or kleep-a-kleep; shrill chorus from big flocks.*
NESTING *Shallow scrape in shingle or sand; 2–3 eggs; 1 brood; Apr–Jul.*
FEEDING *Probes for molluscs and marine worms; prises bivalve molluscs from rocks and seaweed; eats earthworms inland.*
SIMILAR SPECIES *Avocet, Black-tailed Godwit.*

Stone-curlew

Burhinus oedicnemus

This semi-nocturnal wader is hard to locate by day, when it spends time standing or squatting stock-still, its camouflaging plumage blending into the background of soil, stones, or sand. If seen, it is easy to identify, with its big, pale, goggle-like eyes, long, strong, yellow legs, and two-tone bill. Breeding birds are very noisy after dark.

BREEDS ON *heaths, arable fields with light, stony soil and sparse crops; most coastal populations extinct.*

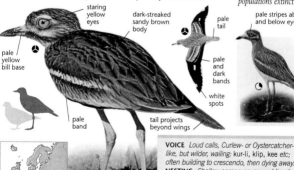

staring yellow eyes

dark-streaked sandy brown body

pale yellow bill base

pale tail

pale and dark bands

white spots

pale stripes above and below eye

pale band

tail projects beyond wings

VOICE *Loud calls, Curlew- or Oystercatcher-like, but wilder, wailing: kur-li, klip, kee etc; often building to crescendo, then dying away.*
NESTING *Shallow scrape on ground lined with stones etc; 2 eggs; 1–2 broods; Apr–Aug.*
FEEDING *Runs and tilts like plover to pick up beetles, worms, snails, lizards, or mice.*
SIMILAR SPECIES *Curlew, female Pheasant.*

Whimbrel 🔊

Numenius phaeopus

This smaller cousin of the Curlew is more compact and darker-plumaged, with a distinctively striped head. Unlike the common and widespread Curlew, the Whimbrel breeds only in the north, being just a spring and autumn migrant elsewhere.

BREEDS ON *boggy moors and tundra. Migrants stop off to feed and rest on tidal mudflats, rocky shores, and coastal fields.*

TIP

Distinctly shorter-billed than Curlews, Whimbrels look dumpier in flight, and have faster wingbeats. Their stuttering calls are the best distinction.

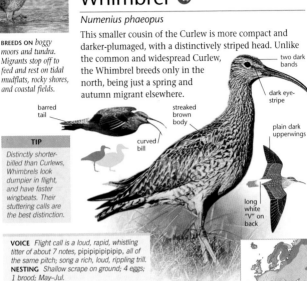

barred tail

streaked brown body

curved bill

two dark bands

dark eye-stripe

plain dark upperwings

long white "V" on back

VOICE *Flight call is a loud, rapid, whistling titter of about 7 notes, pipipipipipipip, all of the same pitch; song a rich, loud, rippling trill.*
NESTING *Shallow scrape on ground; 4 eggs; 1 brood; May–Jul.*
FEEDING *Probes and picks up insects, snails, earthworms, crabs, and marine worms.*
SIMILAR SPECIES *Curlew, Bar-tailed Godwit.*

Curlew 🔊

Numenius arquata

Europe's largest wader, the Curlew is widespread on all coasts and, especially when breeding, inland too. With its very long, downcurved bill, distinctive calls, and lovely song, it is hard to mistake for any common bird apart from a Whimbrel, although distant flying birds can look gull-like.

WINTERS *mainly on big, muddy estuaries; breeds on bogs, wet moorland or meadows, and northern shores and islands.*

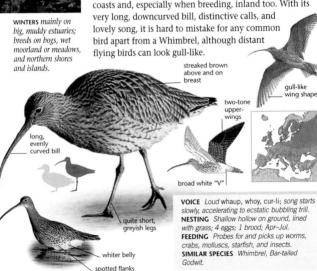

streaked brown above and on breast

gull-like wing shape

two-tone upper-wings

long, evenly curved bill

broad white "V"

quite short, greyish legs

whiter belly

spotted flanks

VOICE *Loud whaup, whoy, cur-li; song starts slowly, accelerating to ecstatic bubbling trill.*
NESTING *Shallow hollow on ground, lined with grass; 4 eggs; 1 brood; Apr–Jul.*
FEEDING *Probes for and picks up worms, crabs, molluscs, starfish, and insects.*
SIMILAR SPECIES *Whimbrel, Bar-tailed Godwit.*

Little Bittern

Ixobrychus minutus

Living among dense wetland cover, this tiny, secretive heron is normally difficult to see. However, during its short, low flight, on rapidly beating wings, the big, oval, pale wing patches – the most obvious feature of the plumage of both adults and juveniles – are a giveaway. The occasional individual that perches high on a reed stem or on a branch overhanging the water reveals its subtle pattern, especially delicate in the male, including subtle stripes on the neck.

SUMMER *visitor to south and central Europe, breeding in reedbeds, marshes, riversides, as well as small pools and flooded willow thickets. Rare spring migrant to UK.*

greenish gloss to black upperparts

black extends to head as a cap

yellow dagger-like bill

♂

bright buff neck

strong greenish legs

large, creamy buff wing patch

♂

trailing legs

narrow streaks on neck

streaked brown back

duller wing patch

streaked pale brown

♀

striped chest

TIP

Although it may be easier to see than its much larger relative the Bittern, the Little Bittern is generally unobtrusive. Especially where common, it is more likely to reveal itself at and after dusk by its short nasal calls and monotonous "song". However, these are often hard to pick out against a background of calls from other waterbirds and frogs.

VOICE Nasal kwekwekwe flight call, shorter kuk or kek calls; nocturnal "song" is a monotonously repeated, deep, single croak.
NESTING Small nest of stems among dense reeds or bush; 2–7 eggs; 1 brood; May–Jul.
FEEDING Catches fish, frogs, aquatic insects, and freshwater shrimps, by stealthy stalking or waiting followed by a sudden forward lunge.
SIMILAR SPECIES Squacco Heron, Night Heron; juveniles similar to juvenile Little Bittern.

Night Heron

Nycticorax nycticorax

Although they may hunt for food during daytime when breeding, Night Herons are mainly active at dusk and dawn. At their communal roosts, they spend much of the day motionless, perched on branches of trees and shrubs, resembling pale spots at a distance.

broad wings

thin white plumes

chest streaks

pale spots above

FEEDS AT *the edge of ponds, lakes, rivers, reedbeds, and other wetlands; roosts and breeds in trees and bushes.*

grey wings

dark brown wings and back

black cap and back

short, thick bill

yellow legs; red in spring

VOICE *Brief, low-pitched, crow-like croaks, especially at dusk.*
NESTING *Small nest of sticks in tree or bush; 3–5 eggs; 1 brood; Apr–Jul.*
FEEDING *Suddenly seizes small fish, large insects, and amphibians, mainly at night.*
SIMILAR SPECIES *Little Bittern, Bittern (similar to but much bigger than juvenile).*

Bittern

Botaurus stellaris

This very secretive, large, bulky bird is more often heard than seen, when males proclaim their territories by a remarkable booming "song", audible up to 5 km (3 miles) away. Restricted to large wet reedbeds, the Bittern is very local and scattered across its European range.

BREEDS IN *large, wet reedbeds. More widespread in winter, when it may be forced by frost to feed in smaller patches of reed or open water.*

mottled brown body

blackish crown

broad, bowed wings

paler panel

black stripe

dagger-like bill

streaked neck

short legs and very long toes

VOICE *Repeated, deep, rhythmic boom, ker-whooomp! like the sound made by blowing over the top of a bottle; nasal flight call.*
NESTING *Broad nest of reed stems hidden in dense reedbed; 4–6 eggs; 1 brood; Apr–May.*
FEEDING *Catches fish, especially eels.*
SIMILAR SPECIES *Purple Heron, juvenile Little Bittern.*

Squacco Heron

Ardeola ralloides

This smallish, squat-bodied heron can be easily overlooked on the ground, as its buff plumage blends into the background. However, it is transformed when it takes flight, as it reveals its brilliant white wings, rump, and tail. This is very much a southern bird in Europe, occurring only rarely as a vagrant further north.

BREEDS IN *freshwater swamps and marshes, from reedbeds to weed-fringed riversides; when looking for prey, often in overgrown ditches or streams.*

white wings

streaked head and neck

blue-grey bill with black tip

long, streaked plumes

duller back

heavy streaks

pale forewings

tawny-buff

VOICE *Generally silent, but may utter shrill, harsh karr of alarm at dusk or frog-like croaks.*
NESTING *Small nest of branches, twigs, grass or reeds, low in reeds; 4–6 eggs; 1 brood; Apr–Jun.*
FEEDING *Stands on floating weeds or among dense cover, snatching fish, frogs, and insects.*
SIMILAR SPECIES *Cattle Egret, Little Bittern.*

Cattle Egret

Bubulcus ibis

Unlike most members of the heron family, which feed mainly on fish, the Cattle Egret specializes in accompanying large animals and snapping up the insects disturbed by their hooves. In Africa, they join buffaloes and other wild herbivores, but in southern Europe they usually follow cattle, generally in small groups.

rich buff crown

reddish bill (spring)

rich buff

FEEDS BY *following cattle in fields, also finds food at refuse tips; roosts and breeds in thickets of trees and bushes near water.*

looks all-white in flight

white body and wings

golden buff plumes (spring)

all white body

dark, trailing feet

VOICE *Harsh, double croaks at roosts and breeding colonies; otherwise usually silent.*
NESTING *Shallow nest of sticks and reeds in tree or bush; 4–5 eggs; 1 brood; Apr–Jun.*
FEEDING *Seizes insects disturbed by cattle, sheep, or other livestock; also eats small reptiles, frogs, and mice.*
SIMILAR SPECIES *Squacco Heron, Little Egret.*

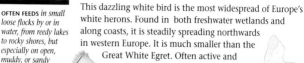

Little Egret

Egretta garzetta

OFTEN FEEDS *in small loose flocks by or in water, from reedy lakes to rocky shores, but especially on open, muddy, or sandy shores.*

This dazzling white bird is the most widespread of Europe's white herons. Found in both freshwater wetlands and along coasts, it is steadily spreading northwards in western Europe. It is much smaller than the Great White Egret. Often active and agile in search of prey, it also spends much time wading slowly or standing still.

long plumes on nape

all-white plumage

slim, sharp dark bill

pointed breast plumes

rather bowed wings

no head or back plumes

black legs

yellow feet

VOICE *Usually silent except when breeding, when it utters snarling and croaking calls.*
NESTING *Stick nest in tree, often with other herons and cormorants; 3–4 eggs; 1 brood; Apr–Jul.*
FEEDING *Eats small fish, frogs, and snails.*
SIMILAR SPECIES *Great White Egret, Cattle Egret.*

Great White Egret

Ardea alba

PERCHES IN *trees overlooking wetlands; nests mainly in reeds, sometimes in low trees. Feeds in drier grassy areas as well as wetter habitats.*

This is a well-named bird, standing as tall as or even a little taller than a Grey Heron. Its size, and its dazzlingly white plumage, make this elegant, slim, angular bird easy to see at a distance. In spring at its breeding colonies, it spreads its long back plumes in a dramatic courtship display; its dagger-like bill is then blackish and its upper legs reddish.

long legs

arched wings

long yellow bill

very long, slim neck

all-white plumage; long back plumes in summer

slower, heavier flight than Little Egret

legs all-blackish or dull yellow mainly above joint; feet dark

VOICE *Mainly silent, but cawing calls at breeding colonies.*
NESTING *Shallow platform of reeds or twigs, lined with finer material; nests in colonies; 2–5 eggs; 1 brood; Apr–Jul.*
FEEDING *Hunts for fish, frogs, and small mammals in typical heron fashion.*
SIMILAR SPECIES *Little Egret.*

Spoonbill

Platalea leucorodia

This big waterbird is unmistakable in
Europe once its remarkable spatula-shaped
bill is visible. Though rather like a
large white egret, it is distinguished
by its habit of striding
with a strangely
human-like walk through
the shallows and sweeping its
bill from side to side. Its head is
outstretched in flight.

black
wingtips

outstretched
head

FEEDS ON *saltpans,
marshes, other shallow
wetlands; breeds at
reedy lakes with fringing
bushes or trees.*

ochre on chin
and base of neck

flattened, broad-
tipped, black bill,
yellow at end

pinkish
bill

white
underwings

long, thick
black legs

VOICE *Normally silent.*
NESTING *Platform of sticks or reed in colony
in reeds or tree; 3–4 eggs; 1 brood; Apr–Jul.*
FEEDING *Sweeps partly open bill through
water from side to side to snap up small fish,
molluscs, and crustaceans.*
SIMILAR SPECIES *Mute Swan (similar in
flight), Little Egret.*

Black Stork

Ciconia nigra

Slimmer than the White Stork, the
Black Stork is a far shyer, rarer bird,
restricted to wilder habitats with
extensive tracts of forest, marshes,
and isolated crags. Some can be
seen in the Pyrenees on migration
to winter in Africa; few
turn up outside the
normal range.

white wingpits

red around
eye

NESTS IN *remote areas
in forests, marshes,
and rocky areas, not in
towns or villages like
White Stork.*

dagger-like
red bill

purple and green
gloss to black
plumage

dull greenish bill

duller

long
"fingers"

paler
legs

white
belly

long red
legs

VOICE *Silent apart from rasping calls and
bill-clappering when at nest.*
NESTING *Big, bulky, platform of sticks on
rock ledge or high in large tree; 2–4 eggs;
1 brood; May–Jul.*
FEEDING *Eats amphibians and insects.*
SIMILAR SPECIES *White Stork and juvenile
Cormorant (in flight).*

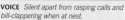

White Stork

Ciconia ciconia

OFTEN NESTS *on rooftops, with the huge pile of sticks and the large birds visible at great range. Feeds on open land near rivers, lakes, and marshes.*

Although widespread, the White Stork is declining in most of its range, due to intensification of farming and drainage or pollution of wetlands. Among Europe's largest birds, White Storks form a dramatic spectacle when thousands of birds gather in swirling flocks to fly migration to Africa, soaring on long, broad wings.

red bill

long "fingers"

white body

black flight feathers

outstretched head

trailing legs

holds wings flat when gliding

long, sturdy red legs

VOICE *Silent, apart from loud bill-clappering at nest.*
NESTING *Great bulky nest of sticks on tower, house roof, or pole, or in tree; 2–4 eggs; 1 brood; Apr–Jun.*
FEEDING *Snaps up insects, rodents, small fish, and amphibians.*
SIMILAR SPECIES *Grey Heron, White Pelican.*

Purple Heron

Ardea purpurea

SEARCHES FOR *food in reed swamps, sedge beds, or wet meadows. Migrants found north of breeding range in similar wetlands with cover.*

Slimmer, darker than the Grey Heron, with a thinner, more kinked neck, the Purple Heron is a far more secretive bird, spending long periods hidden among dense reeds. When it takes flight, its wings show a more curved trailing edge and narrower base than its larger, far more widespread relative.

grey midwings

less striped

snake-like head and neck

paler neck

brown body

deep neck bulge

reddish underwing coverts

ginger neck with dark stripes

rusty shoulder patch

dark back with paler buff plumes

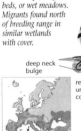

VOICE *Simple, brief, harsh krekk.*
NESTING *Large pile of reed stems and other vegetation, often in reeds, sometimes in trees; 4–5 eggs; 1 brood; Feb–Jun.*
FEEDING *Seizes small fish and frogs, as well as aquatic invertebrates in its long, slim, spear-like bill.*
SIMILAR SPECIES *Grey Heron, Bittern.*

Grey Heron

Ardea cinerea

Standing still as a statue or walking slowly through the shallows before suddenly straightening its neck with lightning speed to seize a fish in its powerful bill, this big, grey heron is easy to identify. It may also be slimmer or hunched, and can perch in a tree or perform dramatic aerobatics.

FEEDS IN *fresh and salt water habitats, from estuaries and rocky shores to lakes, floods, and even garden ponds in towns and cities.*

dagger-like yellowish bill; orange in spring

head with grey cap; lacks crest

grey sides of head and neck

wispy black plume

pale grey body

black streaks on white foreneck

broad, bowed, grey and black wings

long yellowish legs, reddish in spring

VOICE Loud, harsh *fraink*; squawking, croaking, and bill-snapping at nest.
NESTING Large nest of stout sticks, usually in treetop colony; 4–5 eggs; 1 brood; Jan–May.
FEEDING Seizes fish, frogs, small mammals, and other prey in its bill, typically after long, patient stalk before sudden strike.
SIMILAR SPECIES Purple Heron.

Greater Flamingo

Phoenicopterus roseus

The only one of the world's five species of flamingo to occur in the wild in Europe, this is one of our most exotic-looking birds. Its strangely shaped, angled-down bill, extremely long neck and legs, and lovely pastel plumage make it easy to recognize. It usually lives in large flocks.

BREEDS ON *a few big salty lakes scattered across Mediterranean countries; more widespread as a non-breeder, on salt pans and exposed lakes.*

very long trailing legs

very long curved neck

red patch on narrow wing

grey bill

greyish body

dark grey legs

bent, pink bill with black tip

very long pink legs

whitish to pale pink plumage

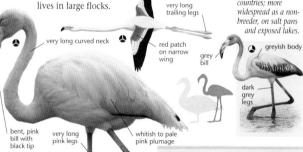

VOICE Loud, deep honking and cackling.
NESTING Small mud pillar in shallow water; 1 egg; 1 brood; Apr–May.
FEEDING Sweeps bill upside down through water to catch tiny crustaceans, as it wades in shallows, belly deep or swimming like a swan.
SIMILAR SPECIES Other flamingos; single birds are often escapes from captivity.

Waterfowl

This large group of water birds consists mainly of one family –
ducks, geese, and swans (commonly known as wildfowl).
It also includes other birds with an aquatic lifestyle –
diving birds like grebes and divers, and two rails, the Coot
and the Moorhen. Most are found in freshwater wetlands
and possess waterproof plumage, quite short, specialized
bills, and, in the case of wildfowl, webbed feet. All are good
swimmers, although many spend much of their time on dry
land. The ducks can be divided into two groups: diving ducks
such as the Tufted Duck, which dive from the surface to feed
underwater, and surface feeders (or dabblers) like the Mallard.
Geese are larger and longer-necked, feeding on dry land or
marshes, but returning to water each night for
a safe roost. Swans are largest of all, and
feed on both water and land.

COOT   MUTE SWAN   GREYLAG GOOSE   MALLARD

Moorhen

Gallinula chloropus

Widespread and common on and near all kinds of waters from wet ditches to large lakes, the Moorhen is easily distinguished from the similar Coot by its red and yellow bill and green legs. It has an oddly nervous manner, and usually runs or swims into cover at any hint of danger.

BREEDS *on small ponds with overgrown edges; feeds near ponds, lakes, and rivers, on open, wet, grassy ground.*

red eye

rich brown back

red bill with yellow tip

slate-grey below and on head

brown head; bill greenish-yellow

brown body

white under tail

green legs

long green toes

diagonal white stripe

VOICE *Loud, throaty or metallic notes, kurruk or kittik, high kik, stuttering kik-kikikikik-ik.*
NESTING *Shallow bowl of leaves and stems in vegetation, usually just above water; 5–11 eggs; 2–3 broods; Apr–Aug.*
FEEDING *Picks seeds, fruit, shoots, snails, and insects from damp ground or shallows.*
SIMILAR SPECIES *Water Rail, Coot.*

Coot

Fulica atra

Bigger and more sturdily built than its relative the Moorhen, the quarrelsome Coot also differs in having lobed toes, like grebes. It forms larger, more cohesive feeding flocks, which dive often to feed underwater, bobbing up to the surface like corks.

BREEDS MAINLY *on lakes and flooded pits, with fringing vegetation or overhanging branches. Winters on larger, more open lakes.*

pale trailing edge

white facial shield and bill

intensely black head

slate-black body

rounded rump

red eyes

VOICE *Loud kowk! high-pitched, metallic pik or teuwk; juvenile gives loud whistles.*
NESTING *Bowl of vegetation in reeds, on overhanging branch or on mound of semi-floating debris; 6–9 eggs; 1–2 broods; Apr–Aug.*
FEEDING *Eats grass, aquatic plants, seeds, tadpoles, and other small aquatic animals.*
SIMILAR SPECIES *Moorhen, small grebes.*

yellowish bill

whitish face and throat

big grey feet with lobed toes

Little Grebe

Tachybaptus ruficollis

The smallest European grebe, this dark, short-billed, rotund, and almost tailless bird swims buoyantly and dives often. Longer-necked and less portly in winter, it can look like a Black-necked Grebe. In summer, its whinnying trills are a good clue to its presence.

BREEDS ON *freshwater lakes, ponds, flooded pits, canals, and rivers. Winters on larger waters or sheltered coastal waters.*

all-dark wings

trailing feet

blackish cap

rufous on face and neck

pale yellow spot on short bill

buff foreneck

buffish face

"sawn-off" rear end due to very short, buff tail

VOICE *When breeding, distinctive high-pitched, rapid trill that fades away.*
NESTING *Floating mound of weed, anchored to branch; 4–6 eggs; 1 brood; Apr–Jun.*
FEEDING *Dives to catch small fish, insects, and molluscs.*
SIMILAR SPECIES *Black-necked Grebe, Moorhen.*

Black-necked Grebe

Podiceps nigricollis

Widespread but very local as a breeding bird, since it is restricted to nutrient-rich, low-lying lakes, the Black-necked Grebe is more often seen on fresh water in winter than the Slavonian Grebe. It is best distinguished from the latter by its finer, slightly uptilted bill, peaked crown, and steep forehead.

NESTS AMONG *dense vegetation on low-lying lakes and pools; winters on coastal bays, estuaries, and fresh waters.*

peaked crown

red eyes

fine, uptilted bill

fan-shaped golden ear plumes

black neck

coppery red flanks

trailing legs

white patch on slim wings

dusky cheeks

grey foreneck

pale "hook"

VOICE *Chattering and soft, high whistling calls in breeding season; silent in winter.*
NESTING *Semi-floating mound of wet weed fixed to vegetation; 3–4 eggs; 1 brood; Mar–Jul.*
FEEDING *Catches insects, molluscs, and small fish in long dives underwater.*
SIMILAR SPECIES *Slavonian Grebe, Little Grebe.*

Slavonian Grebe

Podiceps auritus

This handsome bird is easy to identify at its remote northern breeding sites in summer, but in winter is more difficult to distinguish from other small grebes, especially the Black-necked Grebe. Much more tied to coastal waters in winter, it has a different head shape, bill shape, and a sharper contrast between dark and white.

BREEDS ON *remote, cold pools with some fringing vegetation. Winters mainly on muddy estuaries, and more rarely on inland waters.*

flat black crown

straight, pale-tipped bill

stiff golden wedge

rust-red neck

white shoulder patch

rust-red flanks

white cheeks and foreneck

1ST

black cap
large white cheeks

VOICE *Fast, high, whistling trill when breeding; usually silent in winter.*
NESTING *Semi-floating pile of wet weed anchored to stems; 4–5 eggs; 1 brood; Apr–Jul.*
FEEDING *Dives to catch small fish; eats mainly insects and crustaceans in summer.*
SIMILAR SPECIES *Black-necked Grebe, Red-necked Grebe.*

Red-necked Grebe

Podiceps grisegena

A widespread and typical breeding bird of large fresh waters in northeast Europe, the Red-necked Grebe migrates in autumn to spend winter in western Europe. In the British Isles for instance, it is generally much scarcer than the usually slimmer-looking, paler Great Crested Grebe.

BREEDS ON *reedy lakes or slow rivers; winters mainly on sheltered estuaries or coastal bays, sometimes on fresh waters inland.*

black cap extends below eye

yellow base to stout, dagger-like bill

grey face with white upper edge

dark chestnut neck and breast

white patches

slightly drooping neck

VOICE *Growls, squeals, and wails when breeding; silent in winter.*
NESTING *Semi-floating heap of wet weed attached to stems; 3–4 eggs; 1 brood; Apr–Jun.*
FEEDING *Mainly fish caught by diving, also eats crustaceans and insects in summer.*
SIMILAR SPECIES *Great Crested Grebe, Slavonian Grebe.*

striped cheeks

dusky foreneck

Great Crested Grebe

Podiceps cristatus

COURTS AND breeds
on flooded gravel pits,
reservoirs, or big lakes
and rivers; winters
on fresh waters
or sheltered
coastal waters.

Largest of European grebes, this is a striking bird in spring and summer, when pairs use their spectacular head ruff and spiky head tufts in face-to-face head-shaking courtship displays. They also dive, surfacing with weed in their bills to offer one another. Winter birds are hard to distinguish from scarcer Red-necked Grebes.

black head plumes

dagger-like pink bill

unique ruff

slender white neck and white breast

drooping neck

two bold white patches

VOICE *Loud growls and barks while courting and nesting; juveniles make loud, fluty whistles.*
NESTING *Semi-floating pile of wet weed, anchored to vegetation; 3–4 eggs; 1 brood; Feb–Jun.*
FEEDING *Dives to catch mainly fish, also aquatic insect larvae and small amphibians.*
SIMILAR SPECIES *Red-necked Grebe.*

striped head

pink bill

pale greyish

white over eye

white foreneck

Red-throated Diver

Gavia stellata

BREEDS BY *remote*
moorland pools and
lakes, but feeds at sea
daily in parts of range.
Winters on coasts
and estuaries.

As with other divers, this is a long-bodied, skilled swimmer and diver that usually has a low profile in the water, and is rarely seen on land except at the nest. The smallest diver, it is distinguished by its slimmer bill, held angled upwards. In summer, it is often seen commuting to and fro between its nest and the sea, flying high with outstretched head and legs, calling loudly.

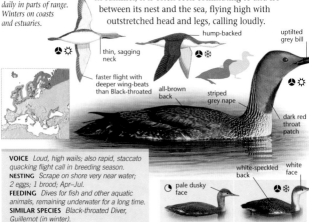

thin, sagging neck

hump-backed

uptilted grey bill

faster flight with deeper wing-beats than Black-throated

all-brown back

striped grey nape

dark red throat patch

VOICE *Loud, high wails; also rapid, staccato quacking flight call in breeding season.*
NESTING *Scrape on shore very near water; 2 eggs; 1 brood; Apr–Jul.*
FEEDING *Dives for fish and other aquatic animals, remaining underwater for a long time.*
SIMILAR SPECIES *Black-throated Diver, Guillemot (in winter).*

white-speckled back

white face

pale dusky face

Black-throated Diver

Gavia arctica

Easily distinguished in its beautifully patterned breeding plumage, the Black-throated Diver is duller in winter and harder to separate from the smaller Red-throated or larger Great Northern Diver. Useful clues are the Black-throated's white flank patch, slim, straight bill, quite bulbous head, and greyish nape, paler than the back.

NESTS MAINLY *on islets in large, remote lakes. Winters in coastal waters and large estuaries, rarely inland.*

grey head

head less sagging than Red-throated

striped neck

black throat

oval patch of white bars on each side

dark above

grey nape

dark cap

white flank patch

scaly back

1ST

VOICE *Loud, wild, rhythmic wailing "song" and croaking calls in breeding season; silent in flight and during winter.*
NESTING *Shallow scrape by water's edge; 2 eggs; 1 brood; Apr–Jul.*
FEEDING *Catches fish in long, deep dives.*
SIMILAR SPECIES *Red-throated Diver, Great Northern Diver.*

Great Northern Diver

Gavia immer

Largest of the common European divers, the Great Northern has boldly chequered upperparts and a black head in breeding plumage. In winter, it is best distinguished by its size, very broad body, heavy bill, thick neck, and big head with a steep forehead. It also has a dark nape and neck collar. It usually swims low in the water, its back often awash.

WINTERS ON *coastal waters, including broad estuaries and bays, typically farther from shore than the two smaller divers.*

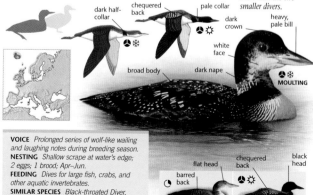

dark half-collar

chequered back

pale collar

dark crown

heavy, pale bill

white face

broad body

dark nape

MOULTING

flat head

barred back

chequered back

black head

VOICE *Prolonged series of wolf-like wailing and laughing notes during breeding season.*
NESTING *Shallow scrape at water's edge; 2 eggs; 1 brood; Apr–Jun.*
FEEDING *Dives for large fish, crabs, and other aquatic invertebrates.*
SIMILAR SPECIES *Black-throated Diver, immature Cormorant.*

Teal

Anas crecca

The Teal is the smallest of the common European surface-feeding ducks. Outside the breeding season, it is usually seen in smallish flocks. Taking off almost vertically, the fast-flying birds wheel and turn with great agility, co-ordinating their actions precisely like a flock of small waders.

BREEDS ON *freshwater marshes and on boggy heathland and moorland. Winters mainly on fresh waters and estuaries.*

cream-edged green band

chestnut head

narrow, horizontal, white band along side

white midwing bars

white centre to underwings

green patch

♂ ❄

finely barred grey body

grey bill

♂ ❄

pale streak by tail

♀

streaked brown

> **VOICE** Male has far-carrying, high-pitched, piping *crik crik*; female utters high quacks.
> **NESTING** Down-lined hollow near water; 8–11 eggs; 1 brood; Apr–Jun.
> **FEEDING** Dabbles and upends mainly for seeds, but also small snails, fly larvae, and other aquatic animals in breeding season.
> **SIMILAR SPECIES** Garganey, male Wigeon.

Garganey

Anas querquedula

Almost as small as the Teal, the Garganey is generally much scarcer; it is unique among ducks in Europe as it is only a summer visitor, wintering in Africa. Males in their breeding plumage are easy to distinguish from Teals, their white head stripe noticeable at long range, but mottled brown females and males in autumn are trickier to separate.

BREEDS IN *wet, grassy marshes and flooded grassland with good cover; migrants are seen in small numbers in autumn on lakes.*

♀

pale fore-wings

♂ ❄

two equal white bars on dark hindwings

bold white crescent

pale spot

dark leading edge

pinkish brown

♂ ❄

♀

pale line

white spot

chestnut breast and head

pale side

♂ ❄

blotchy brown

> **VOICE** Male has brief, dry rattle; female may utter short, high quacks but is often silent.
> **NESTING** Down-lined hollow in vegetation near water; 8–11 eggs; 1 brood; May–Jun.
> **FEEDING** Eats insects, larvae, and other small invertebrates, or roots and seeds, by dabbling and upending.
> **SIMILAR SPECIES** Teal, female Shoveler.

Wigeon

Anas penelope

Although it often nests far from the sea in its northern breeding grounds, the Wigeon is a characteristic duck of coastal estuaries and salt marshes in winter, where it can feed on short grasses like a miniature goose. The often large, colourful, grazing flocks advance across the ground in a tightly packed mass, all the birds usually facing in the same direction. Popular targets for wildfowlers, the flocks have good reason to be wary, and are quick to take to the wing, wheeling about as the males give their wonderfully wild, far-carrying, whistling calls. Squat and short-legged on the ground, Wigeon are transformed into swift and elegant birds in flight.

BREEDS ON *edges of moorland pools and lakes, in Northern Europe and UK. Winters on estuaries, freshwater marshes, or around reservoirs.*

dull grey wings

♀

sharp tail

reddish flanks contrast with white belly

♂❄

bold white wing panel

yellow forehead

greyish bill with black tip

rounded grey body; paler than male Teal's

chestnut head and neck

♂❄

black-and-white stern

pinkish breast

white belly

TIP

In flight, Wigeon are short-necked, with pointed wings and tail and a bulbous head on a pinched-in neck. The males' white wing panels flash prominently.

white band on wings

retains white on wing ♂❄

redder than female

♀ mottled greyish to rust-brown body

round head

VOICE *Male has loud, explosive, musical whistling whee-oo; female gives deep, abrupt, harsh growls.*
NESTING *Down-lined hollow on ground among tallish vegetation, near water; 8–9 eggs; 1 brood; Apr–Jul.*
FEEDING *Grazes on short grasses, especially beds of eelgrass, often in dense flocks; also feeds by dabbling and upending in shallow water, taking mainly seeds, shoots, and roots.*
SIMILAR SPECIES *Male Teal, female Mallard, and female Gadwall.*

Shoveler

Anas clypeata

FEEDS ON *and breeds by reedy pools, mainly in lowlands; winters on lakes, reservoirs, inland marshes, and sheltered estuaries with grassy salt marshes.*

Male Shovelers in breeding plumage look superficially like male Mallards with the colours rearranged into a different pattern. However, they are easily distinguished by their low-slung bodies, gleaming white breasts (visible at long range) that contrast with the dark green head and chestnut flanks, and above all, by their outsized, broad, shovel-like bill. The bill is also a feature of female Shovelers and, along with their body shape, helps separate them from females of Mallard and other dabbling ducks. Both sexes look front-heavy and short-tailed in their fast flight, in which they show pale forewings.

grey forewings

pale blue forewings

♀

♂

bold pattern on underparts

green head; looks black at distance

dark rufous flanks

striking yellow eyes

♂❄

huge, long, broad bill

dazzlingly white breast

streaked, pale brown body

♀

huge, shovel-like bill with orange sides

rufous-tinged flanks

dark head

♂☼

pale crescent

TIP
Shovelers often feed in small groups that swim in circles. Each bird's bill almost touches the next one's tail, and is pushed through the water to sieve food particles from the sediment stirred up by the feet of the bird ahead. They also upend to feed, making their orange legs and pointed wings visible.

VOICE Often silent birds, although rival males give quiet, deep, gruff, nasal took took calls when they chase one another, and females may utter soft, deep quacks; wings make "woofing" noise on taking flight.
NESTING Hollow lined with down and sometimes with grasses or other leaves, in vegetation near water; 8–12 eggs; 1 brood; Mar–Jun.
FEEDING Dabbles on surface for seeds and invertebrates with bill thrust onto the water surface or beneath it with the bird's back almost awash.
SIMILAR SPECIES Mallard. Female Garganey similar to female Shoveler.

Pintail

Anas acuta

Arguably the most elegant of all the surface-feeding ducks, the Pintail is a big, slim, long-necked bird. It is generally scarcer than some of its relatives during winter, when birds from the main breeding populations in eastern and northern Europe disperse widely to milder areas in the west and south, often in ones or twos among large groups of more common ducks. Large flocks are found, however, on a few traditional wintering sites on estuaries and freshwater marshes. The striking breeding plumage of the males, acquired as with other ducks in winter, is unmistakable, but females and immatures need separating from those of other dabbling ducks. Good clues are the long neck, slim bill, and more pointed tail.

FEEDS AT *wintering sites on estuaries and fresh marshes; breeds by tundra and upland pools or lowland coastal marshes. Breeds sporadically in west.*

TIP

The males' long central tail feathers are often raised, but may sometimes be lowered – as when the birds are up-ending for food or when they are nervous. In the autumn "eclipse" plumage, these are lost for a few weeks.

TIP

In flight, female Pintails can be distinguished from females of other dabbling ducks by the bold white rear edge to the wings, visible at long range.

long, narrow, pointed wings

bold head pattern

long, pointed tail

♂※

bold white trailing edge to wing

pointed tail

small head on long, slim neck

♀

chocolate brown head

gleaming white neck-stripe and breast

grey bill with black sides

long, spiky black and buff feathers

♂※

black central tail feathers form long spike

longer feathers than female

creamy patch in front of black undertail

plain tawny head

♀

dull greyish body

pale breast

two-tone bill

♂☼

mottled grey-brown body

grey bill

VOICE *Male has low, short whistling call, lower-pitched than male Teal's, female has quack rather like that of female Mallard but quieter.*
NESTING *Hollow lined with leaves and down on ground among vegetation; 7–9 eggs; 1 brood; Apr–Jun.*
FEEDING *Mainly dabbles or upends for seeds, other vegetation, tiny snails, and other animals; also grazes on grass, marshes, and cereal fields for spilt grain and other crops.*
SIMILAR SPECIES *Mallard, female Gadwall, male Long-tailed Duck.*

Gadwall

Anas strepera

An elegant, exquisitely marked bird at close range, the Gadwall can appear rather drab-looking at a distance. It has a smaller, squarer head than the rather similar Mallard, which gives it a different character; the male also has a darker, greyer body than a Mallard or Wigeon. Gadwalls feed at the surface in shallow water, and in autumn and winter often flock on reservoirs and flooded pits, where they associate with Coots to benefit from the food that the Coots bring up from the bottom when they dive. In spring, pairs are often seen flying over their territories, calling loudly.

FEEDS AND *breeds on lakes and rivers with reeds or wooded islands. Winters on open waters, such as large lakes, flooded pits, and reservoirs; more scarcely on quiet estuaries and salt marshes.*

protruding head

♂❄

white patch near base of wings

white belly

orange-sided bill

♂☼

mottled brown body

white patch

TIP

Both the male and female Gadwall have a small square patch of white at the base of the hind-wing, which shows up well in flight and is often visible while the birds are settled on the water.

paler head than Mallard

white patch

dark bill with orange sides

♀

steep forehead

pale brown head

narrow, straight, black bill

♂❄

pale area

black stern

grey body

pale, yellowish orange legs

VOICE *Male has high, nasal, whistling pee and deep, short, croaking ahrk; female gives loud quack, like female Mallard's but often higher.*
NESTING *Nest is down-lined hollow on ground near water; 8–12 eggs; 1 brood; Apr–Jun.*
FEEDING *Mostly feeds in shallow water, dabbling and upending for seeds, roots, and shoots of aquatic plants, plus insects and other small aquatic animals.*
SIMILAR SPECIES *Mallard, female Wigeon.*

Mallard

Anas platyrhynchos

Common, widespread, and adaptable, able to thrive in all kinds of environments from town parks to coastal marshes, the Mallard is the most familiar of all the ducks. The breeding male's glossy green head and white neck-ring are instantly recognizable, and both sexes sport a characteristic purple-blue wing patch or speculum throughout the year. Most farmyard ducks are derived from the Mallard, and interbreeding has produced a range of variants on the original plumage pattern that can be confusing. Yet they still have their basic Mallard character, and are often easy to identify.

BREEDS ON *and near all kinds of waters, from urban ponds to remote moorland pools. Feeds on arable land and muddy lake margins.*

TIP

Mallard plumage is very variable owing to interbreeding with domestic forms, but most of these hybrids retain the blue wing patch and male's curly tail.

blue hindwings

white underwings

♂

orange legs

yellow bill

glossy green head

♂✻

blue hindwings

♀

dark belly

white neck-ring

pale body

curly central tail feathers

brown breast

purple-blue, white-edged speculum

brown bill

streaked brown body

blue speculum

♀

white tail

brown head

becomes browner

♂✿

VOICE *Male whistles quietly; female gives loud, raucous, descending quacks, quark quark quark.*
NESTING *Usually on ground in down-lined hollow, but sometimes in bush or tree; 9–13 eggs; 1 brood; Jan–Aug.*
FEEDING *Takes small aquatic invertebrates, seeds, roots, shoots, and grain from shallow water while upending or dabbling; also feeds on dry ground, such as stubble fields.*
SIMILAR SPECIES *Gadwall, Shoveler, Pintail.*

Shelduck

Tadorna tadorna

FEEDS AND *breeds on sandy or muddy shores, especially on sheltered estuaries; some breed near inland lakes and reservoirs.*

TIP

Shelducks in drab summer plumage can be confusing, but they usually retain traces of the distinctive chestnut chest band and black belly stripe.

Looking black and white at a distance, but revealing rich chestnut patches and a bright red bill at close range in breeding plumage, the Shelduck is a handsome, erect, rather goose-like duck that lives mainly on coasts and estuaries. In eclipse plumage, it is less distinctive, but still easy to identify. Usually seen in pairs or small, loose flocks, its bright white plumage is easily visible at great range against the dark mud of an estuary at low tide. Its pattern is also striking during its strong, fast, but rather heavy flight. Family groups gather together in late summer, when most of the adults fly to the North Sea to moult.

bold black wingtips

black belly stripe

red knob

brown-black cap

white below

pink or grey bill

tawny orange band

no knob on bill

glossy, green-black head

bright red bill

broad chestnut-orange band around chest

white lower neck

black on wings

white body

pink legs

VOICE Goose-like *a-ank* and growled *grah grah; various whistling notes from male and rhythmic* gagagagaga *from female in spring.*
NESTING *In holes on ground, under brambles, between straw bales, in old buildings, and also in trees; 8–10 eggs; 1 brood; Feb–Aug.*
FEEDING *Typically sweeps bill from side to side over wet mud to gather algae, small aquatic snails, and small crustaceans; also grazes and upends in shallow water.*
SIMILAR SPECIES *Male Mallard.*

Ruddy Duck

Oxyura jamaicensis

Accidentally introduced to Britain through escapes from wildfowl collections in the 1950s, the Ruddy Duck is a native of North America that is spreading fast in Europe, despite attempts to control it. The breeding male is striking and distinctive, with his chestnut body, white cheeks, and gaudy blue bill. During his dramatic courtship display, he vibrates his bill against his breast, creating a flurry of bubbles on the water surface. The Ruddy Duck is a strictly freshwater bird, typically feeding in family parties on the reedy shores of small lakes in summer. It moves to larger stretches of water for the winter, gathering in large flocks of several hundreds on favoured moulting and wintering sites.

BREEDS ON *reedy pools, flooded gravel pits, and sand pits, moving to larger, more open lakes and reservoirs in autumn and winter. Found mostly in a few flocks at regular sites, and in ones and twos elsewhere.*

large round head

black cap and nape

bright blue bill

pure white cheeks

rounded back

rufous body plumage

♂☀

stiff tail, laid flat or angled upward

TIP

Female Ruddy Ducks and males in eclipse plumage are far less distinctive than breeding males, but they share or retain the big-headed, dumpy profile and long, stiff tail. These are more reliable identification features than the dark bill and pale face, which are shared by other species such as the female Common Scoter and Long-tailed Duck.

all-dark wings

white face

♂☀

dull grey-brown body

blackish bill

♂❄

dull, dark grey-brown body

dark cap

cheek stripe

dark grey bill

♀

VOICE *Mostly silent, but male grunts and slaps bill against chest during display, making hollow rattle; female gives hisses and squeaks.*
NESTING *Large, floating pile of vegetation in tall reeds, often roofed over by meshed stems; 6–10 eggs; 1 brood; Apr–Jun.*
FEEDING *Dives for insect larvae and seeds from surface, reappearing like bobbing cork.*
SIMILAR SPECIES *Smew, Red-crested Pochard, Common Scoter, and female Long-tailed Duck.*

Tufted Duck

Aythya fuligula

The drooping crest and black-backed, pied plumage of the male Tufted Duck are distinctive in winter, but females and summer males are dark, dull, and easy to confuse with Scaup. A Tufted Duck has a larger black tip on the bill, which helps to identify it at close range.

♀
bold white wingbars

slight tuft
dull brown body
♂ ☼

golden eyes

short crest ♀

blue-grey bill with large black tip

long, wispy tuft on nape

black body with white flanks

♂ ✳

VOICE *Deep, grating growl; male gives nasal whistles during courtship.*
NESTING *Down-lined hollow concealed in dense, tall vegetation close to water; 8–11 eggs; 1 brood; May–Jun.*
FEEDING *Dives underwater from surface to find molluscs and insects.*
SIMILAR SPECIES *Scaup, female Pochard.*

Pochard

Aythya ferina

Pochard often appear in large flocks on lakes in autumn, feed for a day or two and then move on. A winter male is striking, with a rich red head, black breast, and grey body; the female is greyish with pale "spectacles", but has a similar grey-patched bill. Often sleepy by day, they sit on the water in tight, frequently single-sex flocks.

pale grey wingbars

peaked crown
dull grey-brown
dark cap
♐

rich red head

dark bill with pale patch

pale grey back

brown with pale flanks ♀

♂ ✳

dull head
♂ ☼

black breast

brownish red head
♂ ♄

VOICE *Wheezing rise-and-fall call from displaying male; purring growl from female.*
NESTING *Large pad of leaves and down on ground near water, often in reeds; 8–10 eggs; 1 brood; Apr–Jul.*
FEEDING *Dives from surface, taking seeds, shoots, and roots; often feeds at night.*
SIMILAR SPECIES *Scaup, female Tufted Duck.*

Scaup

Aythya marila

Resembling the Tufted Duck, but with a rounder crown and no trace of a tuft, the Scaup is far more marine in its habits and only appears inland in small numbers. The black head of a breeding male has a green gloss in good light, while the back is a pale, marbled grey rather than black. Winter flocks of Scaup favour sheltered waters, where the clear white flanks of the males show up well against the dark sea.

WINTERS IN *flocks on quiet coastal waters such as sea lochs and estuaries. Breeds by lakes and pools on tundra and moorland.*

pale patch at bill base

broad white wingbars

♂❄

pale cheeks

♀☀

TIP

A female Scaup is bigger than the very similar Tufted Duck. It also has a larger white area at the base of the bill, and the bill itself has a smaller black tip.

white blaze

rich brown head

♀❄

dull dark head

greyer back

♂☀

steep forehead

yellow eyes

black head with green gloss

blue-grey bill with black tip

pale grey back

white flanks

black around tail

♂❄

VOICE *Male produces low whistles in display, but is otherwise mostly silent; female has deep growl.*
NESTING *Uses hollow on ground, lined with feathers and down, near water; 8–11 eggs; 1 brood; Apr–Jun.*
FEEDING *Dives from surface in coastal shallows to find molluscs, crustaceans, and other invertebrates, as well as aquatic plants and waste grain on lakes and other fresh waters.*
SIMILAR SPECIES *Tufted Duck, male Pochard.*

Goldeneye

Bucephala clangula

FEEDS ON *coasts, lakes, reservoirs, large rivers, and estuaries; breeds in wooded areas beside cold freshwater lakes. In winter, widespread on lakes, reservoirs, and estuaries.*

A bulky, short-necked diving duck with a high-peaked head and triangular bill, the Goldeneye is an active, wary bird that spends most of its time on the water, repeatedly diving for food. The yellow eye (golden in the male) is hard to see at a distance, but the winter male's pied plumage and bold white head patch are eye-catching. The female is basically grey with a chocolate-brown head and a white collar; summer males are similar, but without the collar. Feeding Goldeneyes are shy and easily disturbed, flying off in tight groups with a loud whistling noise from their wings. They fly fast and direct with deep wing-beats, their large white wing patches showing up well.

extensive white on wings

♀

golden yellow eyes

high-peaked, triangular head

bold white spot

green-glossed black head plumage

♂❄

large white belly

black marks on sparkling white body

triangular dark bill

TIP

Goldeneyes are expert divers and spend much of their time underwater. A flock seen on the water tends to multiply if disturbed, as the submerged birds surface and take to the air.

face develops white spot in winter

gets whiter with age ❂♂

TIP

Flocks of Goldeneyes are mostly made up of females and immatures, although more adult males may appear in spring. During the summer, the males are almost indistinguishable from the females, and the difference only becomes apparent when a female raises its head to reveal its white collar. The similar female Velvet Scoter is browner, with no grey.

grey and yellow bill

dark brown head

grey body

white collar

♀

VOICE *Male gives frequent nasal, mechanical ze-zeee in display; female has grating double note.*
NESTING *Cavity lined with down from female typically in tree hole, sometimes in abandoned rabbit hole or artificial nest box; 8–11 eggs; 1 brood; Apr–Jun.*
FEEDING *Dives constantly from the surface to gather molluscs, insect larvae, and crustaceans.*
SIMILAR SPECIES *Male Smew, female Velvet Scoter.*

Long-tailed Duck

Clangula hyemalis

Many ducks feed both at sea and in fresh water, but the Long-tailed Duck is essentially a marine species that is found on lakes and similar waters only during the breeding season. Winter males are striking, with largely white plumage set off by blackish markings and a pair of long, dark central tail feathers. Females are darker above but pale below, with no long tail; summer males are similar, losing their long tails and becoming duller in late summer. Generally lively and active at sea, Long-tailed Ducks often fly low over the water, splash down, and take off again. They feed in flocks, often associating with scoters, and spend long periods underwater.

BREEDS ON *lakes and pools on moorland and tundra. Winters at sea, typically well offshore but often drifting into bays and estuaries with tide, especially in early spring.*

TIP

Winter male Long-tailed Ducks are distinctive, but other plumages can be confusing. The dark wings, dumpy body, and stubby dark bill are good clues.

dark wings

♀ ☀

white breast, dark in summer

♂ ☀

long, flexible tail point

♂ ☀

white and pale grey body

dark cheek patch

grey around eyes

pink band on stubby dark bill

☾ ☀ blurred white band around eyes

♀ ☀ pale flanks

dark cheek patch

♂ ☼ rich brown body

white face patch

♀ ☼ white neck

VOICE *Male makes loud, rhythmic, musical yodelling calls, a-ahulee; female gives low, barking quacks and growls.*
NESTING *Down-lined hollow on ground near water; 4–6 eggs; 1 brood; May–Jun.*
FEEDING *Dives from the surface to take molluscs, crustaceans, marine worms, and sea urchins; eats aquatic insects in summer on northern breeding grounds.*
SIMILAR SPECIES *Female Goldeneye, male Pintail.*

Common Scoter

Melanitta nigra

WINTERS AT *sea around coasts, often well off-shore. Breeds on shores of moorland lakes and pools. Occurs in large flocks at regular sites.*

A dark, large-bodied, slim-necked sea duck with a pointed tail, the Common Scoter gathers in large sociable groups out at sea, swimming buoyantly or flying low over the waves. The male is the only totally black duck; the female is browner with a pale face, but has no truly white body plumage.

♀ dark brown body — dark cap — grey face

round head — pointed bill with yellow patch

black body with duller or paler wings

♂ ✳

thin neck

long, pointed tail, often raised

pale tip to underwings

♂

slim neck

VOICE *Male has musical, piping whistle; female makes deep growls.*
NESTING *Hollow near water, lined with leaves and down, often on island; 6–8 eggs; 1 brood; Mar–Jun.*
FEEDING *Dives from surface to find shellfish, crustaceans, and worms.*
SIMILAR SPECIES *Velvet Scoter, Ruddy Duck.*

Velvet Scoter

Melanitta fusca

WINTERS AT *sea off sheltered coasts. Breeds along northern coasts and by tundra pools.*

With its large body and wedge-shaped face, the Velvet Scoter looks almost Eider-like, but much darker. It is usually seen in small numbers among flocks of the smaller Common Scoters, where it can be difficult to pick out – although the white wing-patches are distinctive. The white eye-spot of the black male is hard to see at long range.

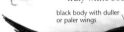

brown body — white spots ♀

white eye-spot

wedge-shaped face

thick neck

bill with yellow sides

black body

♂ ✳

red legs

VOICE *Male whistles, female growls, but generally quiet, especially in winter.*
NESTING *Down-lined hollow near the water; 6–8 eggs; 1 brood; May–Jul.*
FEEDING *Dives from surface to gather molluscs, crustaceans, and marine worms.*
SIMILAR SPECIES *Common Scoter, immature Goldeneye.*

white wing patch ♂

Eider

Somateria mollissima

A big, bulky, entirely marine duck with a characteristic wedge-shaped head, the Eider is usually easy to identify. A winter male is boldly pied black and white, with green patches on its head and a pink flush on its breast. Females have brown plumage with close dark bars that provide suberb camouflage on the nest. Highly sociable, Eiders often form large rafts offshore, but they are equally familiar around coastal rocks.

BREEDS ON *low-lying northern coasts and islands with rocky shores and weedy bays. Winters at sea, often in sandy bays and over mussel beds.*

black outer wings

dark hindwings

white rear flanks

♂

♀

black crown

green patch

wedge-shaped bill

white upperparts

pinkish breast

black underparts

♂☼

white patch

pale line above eye

brown, closely barred body

dark belly

♀

unbarred dark body, often piebald

♂☼

pale band over eye

◑

black stern

TIP

The male Eider is the only duck that combines a white back and breast with black flanks and belly – features that are readily seen at long range.

VOICE Male gives sensuous, cooing aa-ahooh; females respond with deep growls and a mechanical kok-kok-kok.
NESTING Hollow on ground, liberally lined with down, either exposed or well hidden; 4–6 eggs; 1 brood; Apr–Jun.
FEEDING Eats mainly molluscs, especially mussels, diving from surface to gather them from rocks; also crustaceans such as crabs and shrimps, starfish, and marine worms.
SIMILAR SPECIES Velvet Scoter, female Mallard.

Smew

Mergellus albellus

This is the smallest of the sawbilled ducks. The stunning winter male is a scarce bird over much of western Europe but immatures and females regularly winter at favoured sites. These "redheads" are quite distinctive, but the occasional adult male can be hard to spot in an active flock.

WINTERS ON *coastal waters, and on lakes, pools, reservoirs, and estuaries. Breeds by forest lakes and rivers.*

brown cap
white cheeks ♀

orange-brown ♂♀

white crest
black nape
largely white plumage
black face patch
black lines on plumage

large white areas on wings
♀

outstretched head
♂❄

VOICE *Silent in winter, but males often display with raised crests.*
NESTING *Tree hole near water, often of Black Woodpecker; 4–6 eggs; 1 brood; Apr–Jun.*
FEEDING *Dives from surface to catch small fish and insect larvae.*
SIMILAR SPECIES *Ruddy Duck, female Goosander.*

Red-breasted Merganser

Mergus serrator

A long, slim duck with a slender red bill, the Red-breasted Merganser is one of the fish-catching sawbills. The male is striking, with a dark head and a spiky crest; the female is very like a female Goosander, but has no sharp colour change on the neck. It is usually seen in small groups.

WINTERS AT *sea, on sheltered coasts and estuaries. Breeds by northern coasts or along fast rivers.*

ginger-brown head
♀
white wing patch
♂❄

wispy crest on green-black head
black and white above
grey flanks
slim, slightly upcurved red bill
white collar
♂❄

♂☀
brown head
brownish grey body
♀

VOICE *Generally quiet, but may give a low, rolling croak or growl.*
NESTING *In long grass on ground, or among rocks; 8–11 eggs; 1 brood; Apr–Jun.*
FEEDING *Dives from surface to catch small fish and invertebrates.*
SIMILAR SPECIES *Female Goosander, male Mallard.*

Goosander

Mergus merganser

The Goosander is the largest of the sawbills, with a thicker, more strongly-hooked bill than the more delicately built Red-breasted Merganser. The male is also much whiter with a salmon-pink tinge, and has a neater, drooping crest on its green-black head. The smaller female is mostly blue-grey with a dark rufous head and a white throat. It is much more of a freshwater bird than the Red-breasted Merganser; large flocks may gather on big lakes and reservoirs, with smaller numbers on flooded pits and rivers. Usually a shy, wary bird, the Goosander is easily scared off by intruders, even at long range.

FEEDS MAINLY *on fresh water, on reservoirs, lakes, and rivers. In summer, breeding pairs prefer upland reservoirs and shallower, fast-flowing, clear streams with plenty of boulders and stony shores.*

♂✲

large white wing patch

TIP

A female Goosander can be reliably identified by the sharp division of colours on its neck; those of the Red-breasted Merganser are blurred.

♀

elongated look in flight

dark eyes

glossy green-black head

salmon-pink to white body

black back

plum-red, thick-based, hooked bill

long tail ♂✲

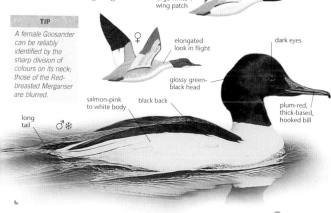

striped face

greyish body

dark brown head

smooth, downward-pointing crest

blue-grey body

♀

sharp division between brown and white

TIP

A male Goosander in eclipse plumage looks almost exactly like a female, but it has a redder bill and a clear division between its darker back and paler flanks. It also has more white on its wings, which shows up in flight and looks like a white flank streak on the water.

VOICE Usually silent, but male gives frog-like double croaks during courtship, also twanging or bell-like notes; female makes cackling notes and harsh *karrr*.
NESTING Usually hole in tree near water, but may nest among heather, among rocks, or in hole in bank; 8–11 eggs; 1 brood; Apr–Jul.
FEEDING Dives from surface, travelling long distances underwater in large lakes, to take fish.
SIMILAR SPECIES Red-breasted Merganser, male Mallard.

Pink-footed Goose

Anser brachyrhynchus

This round-headed, short-billed goose has a shorter neck than other geese, and a strong contrast between its very dark head and pale breast – features that are often obvious in flight. It occurs in tens of thousands at favoured sites, feeding in dense flocks by day and making spectacular mass flights to its roosts in the evening.

FEEDS ON *marshes, pasture, and arable land near coast. Roosts on lakes, estuaries, and low-lying islands.*

small bill with pink band

dark underwings

dark, round head

white-barred, pale grey back

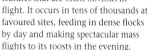

pale grey wings

dark bars on flanks

pale to rich pink legs

pale pinkish breast

VOICE *Resonant* ahng-unk *and frequent, higher* wink-wink.
NESTING *Down-lined nest on open tundra or rocky slope; 4–6 eggs; 1 brood; Jun–Jul.*
FEEDING *Eats grass, waste grain, sugar beet tops, carrots, and potatoes, feeding in flocks.*
SIMILAR SPECIES *Bean Goose, Greylag Goose.*

White-fronted Goose

Anser albifrons

One of the more colourful and lively of the grey geese, the White-fronted Goose has a distinctive white patch at the front of its head and ragged black bars on its grey belly. The Siberian race has a pink bill, while the larger, darker Greenland race (*A. a. flavirostris*) has a longer, heavier orange bill. Both occur in large flocks at regular locations.

WINTERS ON *pastures, coastal marshes, and estuaries. Breeds on northern tundra.*

broad, dark tail-band

grey on wings

white forehead blaze

no black bars

grey-brown body, with black bars on belly

pale bars

A.a.flavirostris

bars broader

VOICE *High, yodelling, yelping notes,* kyu-yu, ku-yu-yu *or* lo-lyok.
NESTING *Makes down-filled nest on the ground on tundra; 5–6 eggs; 1 brood; Jun.*
FEEDING *Grazes on firm ground during steady forward walk, taking grass, roots, some winter wheat, and grain.*
SIMILAR SPECIES *Greylag Goose.*

Bean Goose

Anser fabalis

This large, handsome, sociable goose is darker than other grey geese, with basically dark brown plumage marked with narrow, regular pale bars. There are two forms: one long-necked and long-billed, the other shorter-necked and looking more like a Pink-footed Goose. It sometimes joins flocks of White-fronted Geese, when it can be picked out by its long, dark head and cleanly-barred back.

WINTERS ON *lakes and wet pasture, on sites used year after year. Breeds on northern bogs and tundra.*

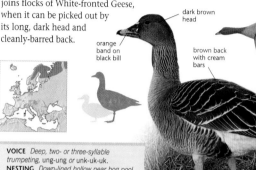

dark brown head

orange band on black bill

broad, dark tail-band

brown back with cream bars

dark grey wings

yellow-orange legs

VOICE *Deep, two- or three-syllable trumpeting, ung-ung or unk-uk-uk.*
NESTING *Down-lined hollow near bog pool on tundra or in forest; 4–6 eggs; 1 brood; Jun.*
FEEDING *Grazes short grass, picks up grain and roots crops from fields.*
SIMILAR SPECIES *Pink-footed Goose, Greylag Goose.*

Greylag Goose

Anser anser

The heaviest of the grey geese, the Greylag looks big and pale in soft light but more contrasted in strong sun. It has a very pale forewing, and its white stern is often conspicuous. The honking calls of the Greylag are familiar, betraying the fact that it is a direct ancestor of domestic geese.

FEEDS ON *coastal marshes, pastures, and farmland in winter. Breeds by lakes and coastal inlets.*

large orange bill

very pale upperwings

brown-grey above

pale patch on under-wings

pink legs

white stern

VOICE *Loud clattering and honking like farmyard goose, ahng-ahng-ahng, kang-ank.*
NESTING *Sparsely lined nest on ground, often on island; 4–6 eggs; 1 brood; May–Jun.*
FEEDING *Plucks grass and cereal shoots, digs for roots and waste grain.*
SIMILAR SPECIES *Pink-footed Goose, Bean Goose, White-fronted Goose.*

Brent Goose

Branta bernicla

This small, very dark goose occurs as two main races, dark-bellied and pale-bellied; the black-bellied North American race is a rare vagrant. All have black heads and a distinctive white neck patch. Flocks often feed on the water, upending like ducks to reach vegetation growing beneath the surface.

WINTERS ON *muddy estuaries and harbours, salt marshes, and nearby arable land. Breeds on tundra.*

black head

black bill

white patch on neck

black chest

DARK-BELLIED

brown underside

pale bars on wings

PALE-BELLIED

uniform wings

DARK-BELLIED

dark grey-brown upperparts

bold white stern

VOICE Rhythmic, deep, throaty rronk rronk, in loud, murmuring chorus from flocks.
NESTING Feather-lined nest on ground near shallow pool; 4–6 eggs; 1 brood; May–Jun.
FEEDING Eats eelgrass and algae on coastal mudflats; increasingly cereals and grass.
SIMILAR SPECIES Barnacle Goose, Canada Goose.

Barnacle Goose

Branta leucopsis

Although clearly related to the Canada Goose, this highly social bird is easily identified by its creamy-white face, black breast, and beautifully barred back. Juveniles are duller, with less even barring. Large flocks winter on the same sites every year, often grazing at night.

WINTERS ON *pastures and salt marshes, on traditional sites. Breeds on northern coasts and Arctic tundra.*

pale grey wings

stubby black bill

cream-tinged white face

glossy black neck and chest

strongly contrasted below

black and white bars

black eye patch

blue-grey back

VOICE Harsh, short bark, creating chattering, yapping chorus from flocks.
NESTING Feather-lined nest on ground or cliff ledge; 4–6 eggs; 1 brood; May–Jun.
FEEDING Large flocks graze on grass, clover, and similar vegetation.
SIMILAR SPECIES Brent Goose, Canada Goose.

Canada Goose

Branta canadensis

A large goose with a black head and neck and a distinctive white "chinstrap", the Canada Goose is a native of North America that has become common and familiar in Britain and other parts of northern Europe. Originally migratory, it is largely resident apart from annual movements to moulting grounds on quiet estuaries.

LIVES ON *lakes, rivers, marshes, reservoirs, and surrounding grassland; also town parks and estuaries.*

white chinstrap

black bill

white rump

black head and neck

brown upperparts

tail held high

pale creamy-buff breast

VOICE *Deep, loud, trumpeting ah-ronk! rising on second syllable.*
NESTING *Down-lined scrape on ground, often on small island; loosely colonial; 5–6 eggs; 1 brood; Apr–Jun.*
FEEDING *Grazes on grass and cereals; takes some aquatic plants.*
SIMILAR SPECIES *Barnacle Goose.*

white stern

black legs

Bewick's Swan

Cygnus columbianus

The smallest of the swans, with a rather stocky look and a relatively thick neck, Bewick's Swan can be distinguished from the larger Whooper Swan by its goose-like shape and shorter yellow bill patch. It is usually seen feeding in flocks on wet fields, their conversational chorus often audible over long distances.

WINTERS ON *flooded fields, lakes, and farmland. Breeds on Siberian tundra.*

pale bill with dark tip

dull grey

concave bill

rounded head

short, yellow bill patch

fairly thick neck

dark legs

all-white plumage

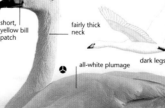

VOICE *Loud, bugling notes; flocks produce soft conversational chorus.*
NESTING *Pile of grass stems at edge of tundra pool; 3–5 eggs; 1 brood; May–Jun.*
FEEDING *Grazes grass or cereals; or eats root crops; feeds less often in water.*
SIMILAR SPECIES *Whooper Swan, Mute Swan.*

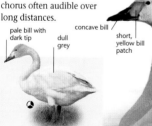

Whooper Swan

Cygnus cygnus

As big as a Mute Swan, but with the goose-like look of Bewick's Swan, this is a wild, usually shy bird with a long, flat forehead and bill. It has more yellow on its bill than Bewick's Swan, and always holds its head horizontal and neck bolt upright when alert.

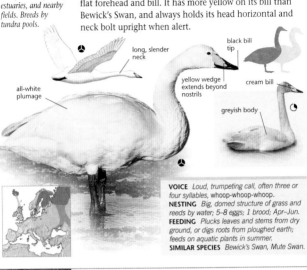

long, slender neck

black bill tip

yellow wedge extends beyond nostrils

cream bill

all-white plumage

greyish body

VOICE Loud, trumpeting call, often three or four syllables, whoop-whoop-whoop.
NESTING Big, domed structure of grass and reeds by water; 5–8 eggs; 1 brood; Apr–Jun.
FEEDING Plucks leaves and stems from dry ground, or digs roots from ploughed earth; feeds on aquatic plants in summer.
SIMILAR SPECIES Bewick's Swan, Mute Swan.

Mute Swan

Cygnus olor

The huge, elegant Mute Swan is one of the most familiar of waterfowl. It holds its neck in a graceful curve, distinctive at long range, and has a longer tail than the two tundra-breeding swans. Territorial pairs are aggressive, driving off intruders with arched wings and loud hisses.

outstretched neck

large black knob; smaller on female

all-white plumage

orange-red bill, angled down

long tail

long, often curved neck

grey-brown plumage

grey bill

VOICE Strangled trumpeting, snorting, and hissing notes; wings throb loudly in flight.
NESTING Huge pile of vegetation at water's edge; 5–8 eggs; 1 brood; Mar–Jun.
FEEDING Plucks plants from short grass and shallow water; upends in deeper water.
SIMILAR SPECIES Bewick's Swan, Whooper Swan.

Seabirds

This chapter profiles birds from different families that are adapted to life at sea. Some, such as storm-petrels, shearwaters, auks, and the Gannet, spend much of their lives at sea, visiting land just to breed, often in huge, noisy colonies. Others – especially members of the large gull family – are more tied to coasts, and some also occur inland. Seabirds are mainly swift fliers, and skilled swimmers and divers. The Gannet, for example, makes spectacular plunge-dives from mid-air to catch fish; skuas are fast, agile, hawk-like birds; gulls and their smaller relatives the terns are also superb fliers, with long, pointed wings. Auks, such as the Guillemot and Razorbill, have small wings, better suited to propelling them underwater than flying in the air – like the Shag and Cormorant they are deep divers.

| ARCTIC TERN | LITTLE GULL | GUILLEMOT | RAZORBILL |

Storm Petrel

Hydrobates pelagicus

LIVES WELL *offshore at sea, only rarely being forced inshore by gales. Breeds on offshore islands and headlands, to which it returns only at night.*

The tiny, delicate-looking Storm Petrel is little larger than a sparrow, yet spends most of its life far out at sea, enduring the most extreme conditions throughout the winter. Generally very dark, but with a bold white rump, it flies very low over the waves with constant, easy but fluttering wing-beats, rolling from side to side or turning and dipping to feed by snatching edible morsels from the surface. It often follows ships in small flocks, and may fly past them at surprising speed before swooping down to the water to investigate another potential meal. It is rarely seen on shore, since it returns to its breeding grounds only at night to avoid predatory gulls and skuas.

white bar on underwings

swept-back wings

sooty black head

steep forehead

rounded tail

sooty black body

all-dark upperwings

white rump

tube-nosed bill

short legs

settles on water with wings raised

TIP

The highly oceanic Storm Petrel rarely comes inshore, and is most likely to be seen from ships. Look for the white underwing bar and rounded tail that distinguish it from Leach's Petrel; the wingbar is the best clue, but is variable and often difficult to see. Apart from its white rump, the Storm Petrel is also very dark, with no pale patches on its upperwings.

VOICE *Soft, purring trill with abrupt ending, at nest; high-pitched squeaking from colonies at night.*
NESTING *Hole among rocks or in old wall, or small burrow made by animal such as rabbit; 1 egg; 1 brood; Apr–Jul.*
FEEDING *Picks up small planktonic invertebrates, tiny fish, fish oil, and scraps of fish offal discarded from ships; feeds in flight, taking food with bill while pattering across surface with feet.*
SIMILAR SPECIES *Leach's Petrel, House Martin.*

Leach's Petrel

Oceanodroma leucorhoa

Although slightly larger than the Storm Petrel, Leach's
Petrel still seems far too fragile to live out on the open
ocean, buffeted by Atlantic gales. It is browner than the
Storm Petrel, with an obvious pale panel on each upperwing, a "V"-shaped white rump, and a notched tail –
although the notch is not always conspicuous. It has
a quick, strong flight, more powerful than that of the
Storm Petrel, and often makes erratic twists, turns,
and changes of speed. While feeding, it dangles its
legs, but is less likely to patter its feet on the
surface. Storm-driven birds occasionally appear
over reservoirs and large lakes far inland.

FEEDS OUT AT *sea, well
offshore throughout
winter, but may be
driven inshore or even
inland by storms.
Breeds on remote
offshore islands.*

pale panel on
upperwings

notched
tail

dark
underwings

long, angled,
arched wings

"V" shaped
white rump with
central dark line

notch in tail
hard to see

TIP

*While the Storm
Petrel flies rather
like a Swallow,
Leach's Petrel is
more tern-like, often
holding its wings
arched with the
inner section raised
and the tips pointing
down to form a
shallow "M". Its
flight is buoyant,
graceful, and
extremely agile.*

steep
forehead

sooty-brown
back

angular
shape

paler wing
plumage

VOICE *Rattling, chattering coo at nest, plus cackling and screeching
from breeding colonies at night.*
NESTING *Burrow or cavity among rocks, sometimes rabbit burrow; one
bird incubates while the other is at sea, returning to nest only at night;
1 egg; 1 brood; Apr–Jul.*
FEEDING *Eats floating pieces of fish offal, fish oil, jellyfish, and other
marine invertebrates, picking them from the surface at night.*
SIMILAR SPECIES *Storm Petrel, Black Tern.*

Little Auk

Alle alle

FEEDS WELL *out to sea, although may be driven inshore by gales. Breeds on coasts of Arctic islands.*

The smallest and most agile of the auks, both on land and in flight, the Little Auk is the size of a Starling but much bulkier, with a round, frog-like head and a very short bill. In Europe, it is usually seen in winter plumage, as a late autumn visitor to the North Sea; the much blacker summer adults are rare.

white streaks on shoulders

white patch curves up behind cheeks

black cap and face

white trailing edge

stumpy black bill

black extends to side of chest

all-black head and breast

VOICE *Shrill twittering or chattering notes or trills at breeding colonies; silent at sea.*
NESTING *Burrow high above shore, often among boulders or scree, in very large colony; 1 egg; 1 brood; Jun–Aug.*
FEEDING *Dives for small fish, planktonic animals, and marine crustaceans.*
SIMILAR SPECIES *Puffin, Razorbill.*

Black Guillemot

Cepphus grylle

BREEDS ON *coasts, on fringes of rocky islets with boulders and rock cavities. Feeds at sea.*

In summer, the unique, striking plumage of the Black Guillemot makes it easy to identify. It is less distinctive in winter, when it is barred black and white above, but adults retain the clean white patches above and below their wings. Less gregarious than other auks, it is usually seen in pairs or small groups.

whitish head, smudged with black

small, sharp, dagger-like bill

smoky black body

bold white wing patch

oval white patch

black bars on wing patch

bright red legs

VOICE *Shrill whistle, often extended into fast trill; quick, thin sip-sip-sip.*
NESTING *Crevice between boulders, or hole in harbour wall; 1 egg; 1 brood; May–Jun.*
FEEDING *Dives underwater to catch small fish and crustaceans.*
SIMILAR SPECIES *Guillemot, Puffin, Slavonian Grebe.*

Puffin

Fratercula arctica

Few seabirds are more instantly recognizable than the Puffin in summer, with its clown-like eye and huge, flamboyantly coloured bill. Even at a distance it is usually distinctive, bobbing on the water or whirring through the air like a clockwork toy. In winter, it is less striking, as the colourful eye ornaments and horny plates at the edges of its bill fall away; its face is also darker, although not as dark as that of a juvenile bird. In summer, Puffins are often to be seen bringing food to their nesting burrows on northern and western coasts, but Puffins in winter plumage are generally rare close inshore.

BREEDS ON *coastal clifftops, mainly on islands, feeding in nearby waters. Winters well out to sea.*

deep, triangular bill, striped bluish, orange, yellow, and red

dark eyes with bluish scale above

grey-white facial disc

black upperparts and neck

white below

grooves on bill increase with age

black back

dusky grey face

vivid orange legs

plain black wings

smaller, duller bill

TIP

A breeding Puffin is hard to mistake for any other bird, but in winter, Puffins usually feed well offshore and may be confused with other auks at long range. One distinctive feature is the grey facial disc; a Puffin also has a dumpier, more front-heavy body than a Guillemot or a Razorbill, and it has all-dark wings with no white trailing edge.

VOICE Loud, cooing growl at nest, aaarr, karr-oo-arr; generally silent outside breeding season.
NESTING Digs or occupies ready-made burrow at or near clifftop, often excavated by rabbit or Manx Shearwater, or finds suitable cavity between boulders; 1 egg; 1 brood; May–Jun.
FEEDING Dives from water surface to catch small fish such as sandeels; also takes small squid, crustaceans, and marine worms.
SIMILAR SPECIES Little Auk, Razorbill, Guillemot.

Guillemot

Uria aalge

A slim, long-bodied auk with a slender, pointed bill, the Guillemot is one of the commonest breeding seabirds at cliff colonies. It often nests alongside the more thickset Razorbill, which has a deeper bill. Guillemots can often be seen flying low and fast off headlands, or swimming in large groups below the cliffs.

BREEDS IN *colonies on narrow ledges on sea-cliffs and flat-topped stacks. Winters at sea, well offshore.*

dark brown to black above

sharp bill

long neck

black eye-stripe

white face

white below

white sides to rump

smudgy greyish streaks on flanks

VOICE *Loud, whirring, growling chorus at colony, arrrr-rr-rr; juveniles make loud, musical whistle at sea.*
NESTING *On bare ledge on sheer cliff, in colony; 1 egg; 1 brood; May–Jun.*
FEEDING *Dives from surface to catch fish deep underwater, propelled by wings.*
SIMILAR SPECIES *Razorbill, Manx Shearwater.*

Razorbill

Alca torda

More heavily built than the very similar Guillemot, and not usually as numerous, the Razorbill has a pointed tail and a distinctive deep, flattened, blade-like black bill with a fine white line near the end. It breeds in company with Guillemots, but less conspicuously because it nests in cavities rather than open ledges.

BREEDS ON *rocky coasts on cliffs with crevices, or among boulder scree, feeding at sea. Winters out at sea, usually far from land.*

broader, longer white sides than Guillemot

deep, white-lined bill

black head

white throat and breast

black cap

black upper-parts

pointed tail, often cocked

white below

VOICE *Prolonged, tremulous growls and grunts at colony, deep urrr.*
NESTING *On sheltered cliff ledge, or cavity between boulders; 1 egg; 1 brood; May–Jun.*
FEEDING *Dives, often very deeply, from surface to pursue and catch fish, using its wings to "fly" underwater.*
SIMILAR SPECIES *Guillemot, Puffin.*

Little Tern

Sternula albifrons

The quick, nervous, and tiny Little Tern is usually easy to identify by its size alone, but it is also paler than other terns, with a white forehead all year round. Its wings have a black streak at the tip on the upper side, and the adult has a distinctive yellow dagger bill with a black tip. Although a widespread summer visitor, the Little Tern is becoming scarce on many coasts because it often breeds on popular leisure beaches; many colonies survive only because they are fenced off and protected. Rising sea levels may also be a threat, since extra-high tides often destroy its eggs and chicks.

BREEDS ON *narrow sand and shingle coastal beaches; also inland in Spain and Portugal and eastern Europe. Winters along coasts of Africa.*

black streak at wingtips

short, white, forked tail

pure white underside

white forehead

black stripe through eye

black cap

black nape

sharp yellow bill with tiny dark tip

black wedge at wingtips

long, narrow wings

pale grey back

orange to yellow legs

streaky crown

dark chevrons on back

TIP
The Little Tern is narrower-winged than other terns, and has a faster, more dashing, frenetic flight with rapid, flickering wing-beats, often calling noisily as it goes. It hovers often, low over the sea, with very quick, whirring wing-beats. So, even if a Little Tern is too distant to assess its size or distinguish its plumage, these features provide a clue to its identity.

VOICE *Sharp, high, rapid, irritated-sounding chattering kirri-kirri-kirri and kitititit.*
NESTING *Shallow scoop on sand or shingle beach, often very near the water; 2–3 eggs; 1 brood; May–Jun.*
FEEDING *Plunge-dives for fish, often into breaking waves off steep shingle beach, with fast, abrupt smack into water, after a whirring hover that is often quite prolonged; repeats dives more quickly than other terns.*
SIMILAR SPECIES *Sandwich Tern, Common Tern, Arctic Tern.*

Common Tern

Sterna hirundo

A typical black-capped, pale-bodied tern, the Common Tern is well named. It is widespread on European coasts from spring to late autumn and is the most likely tern to be seen inland. It closely resembles the Arctic Tern, and often mixes with it, but is rather stouter, with a shorter tail and a longer red bill with a black tip. Towards the end of summer the forehead of the adult turns white, and so resembles the Little Tern's, but since that is a much smaller and paler bird there is little risk of confusion. It typically plunge-dives for prey with little hesitation, swallowing it or carrying it to the nest in its bill.

FEEDS IN *coastal waters, rivers, and lakes. Breeds on coasts, islands, salt marshes, and locally on shingle or gravel banks by fresh waters. Migrants are widespread on coasts, some inland. Winters along coasts in Africa.*

darker wingtip feathers

translucent underwing patch

long neck

♣ ☼

long, black-tipped, bright red bill

black cap

pale grey upperparts

forked white tail

red legs, longer than Arctic Tern's

white body

♣ ☼

white forehead

dark shoulder

dark streaks on outer wings

♣ ❋

dark nape

faint ginger bars

pale bill base

dark shoulder

◑

TIP

While very like the Arctic Tern, the Common Tern has a flatter head with a wider white line between its black cap and longer red bill. When seen in flight from below, only the inner primary feathers on its wings are translucent, creating a pale patch, whereas those of the Arctic Tern are all translucent apart from the dark trailing edge of the outer wing.

VOICE *Grating, thin, falling* kreee-yair *of alarm, sharp* kik kik, *ringing* keeer, *rapid* kirrikirrikirrik.
NESTING *Scrape on ground, in sand, shingle, or dry earth, in colonies near water; 2–4 eggs; 1 brood; May–Jun.*
FEEDING *Dives from air for fish and aquatic invertebrates, plunging into water with a splash after brief hover; also picks some insects and fish from water surface in flight.*
SIMILAR SPECIES *Roseate Tern, Arctic Tern, Sandwich Tern.*

Arctic Tern

Sterna paradisaea

Closely resembling the Common Tern, but slightly more elegant, the Arctic Tern is a more strictly maritime bird that rarely occurs inland. It has a shorter head and neck and a longer tail, giving it a less front-heavy appearance in flight than the Common Tern. Its wings have longer, more pointed wingtips with translucent outer primaries, and a narrow, more tapered dark trailing edge. In autumn, it develops a whiter forehead, and its deep red bill becomes blacker. Uniquely, the Arctic Tern flies all the way from the far north to the far south to spend the northern winter in the Southern Ocean, a strategy that allows it to enjoy more summer daylight than any other bird.

BREEDS ON *northern offshore islands, and sandy and gravelly beaches. Winters in Southern Ocean, as far as Antarctic pack ice.*

very pale outer wings

bill shorter than Common Tern's

short neck

translucent primaries with thin dark trailing edge

very pointed, tapered wingtips

long forked tail

long outer tail streamers

rounded head with black cap

short red bill

grey back

pale grey below

short red legs

white forehead

black bill

dark crescents on back

TIP

In the air, the Arctic Tern is more graceful than the Common Tern, with a relaxed, buoyant flight style. Its feeding technique is similar – employing plunge-diving – but it is more hesitant; it often hovers, drops a little, then hovers again, as if making sure of its target. When it is satisfied, it plunges into the water with a splash, to re-emerge with a fish.

VOICE *Calls similar to Common Tern, but usually higher, including grating, sharp kee-yaah, rising pee-pee-pee, sharp kik, kreer.*
NESTING *Scrape in sand or shingle, or makes use of hollow in rock in colonies; 2 eggs; 1 brood; May–Jun.*
FEEDING *Plunge-dives for small fish such as sandeels, often descending in a series of steps before final dive; also takes some insects from freshwater pools, and small crustaceans.*
SIMILAR SPECIES *Common Tern, Roseate Tern, Whiskered Tern.*

Roseate Tern

Sterna dougallii

BREEDS ON *beaches and vegetated islands, feeding at sea. Winters on West African coasts.*

Named for the pink flush of its pale underparts in spring, the Roseate Tern is similar to the Common and Arctic Terns, but paler, with longer tail streamers. It also has a longer, black bill, with a red base that becomes more extensive in late summer. Populations have undergone serious declines in recent years; the bird is now rare and local in Europe.

no dark trailing edge

all-dark

dark legs

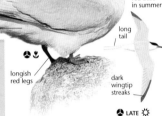

smooth black cap

very pale grey above

black bill; red base in summer

white underside, flushed pink

long tail

VOICE *Harsh croaking notes and quick, musical chu-vik, unlike calls of other terns.*
NESTING *Grassy nest, often in tall vegetation or by tussock; 2–3 eggs; 1 brood; May–Jun.*
FEEDING *Plunges for fish, especially sandeels and sprats, after fast hover.*
SIMILAR SPECIES *Common Tern, Sandwich Tern, Arctic Tern.*

longish red legs

dark wingtip streaks

LATE

Gull-billed Tern

Gelochelidon nilotica

LIVES AROUND *lagoons, marshes, wet fields, and high grassland. Rare migrant on northern coasts.*

A large, pale tern of freshwater marshes and coastal lagoons, the Gull-billed Tern often feeds on flying insects like a giant swallow. It has a stout, all-black bill and black legs, and its rump and tail are pale grey. Its underwings have obvious black trailing edges at the tips.

round black cap

pale grey back

stout black bill

white below

pale grey wing feathers wear darker

black legs

pale grey tail

dark line

white head with black eye patch

thick bill

VOICE *Nasal, deep gur-wik, rattling call, and laughing notes.*
NESTING *Grass-lined hollow on sand or mud near water; 3 eggs; 1 brood; May–Jun.*
FEEDING *Snatches insects on the wing and from ground; also small birds, rodents, frogs.*
SIMILAR SPECIES *Sandwich Tern, Common Tern, Whiskered Tern.*

Sandwich Tern

Sterna sandvicensis

The Sandwich Tern is a large, active, noisy bird with a spiky black crest, a long, sharp bill, and long, angular wings that it often holds away from its body, slightly drooped. It looks very white in the air, diving for fish from high up and hitting the water with a loud smack.

BREEDS ON *sand dunes, shingle beaches, and islands. Winters in coastal waters of Africa.*

long black bill, yellow at tip

black cap, spiky at rear

very pale silver-grey back

very pale silver-grey wings

white tail

white underside

short tail with shallow fork

black legs

dark chequers and bars on "saddle"

dark tail corners

white forehead

dark streaks

VOICE *Loud, harsh, rhythmic ker-ink, short kik or kear-ik!*
NESTING *Shallow scoop in sand or shingle; 1–2 eggs; 1 brood; May–Jun.*
FEEDING *Catches fish, especially sandeels, by plunge-diving from air.*
SIMILAR SPECIES *Common Tern, Gull-billed Tern, Black-headed Gull.*

Caspian Tern

Hydroprogne caspia

The Caspian tern is enormous compared to other terns, with a massive red bill. Yet it is a handsome, well-proportioned bird, and if there are no other terns for comparison its bulk may not be obvious. Now scarce, it can be seen flying steadily and heavily over water, head angled down, looking for fish to catch.

blackish under wingtips

black cap, flecked white

grey upper-parts

BREEDS ON *coasts and low islands, mostly in Baltic; rare migrant on other coasts.*

huge, red bill with black near tip

square head

white breast

long black legs

white flecks on cap

dull bill

VOICE *Deep, explosive kree-ahk; very noisy at breeding colony.*
NESTING *Shallow scrape on ground, in sand or shingle; 2–3 eggs; 1 brood; May–Jun.*
FEEDING *Plunge-dives for fish; may fly long distances from colony to feed.*
SIMILAR SPECIES *Sandwich Tern, Common Tern.*

Black Tern

Chlidonias niger

The marsh terns of the genus *Chlidonias* are smaller, more delicate birds than the sea terns, and customarily feed by dipping to the water surface instead of plunge-diving. The Black Tern is the most widespread species. It lives up to its name in summer by being mainly blackish and smoky grey, with white beneath its tail and pale underwings. It is more common in western Europe in autumn, when its plumage is less distinctive: its body becomes patched with white, and the black on its head and body is reduced to a three-lobed black cap and a dark spot on each side of its chest.

FEEDS ON *marshes, lagoons, salt pans, estuaries, lakes, and reservoirs. Breeds on lakes and marshes. Winters mainly along coasts in Africa.*

greyish black head

dark smoky grey above

pale underwings

blackish bill

white under tail

blackish legs

dark chest spot

three-lobed dark cap

white forehead

browner body

dark chest spot

dark forewings

TIP
Black Terns have a light, buoyant, rather erratic flight style, with frequent swoops and side-slips. When hunting, they often beat slowly into the wind, rising and falling over the water, their heads down, ready to dip down and snatch a small fish or insect from near the water surface.

sharp wings

VOICE *Usually a rather quiet bird, but may give short, low, squeaky, nasal flight calls, kik, or kik-keek.*
NESTING *Nest of stems and waterweed, often in shallow water or on mat of floating vegetation, in marsh or nearby drier land; 3 eggs; 1 brood; May–Jun.*
FEEDING *Dips to take insects, small fish, crustaceans, and amphibians such as frogs from the water.*
SIMILAR SPECIES *Whiskered Tern, Little Gull.*

Whiskered Tern

Chlidonias hybrida

The largest of the marsh terns, the Whiskered Tern has a thick bill and broad wings which give it a rather heavier, stronger look than the closely related Black Tern. It also has a more direct, less airy flight. This makes it easy to confuse with the Common and Arctic Terns in autumn and winter but, unlike them, it rarely plunge-dives for fish. It is a familiar sight over south European marshes and coastal lagoons in summer, but rarely strays far north of its breeding range on migration.

HUNTS FOR *aquatic prey over marshy rivers, reedy marshlands, and coastal lagoons. Winters mainly on inland fresh waters in Africa; some in Mediterranean.*

white rump

brownish scaly bars on back

pale grey rump

mid-grey rump

black cap

white cheeks and throat

dark red bill

mid-grey back

pale upperwing feathers

blackish belly

dark red legs

TIP

A Whiskered Tern in summer plumage could be confused with a Common Tern, but it has a greyer rump and tail. Its bill is also a darker red, with no black tip. In winter plumage, its most distinctive feature is its tail, which is much less forked than that of a Common Tern.

white underwings

black ear coverts

pale grey back

pale body

1ST

VOICE Dry, rasping *cherk*, harsher in alarm; very vocal, particularly at breeding grounds.
NESTING Semi-floating pile of vegetation attached to submerged or emergent water plants in marsh; in loose colony, often in association with grebes; 3 eggs; 1 brood; May–Jun.
FEEDING Dips to water surface in flight to take aquatic insects, crustaceans, small fish, and amphibians.
SIMILAR SPECIES Black Tern, Common Tern.

Manx Shearwater

Puffinus puffinus

FEEDS OVER *open sea, and breeds in colonies on islands and remote headlands. Widespread when migrating off coasts in autumn.*

Ungainly on land, shuffling along on its weak legs, aided by its bill and wings, this is a swift, elegant bird in the air. It is usually seen flying low over the sea with rapid, stiff-winged flaps between long glides, flashing alternately black and white as it banks from side to side.

silvery white

stiff wings

blackish above; browner in strong sun

thin dark bill

white throat

black cap

VOICE *Loud, strangled wailing and chortling sounds at night around breeding colony.*
NESTING *Uses rabbit or Puffin burrow or similar tunnel, or hole in scree; 1 egg; 1 brood; Apr–Jul.*
FEEDING *Flocks take fish and small squid, diving from surface or in short plunge from air.*
SIMILAR SPECIES *Razorbill.*

white flank each side of rump

Cory's Shearwater

Calonectris diomedea

LIVES MAINLY *well out at sea, but sometimes occurs close inshore off headlands and islands. Breeds on many of the Mediterranean islands.*

A big, brown-backed, long-winged ocean bird, Cory's Shearwater has a distinctive yellowish bill and a dark smudge around its eye. It often holds its long wings gently arched, and when extended they show a faint, dark "W" mark. It soars high in the air, then swoops down in lazy, rolling glides, swerving slowly in long, banking arcs.

long, tapered, slightly rounded wings

dark brown above

dull grey head

mainly pale bill with dark tip

all-white below

dark smudge around eye

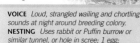

VOICE *Loud, varied wailing sounds near breeding sites; mostly silent at sea.*
NESTING *Hole among rocks or burrow in steep slope; 1 egg; 1 brood; Mar–Jul.*
FEEDING *Takes fish, squid, shrimps, jellyfish, and waste from fishing vessels in shallow dives from surface of sea.*
SIMILAR SPECIES *Immature Herring Gull.*

dark wing edge

white underwings

Fulmar

Fulmarus glacialis

Although it has gull-like plumage, the Fulmar is a tube-nosed petrel more closely related to the albatrosses. It holds its wings straight when gliding, unlike a gull, and has a distinctive thick neck and black eye patch. Fulmars are often seen soaring on updraughts around coastal cliffs, although they spend much of their time at sea.

black eye patch

yellowish white head

short, thick neck

tubular nostrils

hooked bill

pale patch

stiff, straight wings

grey wingtips

pale grey rump and tail

weak legs (cannot stand)

FEEDS AT *sea; breeds on steep coastal cliffs or on remote grassy banks near sea.*

VOICE Loud, harsh, throaty cackling.
NESTING On cliff or earth ledge, or rarely on building; 1 egg; 1 brood; Apr–Jun.
FEEDING Takes mostly fish offal from trawlers, small fish, jellyfish, squid, and other marine animals.
SIMILAR SPECIES Herring Gull, Cory's Shearwater.

Long-tailed Skua

Stercorarius longicaudus

This small, slender skua has a graceful, almost tern-like flight, with frequent changes of course and height. Adults have long, whippy central tail streamers in summer. Juveniles lack these – most are paler than Arctic Skuas, but some are very similar. The best distinction is the shorter, thicker, pale-based bill.

black cap

grey-brown above

long central tail spike

dark belly

broad pale bars under tail

short, thick bill

tiny pale flash

white breast

dark trailing edge

thick-necked shape

narrow dark wings

BREEDS ON *northern tundra; winters at sea, with migrants in coastal waters.*

VOICE Wailing, gull-like squeal and high alarm notes in summer; silent at sea.
NESTING Hollow in ground on tundra or high mountain; 2 eggs; 1 brood; Jun.
FEEDING Takes mostly lemmings, voles, and small birds in summer; fish in winter.
SIMILAR SPECIES Arctic Skua, Pomarine Skua.

DARK FORM

Arctic Skua

Stercorarius parasiticus

FEEDS NEAR COASTS *on migration; winters out at sea. Breeds on coastal moorland and northern tundra. Generally the most commonly seen skua in Europe.*

The slender, sharp-winged Arctic Skua is a very variable but always elegant bird. Bigger and heavier than the Long-tailed Skua, but lighter than the Pomarine, it is one of the most beautifully shaped seabirds in flight. It occurs in both pale and dark forms, which can be confusing, but its clean-cut profile is distinctive. It obtains a lot of its food by piracy, harassing terns and small gulls until they disgorge fish. The swift, acrobatic pursuit can be spectacular. On its northern breeding grounds, it has a fast, swooping, high display flight; it also attacks human intruders with great courage.

white wing flash

breast band

PALE FORM

white wing flash

sharp central tail spike

DARK FORM

dark cap

brown back

grey-brown or yellowish breast band

whitish underside

PALE FORM

TIP

The long-winged Arctic Skua has a fast, fluent, rather erratic flight that can make it look rather falcon-like in the air, especially when it is in pursuit of other birds. Occasionally, it may even kill and eat small birds in flight like a true falcon, but it usually chases other birds to steal their food.

slimmer bill than juvenile Arctic or Long-tailed Skuas

sooty brown

DARK FORM

TIP

The Arctic Skua has a variety of plumages, from pale to dark, with a range of intermediate forms. All have white flashes near the wingtips, both above and below, and the elongated central tail feathers of the adults are straight and pointed, rather than blunt like those of the Pomarine Skua. A juvenile has a very short pointed tail spike.

VOICE *Gives loud, nasal wailing in summer, ahh-yeow, eee-air, ka-wow; silent at sea.*
NESTING *Shallow scrape on ground in moss or heather, in small colony; 2 eggs; 1 brood; May–Jun.*
FEEDING *Robs terns and gulls of fish; also catches fish, small birds, and voles; eats some berries and insects.*
SIMILAR SPECIES *Pomarine Skua, immature Common Gull, immature Herring Gull.*

Pomarine Skua

Stercorarius pomarinus

Resembling a larger, stouter, deeper-bellied version of the Arctic Skua, in both its pale and dark forms, the Pomarine Skua is distinguished in summer by its broad, spoon-like tail streamers. Juveniles can be mistaken for those of Arctic Skuas, but have clearer barring on the under- and upper-tail, and heavier, pale-based bills.

FEEDS OR *rests on beaches after gales on migration, but mainly well out to sea. Breeds on Arctic tundra.*

black cap
yellow tint
brown back
patchy breast band
PALE FORM
dark breast band
DARK FORM
pale base to bill
blunt, spoon-shaped, twisted tail streamers
PALE FORM
blunt tail
broad bars
DARK FORM

VOICE *Loud, laughing waer-waer-waer on breeding sites; usually silent elsewhere.*
NESTING *Shallow scrape on open ground on Arctic tundra; 2 eggs; 1 brood; Jun.*
FEEDING *Eats lemmings and seabirds in summer; otherwise stolen fish and scraps.*
SIMILAR SPECIES *Arctic Skua, Great Skua, immature Herring Gull.*

Great Skua

Stercorarius skua

The largest, heaviest, boldest, and most predatory of the skuas, the Great Skua is always dark brown with pale buff streaks and big white wing patches. Able to steal from a Gannet and kill a Kittiwake, its success in recent years has caused problems for other seabirds.

BREEDS ON *northern moors near sea; at other times usually lives well offshore, but sometimes near coasts.*

dark cap
pale streaks on neck
tapered wings
streaked dark brown above
stout, hooked, dark bill
bold white wing patch
dark underparts
thick blackish legs

VOICE *Barking uk-uk-uk, also deep tuk-tuk; silent at sea.*
NESTING *Simple hollow on ground on moorland; 2 eggs; 1 brood; May–Jun.*
FEEDING *Steals fish from other seabirds; kills birds, takes eggs, or scavenges for carrion.*
SIMILAR SPECIES *Pomarine Skua, Arctic Skua, immature Herring Gull.*

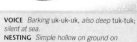

Little Gull

Hydrocoloeus minutus

BREEDS ON *marshland; at other times feeds on coasts, estuaries, coastal lagoons, lakes, and reservoirs.*

The smallest of the gulls, this delicate, elegant, small-billed bird combines the "hooded gull" sequence of plumages with a strongly contrasted immature pattern like that of a Kittiwake. In summer plumage, its hood completely covers its head, with no pale eye-ring, unlike the larger Black-headed and Mediterranean Gulls. It feeds over open fresh waters by dipping for prey like a Black Tern. Like the terns, it tends to appear over lakes and reservoirs in small groups in spring and autumn, but immatures may linger for weeks in the summer, often feeding alongside other gulls.

dark markings on head increase in spring

pale head

delicate dark bill

pale grey back

pale wingtips

black on underwings may be visible

TIP

An immature Little Gull resembles an immature Kittiwake, with a black zigzag on its upperwings, but there are differences. A juvenile has a dark back, a dark rump, and when it moults to first-winter plumage it retains a broad dark nape that extends to the sides of its chest. A Kittiwake has a narrower nape patch and a white rump.

no black on upperwings

blackish underwings with white rims

dark cap and ear patch

blackish zigzag on upperwings

dark ear spot

1ST

underwings paler than adult's

2ND

black hood

pearly grey

VOICE *Low kek-kek-kek call, also hoarse, rapid, rather tern-like call, akar akar akar.*
NESTING *Grassy scrape on ground, or among dense marsh vegetation; 3 eggs; 1 brood; May–Jun.*
FEEDING *Mostly picks up insects, aquatic invertebrates, and small fish from surface of water in dipping flight.*
SIMILAR SPECIES *Black-headed Gull, Mediterranean Gull, immature Kittiwake.*

Black-headed Gull

Chroicocephalus ridibundus

Common and familiar, this is a small, agile, very white-looking gull. It is never truly "black-headed", because in breeding plumage its hood is dark chocolate brown and does not extend to the back of its head. In other plumages, it has a pale head with a dark ear spot. Its dark underwing gives a flickering effect in flight. It has always been a frequent bird inland, but numbers have increased still further in response to abundant food provided by refuse tips and safe roosting sites on reservoirs and flooded pits.

FEEDS ON *coasts, lakes, reservoirs, farmland, refuse tips, and along rivers. Common in towns and cities. Breeds from coastal marshes to upland pools, widespread but local.*

> **TIP**
>
> *Look out for a striking white wedge-shaped marking along the leading edge of each outer wing; no other common gull has this feature.*

dark brown hood

deep red bill

white eye-ring

very pale grey back

deep red legs

brown on neck and back

black-tipped

neck and back become grey

dark hind edge

♦1ST ❊

♦1ST ❊

white leading edge

dark grey underwings with white outer edge

black trailing edge

dark spot

vivid red bill with black tip

vivid red legs

VOICE *Loud, harsh, squealing, laughing, and chattering calls, kwarrr, kee-arr, kwuk, kuk-kuk; particularly noisy at breeding colonies.*
NESTING *Pile of stems on ground in vegetation in marshland, in colony; 2–3 eggs; 1 brood; May–Jun.*
FEEDING *Takes worms, seeds, fish, and insects from ground and water, often picking them from farmland disturbed by ploughing; also catches insects in flight.*
SIMILAR SPECIES *Mediterranean Gull, Common Gull, Little Gull.*

Mediterranean Gull

Larus melanocephalus

Although more common in southeast Europe, this beautiful gull has spread west, far beyond its original range. Bigger than the similar Black-headed Gull, with a heavier bill, it has white wingtips instead of black, and a jet-black rather than dark brown hood in summer.

BREEDS ON *shallow lagoons and coastal marshes. Winters on estuaries, beaches, and rarely on lakes.*

white wingtips

white underwings

dark patch around eye

thick, red to black bill

red to black legs

mottled back

black spots

2ND

black hood

VOICE *Nasal, far-carrying, rising, and falling eeu-err eeu-err.*
NESTING *Grass-lined nest on sand, shingle, or in marsh; 3 eggs; 1 brood; May–Jun.*
FEEDING *Forages for fish, worms, aquatic invertebrates, and offal on beaches and land.*
SIMILAR SPECIES *Black-headed Gull, Common Gull.*

Kittiwake

Rissa tridactyla

One of the most maritime of gulls, the Kittiwake comes to land only to breed in noisy colonies on sheer cliffs. Its very white head and black wingtips are distinctive in flight, and its call is unmistakable. In winter, the adult has a grey nape and a dark ear patch.

BREEDS ON *coastal cliffs. Winters at sea, when scarce on coasts. Rare but regular inland on migration.*

pale yellow-green bill

white head and breast

blue-grey back

short blackish legs

black triangle

grey collar

pale outer wings

black collar

1ST

black zigzag

1ST

dull plumage

black zigzag

dark spot

VOICE *Ringing, nasal, rhythmic kiti-a-wake! often repeated; also high, thin, mewing note.*
NESTING *Nest of weed on ledge on cliff or seaside building; 2–3 eggs; 1 brood; May–Jun.*
FEEDING *Takes mostly fish in shallow dive or from surface; also fish offal from trawlers.*
SIMILAR SPECIES *Common Gull, Little Gull, Herring Gull.*

Common Gull

Larus canus

Rather like the Herring Gull in its general pattern, but much smaller, the Common Gull has a smaller bill with no red spot, a rounder head, and a dark eye, giving it a more gentle expression. Compared to the slightly smaller Black-headed Gull, it has no dark hood or ear spot, and no white leading edge on its outer wing. It is not as common as either species, with a curiously patchy, local distribution despite its wide range.

BREEDS ON *coasts and moors; winters on coasts, farmland, lakes, and reservoirs.*

yellow-green bill with no red

grey-brown on head

mid-grey back

white spots on black wingtips

bold white crescent

🐦 1ST ❄

brown wings, fading to buff

black band

dark brown

grey

brown wingtips

🐦 1ST ❄

mid-grey back

wings fade paler

🐦 1ST ☀

long, slim shape

buff-grey bill with black tip

dark eye on white head

green legs

green to yellow-green legs

large white spot on black wingtip

all-white tail

TIP

At a distance, the Common Gull can be distinguished from the bigger Herring Gull by the larger white patches on its black wing-tips, and its more fluent, easy, relaxed flight style, with relatively little soaring or gliding.

VOICE *Loud, shrill, nasal squealing ke-ee-ya, kee-ar-ar-ar-ar, higher-pitched than Herring Gull's calls; also a short gagagaga.*
NESTING *Pad of grass or seaweed on ground or on low stump, in colony; 2–3 eggs; 1 brood; May–Jun.*
FEEDING *Takes worms, insects, fish, and molluscs from ground or water; also scavenges for scraps.*
SIMILAR SPECIES *Herring Gull, Yellow-legged Gull, Black-headed Gull, Mediterranean Gull.*

Herring Gull

Larus argentatus

The big, noisy Herring Gull is mainly a bird of sea cliffs in summer, but roams over all kinds of shores and far inland in winter, when its white head and neck are streaked brownish. Paler than the Yellow-legged Gull, with pink legs, it has fierce-looking pale eyes.

FEEDS ON *beaches, estuaries, reservoirs, and refuse tips. Breeds on cliffs, islands, and rooftops.*

yellow bill with red spot

pale grey back

blotched brown

grey-brown streaks

white spots

pale pink legs

VOICE Loud, squealing notes, yelps, barks, kyow, kee-yow-yow-yow, ga-ga-ga, kuk-kuk.
NESTING Grass-lined nest on ground, cliff ledge, or building; 2–3 eggs; 1 brood; May.
FEEDING Takes fish, molluscs, insects, fish offal, and scraps from ground or water.
SIMILAR SPECIES Yellow-legged Gull, Common Gull, Lesser Black-backed Gull.

Yellow-legged Gull

Larus michahellis

Formerly regarded as a southern race of the Herring Gull, this bird has a darker back, less white at the wingtips, and yellow instead of dull pinkish legs. Its head remains white in winter, but is streaked pale grey in autumn. In a few places, the two species breed side-by-side, without hybridizing.

BREEDS ON *rocky islands and offshore stacks. Often scavenges around docks and towns.*

vivid yellow bill with large red spot

mid-grey back

all-white tail

brown body

black bill

extensive black and white

1ST

white spots wear off in summer

long black wingtips

white below

pale to deep yellow legs

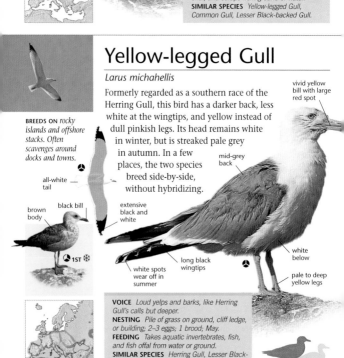

VOICE Loud yelps and barks, like Herring Gull's calls but deeper.
NESTING Pile of grass on ground, cliff ledge, or building; 2–3 eggs; 1 brood; May.
FEEDING Takes aquatic invertebrates, fish, and fish offal from water or ground.
SIMILAR SPECIES Herring Gull, Lesser Black-backed Gull.

Lesser Black-backed Gull

Larus fuscus

In spring and summer, this is one of the most handsome European gulls, immaculate in slate-grey and pure white, with vivid yellow legs and bill. It is almost as big as a Herring Gull, but slimmer and darker. Scandinavian birds are particularly dark, with those of the northern race having black rather than slate-grey backs.

BREEDS ON *cliffs, islands, moorland, and rooftops. Feeds on beaches, refuse tips, reservoirs, and fields.*

The Lesser Black-backed Gull used to be a summer visitor to western Europe, but it has now established large wintering populations inland. Despite this, many migrants still occur over land in spring and autumn, flying high overhead.

TIP

Seen from below, it has darker flight feathers than a Herring Gull, with much less contrast between the black wingtip and the dark band that adjoins the trailing edge, which extends all along the underwing.

densely streaked, grey-brown head

slate-grey back

dull yellow legs

one white primary spot on black wingtip

dark grey band on underwings

mottled dark brown body

black bill

turns dark grey

yellow bill with red spot

white head

bright yellow

🌓 1ST YEAR

🌓 2ND YEAR

VOICE Deep, throaty, wailing calls, deeper than Herring Gull, as well as various barks and yelps, kyow, kyow-yow-yow, ga-ga-ga.
NESTING Pile of grass or seaweed on ground, often in cover of thick vegetation; 2–3 eggs; 1 brood; May.
FEEDING Takes fish, worms, molluscs, crustaceans, and edible refuse, from water and from ground; in summer feeds on other seabirds, their young, and eggs.
SIMILAR SPECIES Herring Gull, Yellow-legged Gull.

Iceland Gull

Larus glaucoides

A large, handsome bird the size of a Herring Gull, the Iceland Gull breeds in Greenland but ranges south to Britain in winter. Its plumage is almost identical to that of the Glaucous Gull, but it has a rounder head, a slighter, shorter bill, and longer wingtips.

FEEDS AT *sea, often following fishing boats into harbours, and on beaches, reservoirs, and refuse tips.*

yellow bill with red spot

head and breast clouded buff-brown and grey

buff-ivory wingtips

oatmeal brown

pale grey back

white wingtips

wingtips extend well beyond tail

short pink legs

VOICE *Shrill squealing notes and barking calls, like Herring Gull.*
NESTING *Small grassy nest on cliff ledge or ground; 2–3 eggs; 1 brood; Jun.*
FEEDING *Fish, molluscs, crustaceans, offal, and scraps; from water, fields, and refuse tips.*
SIMILAR SPECIES *Glaucous Gull, immature Herring Gull.*

Glaucous Gull

Larus hyperboreus

Bigger than the Iceland Gull, and distinctly fiercer-looking, the Glaucous Gull has a much larger, longer bill, and shorter wingtips at rest. In Europe, it is usually seen in its less immaculate winter plumage, before it heads north to breed in the Arctic.

FEEDS AROUND *trawlers at sea, on beaches, reservoirs, and refuse tips. Breeds on northern coasts.*

white wingtips

buff wingtips

yellow bill with red spot

clouded grey-brown

pale pink bill with black tip

pale grey above

barred oatmeal brown

mottled brown

short white wingtips

pale pink legs

VOICE *Wailing and yapping notes, much like those of Herring Gull.*
NESTING *Pad of grass and stems on cliff ledge or ground; 2–3 eggs; 1 brood; May–Jun.*
FEEDING *Takes fish, invertebrates, offal, and scraps; more predatory in summer.*
SIMILAR SPECIES *Iceland Gull, immature Herring Gull.*

Great Black-backed Gull

Larus marinus

Huge, powerful, heavy-billed, and fiercely predatory, the Great Black-backed is the world's largest gull. The size of its bill is a good guide to its identity even in immature plumages, when it resembles an oversized Herring Gull. Adults are blacker than the southern races of the Lesser Black-backed Gull, although the black plumage fades browner as it ages. It dominates other gulls, and preys on other seabirds and their young in summer.

BREEDS ON *rocky coasts with cliffs and stacks, often in flocks around coastal pools. Winters on beaches, harbours, reservoirs, and also on refuse tips.*

big, powerful yellow bill with red spot

faint markings on white head

black back

white underside

broad wings

large white patch on wingtips

pale greyish, whitish, or pink legs

TIP

At long range, this big gull can be distinguished from the Lesser Black-backed by the larger white patch on its wingtips, and its heavier flight.

black bill

whitish head

1ST

pale head

chequered back

2ND

pure white head

dark flight feathers

VOICE *Much deeper than other gulls, with barking notes, short hoarse yowk, gruff, guttural ow-ow-ow.*
NESTING *Shallow scrape on cliff ledge or pinnacle, lined with grass or weed; 3 eggs; 1 brood; May–Jun.*
FEEDING *Bold and predatory in summer, eating seabirds and voles; also catches fish, crustaceans, and other invertebrates; scavenges offal and edible scraps from sea, beaches, and refuse tips.*
SIMILAR SPECIES *Lesser Black-backed Gull, immature Herring Gull.*

Shag

Phalacrocorax aristotelis

This large, long-bodied diving bird is very like the closely related Cormorant, but the adult is black overall with an oily green gloss, the only colour being the bright yellow patch at the base of its bill. In summer, both sexes sport a short curly crest. Winter birds are less distinctive and easier to confuse with Cormorants, but a certain slim snakiness gives the Shag a different character. Although sometimes solitary, Shags tend to feed in flocks, favouring the fast tide races and rough water under rocks and cliffs.

FEEDS OFF *rocky coasts and islands; not common around harbours. Breeds on coastal cliffs.*

short crest

slim, slightly hooked bill

TIP

A Shag's head is a different shape from a Cormorant's, with a steep angle between its bill and its sloping forehead. An adult has no white on its face. It rarely strays inland, so any bird of this type seen away from the coast is likely to be a Cormorant.

narrow wings

slender head and neck

oily green-black plumage

white chin

paler below

long, slim body

long tail

white spot

dark brown above

brown below

low in water

VOICE *Grunts, hisses, and coarse, frenzied rattling at nest; silent when feeding at sea.*
NESTING *Heap of grass, sticks, and seaweed on broad cliff ledge, or inside coastal cave; 3–4 eggs; 1 brood; May.*
FEEDING *Catches fish, mainly sandeels and herrings, by pursuing them underwater after dive from surface; often dives with quick, arching, forward leap.*
SIMILAR SPECIES *Cormorant, Black-throated Diver.*

Cormorant

Phalacrocorax carbo

Bigger and bulkier than a Shag, and slightly less snaky in shape, the Cormorant has a thicker bill, a low, flat forehead, and no crest. Its plumage is blackish, glossed with blue and bronze, and in spring it has white streaks on its head, a bold white throat, and white patches on its thighs. Often seen inland, even on small pools, Cormorants swim with their backs almost awash, and typically perch with their wings half-open. They fly strongly with long glides, often high up, in lines or "V" formations over coastal waters and wetlands.

LIVES ON *coasts in sheltered estuaries and bays, and around harbours; also inland on lakes, rivers, and pools. Breeds on cliffs.*

flat forehead

hooked bill

white below

white on face

yellow near bill

neck kinked in flight

blue gloss on head and neck

blackish above, with bronze gloss

> **TIP**
>
> In flight, the neck of a Cormorant has an upward kink while the Shag holds its neck straight. Shags also tend to fly lower, often just above the waves.

bill tilted up

brown above

white below

long, broad tail

VOICE Growling and cackling at nests and communal roosts, but otherwise a quiet bird.
NESTING Bulky nest of sticks in a tree or on a cliff ledge, often marked by white splashes beneath; 3–4 eggs; 1 brood; Apr–May.
FEEDING Catches fish, especially bottom-living flatfish and eels, in long underwater dive from surface, propelling itself with its feet; brings larger fish to surface before swallowing them.
SIMILAR SPECIES Shag, Great Northern Diver.

Gannet

Morus bassanus

BREEDS IN *dense, noisy colonies on rocky islands. Feeds at sea, many moving south for the winter.*

Largest of all European seabirds, the adult Gannet is typically seen offshore as a brilliant white bird with black wingtips, flying steadily, singly or in straggling lines, or circling and diving for fish with spectacular plunges. Juvenile birds, by contrast, are very dark with white specks, gradually becoming whiter over about five years, but their shape is always distinctive. At close range, the breeding adult's yellow-buff head is visible, as well as the dark markings on its face and fine lines on its big, sharp bill.

long rear end and narrow, pointed tail

protruding head

looks dark greyish at distance

yellow-buff head

pale blue eyes

dagger-like bill with fine black lines

long, narrow wings

white band above tail

dark above with white speckling

white plumage

large black wingtips

TIP

The protruding head, pointed bill, and narrow tail of a Gannet are quite unlike any gull's. Its long wings are much narrower, with more black on them.

webbing across all four toes

black wingtips

yellowish head

blackish above with white spots

piebald; turns white with age

VOICE *Rhythmic, throaty chorus of groans, barks, and croaks at nesting colony; otherwise silent, except for cackling from groups feeding at sea.*
NESTING *Pile of seaweed and debris on broad ledge high above sea, in dense, often very large colony; 1 egg; 1 brood; Apr–Jul.*
FEEDING *Catches fish such as mackerel and pollack underwater, in shallow and sloping dive from air, or vertical plunge dive from a greater height; also scavenges from fishing boats.*
SIMILAR SPECIES *Arctic Skua, immature Great Black-backed Gull.*

Owls & Birds of Prey

Of all birds, these are the chief carnivores; most hunt down living prey. Owls are highly specialized, with superb eyesight and hearing. Most, like the Long-eared Owl, are nocturnal, but some, such as the Short-eared Owl, are also active by day. Birds of prey hunt by day. Both groups of birds have acute vision, powerful legs and feet armed with sharp talons for catching prey, and strong, hooked bills for tearing it up. Their range of dietary preferences spans everything from insects (the Lesser Kestrel and Little Owl) or small rodents (Kestrel and many owls) to carrion (vultures), fish (Osprey), other birds (Sparrowhawk), and prey up to the size of a small deer (Golden Eagle). Superb fliers, many remain perched for hours between feeding forays, while others are far more aerial, spending much of the day aloft.

KESTREL   GRIFFON VULTURE   LONG-EARED OWL   GOLDEN EAGLE

Scops Owl 🔊

Otus scops

LIVES AMONG *trees, in villages and small towns, parkland, farmland, and open woodland, often near old buildings. Most winter in Africa.*

The calling of the Scops Owl at dawn and dusk is a common feature of Mediterranean villages and woodlands. Highly nocturnal, it looks pale in the light of a street lamp, with a square-topped head or raised ear tufts. It is more elongated in shape than a Little Owl.

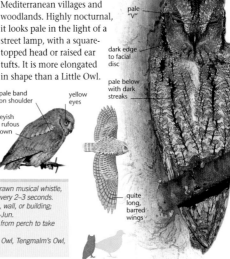

ear tufts raised

pale "V"

dark edge to facial disc

pale below with dark streaks

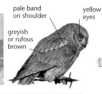

pale band on shoulder

yellow eyes

greyish or rufous brown

quite long, barred wings

VOICE *Single, fluty, indrawn musical whistle, pew or tyuh, repeated every 2–3 seconds.*
NESTING *Cavity in tree, wall, or building; 4–5 eggs; 1 brood; Apr–Jun.*
FEEDING *Mostly drops from perch to take large insects.*
SIMILAR SPECIES *Little Owl, Tengmalm's Owl, Tawny Owl.*

Little Owl 🔊

Athene noctua

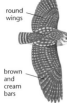

PERCHES ON *posts and branches on farmland, open rocky slopes, and even semi-desert areas with rocks and cliffs.*

The small, chunky, flat-headed, short-tailed Little Owl frequently perches out in the open by day, when it often attracts the noisy attention of small birds. It can look very round and solid – although it may stretch upwards when alarmed and take off in a low, fast, bounding flight, like that of a thrush or woodpecker.

broad head with spotted crown

pale yellow eyes

brown back with cream-buff spots

wavy dark streaks

quite long legs

round wings

brown and cream bars

flattish white eyebrows

VOICE *Loud, musical, plaintive calls, rising keeeoooo, sharper* werro! *short kip kip kip.*
NESTING *In long, narrow hole in tree, bank, or building; 2–5 eggs; 1 brood; May–Jul.*
FEEDING *Mostly takes small rodents, large insects, and worms from ground.*
SIMILAR SPECIES *Scops Owl, Tawny Owl, Short-eared Owl.*

Tengmalm's Owl

Aegolius funereus

Favouring dense forests, and active only at night, this quite small owl is a very difficult bird to see. The combination of its call, size, and habitat helps identify it, since the similar Scops and Little Owls avoid densely wooded habitats. Its "astonished" expression is distinctive in a good view.

bold yellow eyes

high brow

LIVES IN *dense forests, mainly coniferous, with small clearings, staying near breeding site throughout year.*

large, pale facial disc with blackish edge

band of whitish spots next to back

large head

white spots and bars

pale below, mottled soft brown

VOICE *Hoarse chiak; song 5–8 whistles, rising and accelerating, pu-pu-po-po-po-po-po.*
NESTING *Unlined tree cavity or woodpecker hole; 3–6 eggs; 1 brood; May–Jun.*
FEEDING *Watches and listens for voles and similar prey from tree perch within forest canopy; rarely more exposed.*
SIMILAR SPECIES *Little Owl, Tawny Owl.*

Pygmy Owl

Glaucidium passerinum

The smallest European owl, the Pygmy Owl has a small, rounded head with no "ear" tufts. It has small, glaring yellow eyes, a relatively long bill, and a rather long, narrow tail, which it often waves or raises slowly. Often bold, it may be seen closely in daylight, especially at dusk and dawn.

shorter head than Little or Tengmalm's

short white eyebrows

brown bars on flank

BREEDS IN *coniferous and mixed forest, often at edges or in boggy areas; in winter may visit open country.*

no white spots

darker flanks

brown-streaked white underside

narrow, barred tail

VOICE *Male's song is a repeated series of mellow, flute-like notes; calls include (in autumn) series of 5–10 sharp whistles*
NESTING *In tree hole or nestbox; 4–7 eggs; 1 brood; Apr–Jun.*
FEEDING *Small mammals, especially voles, and birds (often larger than the owl itself).*
SIMILAR SPECIES *Little Owl, Tengmalm's Owl.*

Long-eared Owl 🔊

Asio otus

A large, upright owl, with long ear tufts that it raises when alert, the Long-eared Owl is typically strictly nocturnal, with secretive habits that usually make it very hard to see. When relaxed, it can look rounded and bulky, but if alarmed it draws itself up into a slim, erect posture, its ear tufts upright, creating an unmistakable silhouette. Migrants can sometimes be seen by day, when they can be confused with Short-eared Owls, but the Long-eared Owl is slightly less buoyant in flight and never glides on raised wings. The pattern on its wings is less contrasted, with no white trailing edge.

ROOSTS IN *thorn and willow thickets, old hedgerows, and similar thick cover. Breeds mainly in conifer woods or shelter belts.*

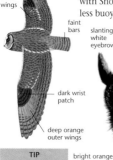

mottled inner wings

faint bars

slanting white eyebrows

long ear tufts, raised

dark wrist patch

deep orange outer wings

TIP

The bird often holds its long ear tufts flat when relaxed, so if there is enough light, look for its slanting white eyebrows and uniformly dark, streaked underside.

bright orange eyes with dark surround

dark, closely streaked underside

ear tufts relaxed

streaking continues on to belly

TIP

Winter roosts in dense thickets are hard to see, but sometimes betrayed by regurgitated pellets and splashes of droppings on the ground below.

VOICE *Song deep, moaning, short hoot, oo oo oo or uh uh; juvenile begs for food with incessant high, sharp "squeaky hinge" eee-ip calls.*
NESTING *Old nest of crow or hawk in tree, squirrel drey, or scrape on ground beneath bushes or thick growth of bracken or brambles; 3–5 eggs; 1 brood; Mar–Jun.*
FEEDING *Hunts from perch or in flight, catching small rodents on ground or (especially in winter) birds roosting in trees.*
SIMILAR SPECIES *Short-eared Owl, Eagle Owl, Tawny Owl.*

Short-eared Owl

Asio flammeus

One of few owls that regularly appears in broad daylight, the Short-eared Owl is often to be seen hunting like a harrier, flying and gliding low over open grassland, heather, or coastal marshland. Its dark-rimmed yellow eyes give it a fierce expression that is often visible at long range, and its blunt head and very buoyant flight make it hard to confuse with a harrier. It is very like the Long-eared Owl in flight, but has a pale belly, strongly barred tail, and white trailing edge to the wings; the Long-eared Owl is also very unlikely to be seen hunting by day.

HUNTS OVER *all kinds of rough grassland, marshes, heaths, upland moors, and young plantations. Erratic breeder in south of range, linked to variations in vole populations.*

whitish underwings

orange-buff to yellowish outer wings

dark wrist patch

bold bars on tail

white trailing edge

pale belly

narrow dark bar

black-rimmed, cold yellow eyes

blunt head

large round head with tiny ear tufts, usually hidden

complex buff marbling on upperparts

buff-white below, with fine dark streaks

scarcely streaked pale belly

TIP

An owl has large wings but low body weight, giving it a very low wing loading that makes it extremely buoyant in the air. This is apparent in the Short-eared Owl, which floats over the ground in long, wavering glides with its wings held up in a shallow "V". It can look very pale, but the dark patches near the end of its wings distinguish it from the even paler Barn Owl.

VOICE *Nasal bark, kee-aw, or hoarse, whip-like ke-ow; male's song a deep, soft, quick booming hoot, boo-boo-boo-boo, given in display flight, often high up, when he also claps his wings quickly below his body.*
NESTING *Unlined scrape on the ground, usually in thick cover; 4–8 eggs; 1–2 broods; Apr–Jul.*
FEEDING *Hunts in flight or watching from perch, often by day; eats small rodents, particularly voles, other small mammals, and some birds.*
SIMILAR SPECIES *Long-eared, Tawny, and Barn Owls; female harriers.*

Tawny Owl

Strix aluco

A big-headed, bulky woodland owl that is generally strictly nocturnal, the Tawny Owl is responsible for the hooting and loud *ke-wick* notes often heard after dark. Beautifully camouflaged, it is hard to spot while roosting in the trees unless betrayed by the mobbing of small birds.

HUNTS IN *all kinds of woodland, wooded famland, and also in urban parks and large gardens with trees, even in big cities.*

large black eyes

obvious facial disc

large, round head

brown back with row of white spots on each side

short wings and tail

pale spots and bars

VOICE *Loud, excited, yapping* ke-wick!, *long, quavering hoot,* hoo hoo-hooo hoo-o-o.
NESTING *Hole in tree or building, or old stick nest of crow; 2–5 eggs; 1 brood; Apr–Jun.*
FEEDING *Drops down to take rodents, frogs, beetles, and worms; also takes roosting birds.*
SIMILAR SPECIES *Long-eared Owl, Eagle Owl, Tengmalm's Owl.*

Eagle Owl

Bubo bubo

The massive, broad-bodied Eagle Owl is well named, for it is one of Europe's most powerful predators. It is almost entirely nocturnal, and surprisingly hard to see when roosting. Although it looks like the Long-eared Owl, it has more widely set ear tufts and is much bigger.

LIVES MAINLY *in forested mountain areas with cliffs, deep ravines, often with caves, big ledges, or big, old trees for nesting.*

pale "V" on face

deep orange eyes

large ear tufts held in shallow "V"

bold black mottling

boldly streaked, pale underside

big, closely barred upper-wings

VOICE *Deep booming hoot,* oo-hu; *barking alarm notes* kvek, kwa, *or* kwa-kwa-kwa.
NESTING *Unlined tree cavity or sheltered cliff ledge; 2–3 eggs; 1 brood; Apr–May.*
FEEDING *Takes mammals from voles to hares, and birds such as crows and pigeons.*
SIMILAR SPECIES *Long-eared Owl, Tawny Owl, Buzzard.*

Barn Owl

Tyto alba

Often seen by day, especially when it has young to feed, this is a strikingly pale owl with a heart-shaped face and black eyes. In western Europe, it has a white breast; in the east, deep buff. It often hunts in flight, flying low over the ground with quick, deep wing-beats.

BREEDS AND *hunts in open country, from farmland to marshes and moorland, and young plantations.*

heart-shaped facial disc

black eyes

thin bars

pale buff upperparts

grey and black spots

white under-wings

buff below

white below

T. a. guttata

legs may dangle

VOICE *Hissing, snoring calls from nest, nasal hi-wit, shrill, rolling shrieks and high squeals.*
NESTING *Big hole in tree, stack of hay bales, or building; 4–7 eggs; 1 brood; May–Jun.*
FEEDING *Hunts from perch or in low flight, for voles, mice, rats, and sometimes birds.*
SIMILAR SPECIES *Short-eared Owl, Tawny Owl.*

Merlin

Falco columbarius

A small, dynamic falcon of open country, the Merlin flies fast and low over the ground in pursuit of prey, with rapid flicks of its wings and a final agile rise to strike. The thrush-sized male is bluish grey above with a dark tail-band, while the bigger female is earthy brown with a cream-barred tail.

BREEDS ON *moorland, in north on tundra and conifer forests. Winters in lowlands on open pasture, and coastal marshes and fields.*

small, square head

dark eyes

barred flight feathers

cream bands on tail

mud-brown above

♀

bluish grey upperparts

orange-buff with dark streaks below

small, chunky body

♂

pale tail with black band

dark, pointed wingtips

♂

VOICE *Male has quick chittering kik-kik-ki-kik; female has deeper, nasal kee-kee-kee.*
NESTING *Bare scrape on ground among heather, or in old crow's nest in tree; 3–6 eggs; 1 brood; Apr–Jun.*
FEEDING *Mostly eats small birds, caught in flight; also eats a variety of large aerial insects.*
SIMILAR SPECIES *Hobby, Peregrine, Kestrel.*

Lesser Kestrel

Falco naumanni

HUNTS OVER *hot, open country in southern Europe. Breeds socially on buildings, ruins, cliffs, and crags and other sites with plenty of nest holes. Very rare wanderer outside its normal range.*

The sociable, mainly insect-eating Lesser Kestrel has suffered a serious decline in recent decades, and is now rather rare. It can be difficult to distinguish from the Kestrel, especially the female. Both species hover to target their prey on the ground, and the smaller size of the Lesser Kestrel is not normally obvious – although its slightly stockier shape and shorter wings may help. The male is easier to identify, thanks to his unspotted back and blue-grey wing panels.

barred, wedge-shaped tail

♀

dark outer wings

white underwings

♂

blue-grey head

blue-grey head without black "moustache"

no spots

unspotted, rich red-brown back

blue-grey panel

♂

central tail feathers protrude as wedge

finely spotted, deep pink-buff chest

♂

white claws

pale cheek spot

♀

brownish head

♀

black bars on back and inner wings

brown tail with black band across wedge-shaped tip

TIP

A hunting Lesser Kestrel does not hover for such long periods as a Kestrel, and has a lighter, quicker flight with much shallower wing-beats.

VOICE *Fast, raucous, triple call, chay-chay-chay, and high, nasal, chattering notes.*
NESTING *On ledges or in cavities, on cliffs or buildings, in loose colonies; 3–6 eggs; 1 brood; Apr–Jul.*
FEEDING *Feeds mainly on insects, chasing them in the air, frequently following swarms, or snatching them from the ground, often after hovering; also takes some small mammals, reptiles, and birds.*
SIMILAR SPECIES *Kestrel.*

Kestrel

Falco tinnunculus

A common and widespread falcon of open spaces, the Kestrel is familiar to most people as the bird that hovers over roadsides for long periods, as if suspended on a wire. In the north of its range, this hovering habit is almost unique: other raptors hover, but not for so long. The smaller male has a blue-grey head and tail while the female's upperparts are all brown, spotted with black. Both show a strong contrast between the pale inner and dark outer wing.

LIVES IN *wide variety of habitats, from cities to remote mountains. Common around woodland, heaths, and over rough grassland.*

♀
pale brown inner wings

paler outer wings than male

rufous inner wings

♂

brown-black outer wings

rufous back, spotted with black

short, round, blue-grey head

dark eyes

♂

dusky moustache stripe

buff below, spotted black

blue-grey tail with black tip

black claws

TIP

A hovering Kestrel is usually unmistakable, especially in northern Europe, beyond the range of the Lesser Kestrel. But Kestrels are also capable of high soaring, and they often hunt from perches or catch small birds in sudden dashes, rather like Sparrowhawks. They always look slimmer than Lesser Kestrels, with longer, more pointed wings.

black-barred back and inner wings

♀

VOICE *Nasal, complaining, whining keee-eee-eeee and variants, especially near nest.*
NESTING *On bare ledges on cliffs, in quarries, on derelict buildings or high window-ledges, in disused crows' nests or tree holes; 4–6 eggs; 1 brood; Mar–Jul.*
FEEDING *Catches small mammals, especially voles, after hovering search, also eats beetles, lizards, earthworms, and small birds.*
SIMILAR SPECIES *Lesser Kestrel, Sparrowhawk, Merlin.*

Hobby

Falco subbuteo

A dynamic aerial hunter with the speed and agility to catch dragonflies, swallows, and even swifts, the scythe-winged Hobby is like a smaller, slimmer version of the Peregrine. No other bird can surpass it for sheer elegance when hunting; it mixes slow, floating glides with deft turns, sudden dashes, and fast dives. An adult is deep grey above, with a black cap and "moustache" that contrast sharply with its pale cheeks and throat.

The dense, dark streaks on its underside can make it appear very dark from below.

NESTS IN *abandoned crows' nests; hunts over open ground, including farmland with scattered trees, heaths, marshes, and especially areas with pools or flooded pits where it can find flying insects to eat.*

whitish cheeks and throat

bold black "moustache"

deep grey upperparts

long, tapered wings

dark head

reddish under tail

bold white neck

browner than adult

buff cheeks

thick black streaks on pale underparts

rufous thighs and undertail coverts

yellow legs

no red under tail

short, narrow, plain tail

TIP

With its long, pointed wings and shortish tail, the Hobby can look almost like a swift in flight. It sometimes dives with folded wings like a Peregrine, but is much narrower across the body, and streaked rather than barred below. It often hunts over marshy ground with pools and flooded pits, catching dragonflies with its feet and eating them in mid-air.

VOICE *Clear, musical, whistled kyu-kyu-kyu-kyu, especially near nest; sharper, rapid ki-ki-ki-ki in flight.*
NESTING *Uses old nest in tree, usually of crow and sometimes other members of the crow family; 2–3 eggs; 1 brood; Jun–Aug.*
FEEDING *Catches fast-flying small birds such as martins and swallows in flight, and eats many large flying insects, such as dragonflies and airborne beetles.*
SIMILAR SPECIES *Peregrine, Merlin, Kestrel.*

Peregrine

Falco peregrinus

The big, powerfully built Peregrine is a bird-killing falcon, famous for the high-speed diving "stoop" that it often uses to kill its prey in mid-air. When hunting, it often patrols at great height, looking like a tiny black anchor in the sky. A closer view reveals its closely barred underparts, yellow legs, pale breast and throat, and the large dark "moustache" patches below its big, black, yellow-rimmed eyes. It spends much of its time perched, when it looks particularly bulky and broad-chested.

BREEDS ON *hills and rocky coasts with cliffs; also, increasingly in cities. Hunts over estuaries and marshes in winter.*

dull black head

yellow eye-ring and bill base

black lobes below eyes

white cheek patch

broad white breast

darker wingtips

blue-grey above

white below, closely barred with grey

broad, pale rump

broad, pointed wings

blue-grey upperparts

blue base to bill

browner than adult with buff feather edges

TIP

The arrival of a Peregrine overhead often causes panic among other birds, any of which may be potential prey. If you notice a sudden commotion, look up.

VOICE *Loud, raucous calls at nest include throaty* haak-haak-haak-haak *and whining* kee-keee-eeeeee *and* wheeee-ip.
NESTING *On broad ledge or earthy scrape on cliff, in quarry, or more rarely on building or on flatter ground; 2–4 eggs; 1 brood; Mar–Jun.*
FEEDING *Kills birds of sizes ranging from thrush to pigeon or grouse, sometimes larger, often rising to take them from beneath, chasing them in level flight, or diving from great height.*
SIMILAR SPECIES *Hobby, Kestrel, Merlin.*

Sparrowhawk

Accipiter nisus

HUNTS IN *wide variety of habitats, from dense forests to cities. Breeds in wooded farmland and forest; winters in more open country.*

The Sparrowhawk is a small, quick, agile bird hunter, adapted for pursuing its prey through forests. It has relatively short, broad wings and a long tail, giving it great manoeuvrability. It often dashes into view at low level with a distinctive flap-flap-glide action, then jinks and swerves to disappear through a tight gap. At other times, it soars over the woods on fanned wings, sweeping them back to a point in fast glides. The male, much smaller than the female, is blue-grey above with bright rusty orange below; the female is browner above and whitish barred with grey below.

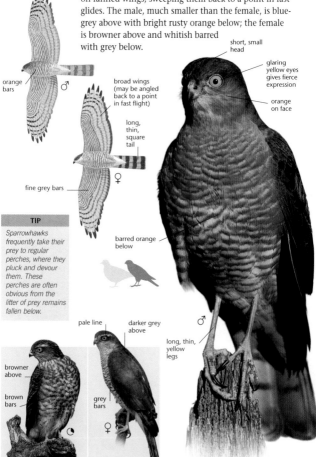

orange bars ♂

broad wings (may be angled back to a point in fast flight)

long, thin, square tail

fine grey bars ♀

short, small head

glaring yellow eyes gives fierce expression

orange on face

barred orange below

TIP

Sparrowhawks frequently take their prey to regular perches, where they pluck and devour them. These perches are often obvious from the litter of prey remains fallen below.

browner above

brown bars

pale line

darker grey above

grey bars ♀

♂

long, thin, yellow legs

VOICE *Repetitive kek-kek-kek-kek-kek, thin squealing peee-ee, but generally quiet away from nest.*
NESTING *Small, flat platform of thin twigs on flat branch close to tree trunk; 4–5 eggs; 1 brood; Mar–Jun.*
FEEDING *Hunts small birds, darting along hedges, woodland edges, or into gardens to take prey by surprise; males take mainly tits and finches, larger females take thrushes and pigeons.*
SIMILAR SPECIES *Kestrel, Goshawk.*

Goshawk

Accipiter gentilis

Essentially a giant version of the Sparrowhawk, with the same adaptations for hunting in forests, the Goshawk – especially the Buzzard-sized female – is powerful enough to kill a pheasant. The male is a lot smaller, about as big as a large female Sparrowhawk. The two can be hard to tell apart, but the Goshawk has longer wings, a bulkier, deeper body, and a less square-tipped tail. Often elusive in dense forest, Goshawks are best looked for in early spring when they soar over breeding territories in courtship display flights.

HUNTS AND *breeds in well-wooded farmland, forests, and uplands; favours tall conifers. A few winter in more open country.*

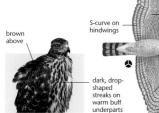

broad wings

S-curve on hindwings

buff below with dark streaks

brown above

dark, drop-shaped streaks on warm buff underparts

flight feathers often only faintly barred

dark cap

pale stripe over eye

orange-red eyes

dark ear coverts

greyish to brownish above

white undertail coverts

whitish below with fine grey barring

♂

TIP

The Goshawk has much more obvious white undertail coverts than a Sparrowhawk, often visible when the birds are soaring overhead.

VOICE *Woodpecker-like, chattering, nasal gek-gek-gek and mewing pi-aah from female begging food.*
NESTING *Remarkably large, flat-topped heap of sticks and greenery close to trunk of tall tree; 2–4 eggs; 1 brood; Mar–Jun.*
FEEDING *Hunts boldly in forest or clearings, catching birds from size of a thrush to crows, pigeons, gamebirds, and other birds of prey; also takes rabbits and squirrels.*
SIMILAR SPECIES *Sparrowhawk, Buzzard.*

Montagu's Harrier

Circus pygargus

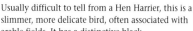

BREEDS ON *heaths, grassland, marshes, and in cereal fields; winters in Africa.*

Usually difficult to tell from a Hen Harrier, this is a slimmer, more delicate bird, often associated with arable fields. It has a distinctive black bar on the inner wing, obvious on the male, but the narrower, long-tipped wings are the best clue to its identity.

long, tapered black wingtips

wingtips angled back ♂

black wingbar

small white rump ♀

barred tail

rufous

pale crescents above and below eye

streaked below ♀

grey head

medium grey above

streaked flanks ♂

VOICE *High, clear yek-yek-yek from male, chek-ek-ek-ek from female.*
NESTING *Nest of stems and grasses on ground; 4–5 eggs; 1 brood; Apr–Jun.*
FEEDING *Catches small mammals, reptiles, and small birds on or near ground.*
SIMILAR SPECIES *Hen Harrier, female Marsh Harrier.*

Hen Harrier

Circus cyaneus

HUNTS OVER *heather moors in summer, coastal marshes or low-lying rough grassland in winter.*

Male and female Hen Harriers look very unlike one another, but very like the slimmer-winged Montagu's Harrier. The smaller, pale grey male is easier to identify than the female. Both tend to glide on flatter wings than other harriers when hunting. The male is the only grey harrier to winter in Europe.

black wingtips ♂

♀

grey with dark bars

barred tail

pale grey head and body ♂

white rump

whitish underside

dark brown ♀

buff with streaks ♀

VOICE *Near nest, irregular week-eek-ik-ik-ik from female; even chekekekekekek from male.*
NESTING *Nest of stems on ground in rushes or heather; 4–6 eggs; 1 brood; Apr–Jun.*
FEEDING *Hunts low over marshes, diving to catch small birds, ducks, rodents, and frogs.*
SIMILAR SPECIES *Montagu's Harrier, Short-eared Owl.*

Marsh Harrier

Circus aeruginosus

This is the biggest and heaviest of the harriers, and also the darkest – it can be taken for a dark Buzzard or a Black Kite when soaring. The male does have some grey in its plumage, but is much browner than a male Hen Harrier. The female is chocolate-brown above with cream head markings; a juvenile male is almost identical, but has no cream wing patch. Marsh Harriers hunt in classic harrier fashion, patrolling slowly at low level with their wings raised in a "V" when gliding, and dropping into reeds or long grass to seize their prey.

SEARCHES FOR *prey on marshland and flat, open country near coasts. Breeds in large reedbeds or among long grass or tall crops.*

broad wings held in "V" when gliding

♀

broad black wingtips

silver-grey

♂

brown wing coverts

square grey tail

creamy cap and throat

cream patch on wings

very dark brown plumage

♀

♀

TIP

Although harder to identify when soaring, the Marsh Harrier has much narrower wings than a Buzzard, and does not twist its tail like a Black Kite.

♂

dark belly

pale markings on head

brown back

grey on wings

♂

pale head

♀

dark brown

VOICE *Shrill kee-yoo in display flight; hoarse chattering kyek-ek-ek-ek or kyi-yi-yi-yi, or high whistles.*
NESTING *Large platform of reed stems among dense reeds over water, or increasingly among crops; 4–5 eggs; 1 brood; Apr–Jul.*
FEEDING *Hunts low over marshes, diving to catch small birds, wildfowl, rabbits and other small mammals, and frogs; also takes eggs and chicks, and scavenges for carrion.*
SIMILAR SPECIES *Hen Harrier, Black Kite.*

Buzzard

Buteo buteo

One of the most common and widespread European birds of prey, the Buzzard is often seen soaring on broad wings in wavering, rising circles as it scans the ground for prey. Its plumage varies from pale cream to blackish brown, but from below its flight feathers are always pale with a dark trailing edge.

SOARS OVER *and hunts and breeds in wooded farmland, on moors, mountains, and other uplands near crags and forests; also on coastal cliffs.*

hunched shoulders

rich brown above

pale "U" below

cream head

soars with wings slightly raised

barred, pale underwings

🔴 PALE

pale, barred tail

short head

dark wrist patch

VOICE *Frequent, loud, high, ringing pee-yaah or weaker mew; calls often while flying.*
NESTING *Stick nest in tree, or beneath bush on cliff ledge; 2–4 eggs; 1 brood; Mar–Jun.*
FEEDING *Catches voles, rabbits, beetles, worms, and some birds; eats a lot of carrion.*
SIMILAR SPECIES *Honey Buzzard, Rough-legged Buzzard, Golden Eagle.*

Rough-legged Buzzard

Buteo lagopus

Named for its feathered legs, this big, broad-winged buzzard is easier to identify by its dark-tipped white tail and "frosted" upperparts. In western Europe, it is usually a rare winter visitor, but more move south in years when prey is scarce in the far north.

HUNTS OVER *moorland, heaths, marshes, and dunes in winter. Breeds in far north on tundra.*

pale head

dark brown above

whitish patches

🔴 pale chest and blackish belly

"frosty" pale feather edges

dark bands on wings and tail

VOICE *Loud, low, plaintive squeal, pee-yow.*
NESTING *Stick nest on cliff or in tree; 2–4 eggs; 1 brood; Mar–Jun.*
FEEDING *Drops onto small mammals, especially voles and small rabbits, either from perch or from hovering flight.*
SIMILAR SPECIES *Buzzard, juvenile Golden Eagle.*

Honey Buzzard

Pernis apivorus

Not a true buzzard at all, this very variable relative of the kites specializes in raiding nests of bees and wasps, using its feet to dig out the grubs and, in the case of bees, the waxy honeycombs. Adults are typically greyish above – with dark trailing edges on the wings and three dark tail bands – and whitish below, with bold "tiger stripes" and dark wrist patches. Juveniles are browner. Elusive when breeding, Honey Buzzards are more often seen on migration, especially at narrow sea crossings like the Strait of Gibraltar.

BREEDS AND *feeds in extensive forest or well-wooded hill country. Concentrates at sea crossings on migration.*

dark head; often whiter on juvenile

yellow eyes; dark on juvenile

tiger-striped underwings and belly

soars with wings flat or drooped

closed tail bulges at sides

dark wrist patches

boldly striped below

three dark bands on tail

narrow, Cuckoo-like head

long tail, widest in centre

VOICE *Infrequent, plaintive, whistling* peee-haa, *or sometimes three-syllable* pee-ee-aah.
NESTING *Small platform of sticks and greenery high in a tree, often built on top of old nest of crow or Buzzard; 1–3 eggs; 1 brood; Apr–Jun.*
FEEDING *Feeds mainly on wasp and bee grubs, beeswax, and honey, which it digs out with its feet; also eats some other adult insects, ant pupae, young birds, eggs, and small mammals and reptiles.*
SIMILAR SPECIES *Buzzard, Rough-legged Buzzard, Black Kite.*

Black Kite

Milvus migrans

FEEDS OVER *rivers, open ground, wooded slopes, and coasts; often on refuse tips. May still be seen around towns in some parts of its range.*

More a dark, dull brown than black, with a paler head and body, the Black Kite is an elegant, long-tailed raptor that glides and circles with its wings slightly bowed and tail often fanned. It frequently forages near rivers, seizing food from the water surface in a fast, sweeping dive and carrying it away in its feet as it feeds in mid-air. It is very adaptable, and in many parts of its wide range it scavenges in towns, snatching scraps from the gutters and even stealing from market stalls. In Europe, it is more likely to join crows and other scavengers feeding at carcasses and rubbish tips.

TIP

A kite has a habit of constantly twisting its fanned tail from side to side in flight. If you see this, and the bird has dark underwings, it's a Black Kite.

glides and soars on bowed wings

dull and dark overall

pale diagonal band on upperwing

long, slightly forked tail

paler underside and head

small pale head

dark area behind eye

long wings

pale buff feather tips appear as contrasting spots above

pale streaks below

usually indistinct pale patch; more noticeable on juveniles

broadly "fingered" wingtips

VOICE High, whinnying peeie-ee-i-ee-i-ee.
NESTING Nest of sticks, earth, and scraps of rubbish in tree; 2–4 eggs; 1 brood; Mar–Jun.
FEEDING Takes a lot of dead or dying fish from water or along shoreline, also small birds, reptiles, and voles; scavenges for carrion and scraps of all kinds, often on refuse tips.
SIMILAR SPECIES Booted Eagle (dark form), Red Kite, female Marsh Harrier, Honey Buzzard (dark form).

Red Kite

Milvus milvus

An agile, long-winged, aerobatic bird of prey, the Red Kite is exceptionally graceful in the air, with a light, buoyant, elastic flight style that has few equals apart from the much darker, drabber Black Kite. Distinguishing the two is no problem, for the Red Kite's rusty plumage, bold white wing patches, and contrasting black wingtips are distinctive. The forked tail often glows almost orange in bright sun. Where common, it may gather in large numbers to exploit good food sources.

BREEDS IN *wooded valleys, hunting over open country. Winters at lower altitude, foraging around towns and refuse tips.*

soars on bowed wings

pale band on upperwings

black flight feathers

forked tail

pale eyes

whitish head

pale tawny to rust-red body

pale

whitish to pale red below tail

bold white patch

TIP

At a distance, the long, narrow wings and flight style separate a kite from a Buzzard. White underwing patches and a reddish body identify a Red Kite.

paler than adult

paler upperwings

rusty-brown, forked tail

VOICE High, long-drawn-out, wailing or squealing weieie-ee-ow, higher pitched than the call of a Buzzard.
NESTING Large nest of sticks, rags, earth, and rubbish in tree, usually well hidden; 2–4 eggs; 1 brood; Mar–Jun.
FEEDING Scavenges from the carcasses of dead animals such as rabbits or sheep; catches birds up to size of crow or gull in surprise dash; also feeds on insects, earthworms, and voles.
SIMILAR SPECIES Black Kite, Buzzard.

Booted Eagle

Aquila pennata

The Buzzard-sized Booted Eagle occurs in both pale and dark forms, but always has dark primaries with a paler inner primary patch visible from below. It also has bright white "spotlights" on its shoulders that show up from head-on. It has straighter wings than a buzzard and holds them flat when soaring.

SOARS OVER *forests and warm, sunny, well-wooded, hilly country with mixed farmland and scrub, often close to villages. Mainly breeds in more remote parts with minimal disturbance.*

PALE FORM

DARK FORM

BOTH FORMS FROM ABOVE

long, whitish tail

pale tail

pale patch

dull brown

white crescent

white spots

pale diagonal band

white forehead

broad, round head

white below

PALE FORM

VOICE *Buzzard-like hi-yaaah and musical, wader-like, whistled kli-kli-kli in display.*
NESTING *Bulky stick nest in canopy of tree, rarely on cliff ledge; 2 eggs; 1 brood; Feb–Apr.*
FEEDING *Catches reptiles, birds, and small mammals on ground, often after steep dive.*
SIMILAR SPECIES *Black Kite, immature Bonelli's Eagle.*

Short-toed Eagle

Circaetus gallicus

HUNTS OVER *high, open slopes and rocky areas with short scrub. Winters in Africa.*

This large, impressive eagle specializes in hunting snakes and lizards, which it targets from a height while soaring, or by hovering with wingtips and tail fanned, before stooping for the kill. Typically grey-brown above, with a dark head and chest, it has silvery-white underwings with variable dark bars. Very pale adults have no dark hood.

broad wingtips

dark hood

yellow eyes

very pale below

rather pale grey-brown above

darker flight feathers

grey-white underside, barred or spotted darker

bare, pale bluish grey legs

long tail

VOICE *A variety of short, abrupt calls, such as kyo, meeok.*
NESTING *Bulky stick nest in crown of large tree; 1 egg; 1 brood; Apr–Jun.*
FEEDING *Catches snakes and lizards, typically diving on them from hovering flight.*
SIMILAR SPECIES *Booted Eagle (pale form), Osprey.*

Osprey

Pandion haliaetus

A big, long-winged, eagle-like bird of prey, yet surprisingly like an immature gull at long range, the Osprey is uniquely equipped for diving into the water to catch fish. It is rarely seen far from water, but like many birds of prey it spends much of its time perched, when its white, black-banded head is usually obvious. Dark brown above, it is white below with a variable dark breastband and bold black wrist patch. It typically holds its wings at a marked angle, kinked at the wrist rather like a gull, and often hovers rather heavily before plunging headlong into the water for its prey.

CATCHES FISH *in lakes, reservoirs, large rivers, estuaries, and in coastal waters. Breeds in tall trees or on cliffs near water.*

black patch on underwings

short, banded tail

variable breast band

glides on kinked wings

black patch

dark brown above

white on head

whitish crown

black stripe through eye

long, broad wings

blackish band along middle of underwings

dark brown above; juvenile has bright buff feather edges

white underparts

close-feathered legs, like tight stockings

TIP

An Osprey in flight can be confused with a gull at long range, but it has a shorter head and broader wings. A gull also has no dark wrist patches.

bluish grey feet

large, sharp claws

VOICE *Loud yelps and repeated, high, liquid, whistled pyew pyew pyew near nest.*
NESTING *Stick nest on tree or cliff, artificial platform or ruined building, re-used and added to each year until it reaches immense size; 2–3 eggs; 1 brood; Apr–Jul.*
FEEDING *Snatches fish from water using feet, after hovering and plunging in a steep dive; sometimes hunts from perch.*
SIMILAR SPECIES *Short-toed Eagle, immature Great Black-backed Gull.*

Bonelli's Eagle

Aquila fasciata

Elegant and powerful, Bonelli's Eagle combines the strength of a large eagle with the speed and dexterity of a bird-catching hawk. As with the Goshawk, its small head serves to emphasize its deep chest. In flight, adults show a distinctive combination of a whitish body and dark wings and upper tail. Juveniles are rufous below, with paler flight feathers that become darker with age. Sadly, this dashing bird of prey is now scarce, with only a few hundred pairs left in Europe.

BREEDS MAINLY *in deep gorges and on crags, and hunts over wooded uplands; immatures hunt at first on lowland plains.*

small, flat-topped head

dark upperparts with distinctive white patch on back

no dark tail tip

rufous below

pale leading edge

blackish band on mainly dark underwings

streaked white below

long, narrow, straight-edged tail, with dark band obvious in flight

dark midwing band

short head, held high

dark tail tip

TIP

Bonelli's Eagle spends much time perched inconspicuously and often hunts low down, snatching birds as they fly up or even chasing them through trees like a giant Sparrowhawk. This makes it hard to see, although it does soar high above its territory at intervals.

VOICE Occasional bark or shrill yelp at nest site, but generally silent.
NESTING Massive stick nest, often re-used and added to over many years, in small cave, on deep ledge, often on sheer cliff, rarely in tree; 2 eggs; 1 brood; Feb–Apr.
FEEDING Hunts mammals such as hares, rabbits, and squirrels, and birds such as partridges, crows, and pigeons; often hunts from perch, but also pounces on prey from low flight, or in stoop from soaring flight.
SIMILAR SPECIES Goshawk, Booted Eagle.

Golden Eagle

Aquila chrysaetos

A huge, supremely elegant raptor, the Golden Eagle favours remote mountains and crags, and is rarely seen as more than a dot in the distance. Despite this, its wide, slow, circling flight is often sufficient to identify it. It holds its long, broad wings in a shallow "V" when soaring, the primaries swept up at the tips. An immature bird has extensive white areas on its wings and tail, which diminish and finally disappear as it grows older.

HUNTS OVER *remote peaks or upland forests and more rarely on steep coasts, far from settlements and roads.*

pale tawny to golden crown

soars with wings raised in shallow "V"

barred dark underwings

dark brown body plumage

white wing patches

white on tail

bulky body and wings

heavily feathered legs

long tail, paler at base

blacker than adult

TIP

At a distance, when its size is not apparent, a Golden Eagle may be mistaken for a Buzzard. But it circles more slowly, has a longer tail, and its head protrudes more. At closer range, its underwings are broader, darker, and less patterned than a Buzzard's.

VOICE Occasional shrill yelps and whistling **twee-oo** of alarm, but generally silent.
NESTING Immense pile of sticks, lined with wool and greenery, on broad cliff ledge or in old pine tree; 1–3 eggs, 1 brood; Feb–Jun.
FEEDING Hunts mainly for grouse, crows, hares, rabbits, and marmots, usually by diving from low-level flight; eats much carrion in winter, chiefly carcasses of dead sheep and deer.
SIMILAR SPECIES Buzzard, White-tailed Eagle, Griffon Vulture.

Egyptian Vulture

Neophron percnopterus

With its black and white plumage, an Egyptian Vulture in flight can look like a White Stork until you notice its much shorter neck. Adults are summer visitors to Europe; dark brown immatures are much rarer, staying in Africa until they gain adult plumage.

SOARS ON *flat wings over wooded mountain regions, gorges, and cliffs, and often feeds at rubbish tips.*

yellow face

thin bill

brownish across wings

dirty white body

white tail

white forewings

narrow head

black hindwings and wingtips

dark brown body

dark wings

VOICE *Silent.*
NESTING *Nest of sticks, bones, and rubbish, on sheltered cliff ledge or in small cave; 1–3 eggs; 1 brood; Apr–Jun.*
FEEDING *Eats all kinds of carrion, offal, and scraps, often at refuse tips; also takes eggs of birds such as pelicans.*
SIMILAR SPECIES *White Stork, Golden Eagle.*

White-tailed Eagle

Haliaeetus albicilla

A huge, heavy-billed bird with very long, broad, plank-like wings and a very short tail, the White-tailed Eagle has a distinctive flight silhouette. Adults have pale heads, big yellow bills, and striking white tails, but immatures are darker overall. This eagle is now rare over most of its former range.

HUNTS ON *rocky coasts, estuaries, and remote marshes in summer; winters mainly on large, damp coastal plains.*

glides on flat wings

dark tail

head and neck protrude

saw-toothed trailing edge

pale head

big yellow bill

short white tail

pale and dark blotches

deeply fingered wingtips

VOICE *Shrill yaps near nest in summer.*
NESTING *Huge pile of sticks on cliff ledge or flat tree crown; 2 eggs; 1 brood; Mar–Jul.*
FEEDING *Picks dead and sick fish, and fish offal, from water with feet; catches seabirds and hares; takes carrion on land.*
SIMILAR SPECIES *Golden Eagle, Griffon Vulture, Black Vulture.*

Griffon Vulture

Gyps fulvus

The Griffon Vulture is a massive, long-winged, short-tailed, soaring bird, which can exploit air currents to travel great distances without beating its wings at all. In flight, it looks distinctively two-tone above and below, with a distinct contrast between its toffee-brown body and wing coverts, and its darker flight feathers. Its near-naked head looks small and pale. It spends much of its time perched quietly on cliffs, especially on still mornings, waiting for the heat of the sun to generate the rising thermal air currents that it needs for effective soaring.

SOARS OVER *all kinds of open country, from lowlands to mountain peaks. Breeds on cliffs or rocky gorges.*

soars with wings in shallow "V"

deeply fingered wingtips

dark brown underwings

narrow light bands on underwings

whitish head and neck

bulbous bill

short pale head

pale toffee-brown back

very short dark tail

rich buff-brown wing coverts and back

ragged plumes

darker flight feathers

TIP

A soaring Griffon Vulture seems to change shape as it circles; from below its broad wings are very square, but from other angles they look pointed.

VOICE Silent, apart from coarse hissing when feeding.
NESTING Pile of twigs, leaves, and grass, on bare but sheltered ledge in gorge or on high cliff, in loose colonies of ten to over 100 pairs; 1 egg; 1 brood; Apr–Jul.
FEEDING Feeds exclusively on carrion, taking soft tissues of dead sheep, goats, and smaller animals such as rabbits; often fed at special feeding stations.
SIMILAR SPECIES Black Vulture, Golden Eagle.

Black Vulture

Aegypius monachus

LIVES IN *mountainous regions and rolling uplands with mixed forest as well as areas of open ground.*

The colossal Black Vulture is one of the world's largest flying birds. It holds its extremely broad, square wings flat as it soars in thermal upcurrents, so it looks like a flying plank – less elegant and shapely than the slightly smaller Griffon Vulture, but with terrific presence in the sky. Its short tail is slightly wedge-shaped, and its pale head and feet are often obvious against its black-brown plumage. Unlike the Griffon Vulture it often perches on trees, rather than cliffs; it also spends a lot of time on the ground, especially near food. But it is most likely to be seen in the air, soaring majestically and effortlessly for hours with barely a beat of its great dark wings.

pale head with black mask

strong bill

soars on flat wings

pale brown ruff; darker on juvenile

broad, square wings

very dark forewings

massive, dark brown body; juvenile paler

TIP

Even at a great distance the Black Vulture can be distinguished from the Griffon Vulture by its flat-winged soar; the Griffon soars with its less rectangular wings raised in a "V".

VOICE *Mostly silent, but croaks and hisses when feeding at carcasses, and gives mewing or roaring calls in breeding season.*
NESTING *Huge stick nest in crown of flat-topped tree, sometimes on ledge; 1 egg; 1 brood; Apr–Jun.*
FEEDING *Feeds mainly on carrion taken from medium to large carcasses; occasionally catches live prey, usually weak or sick animals; also feeds at special feeding stations.*
SIMILAR SPECIES *Griffon Vulture, Golden Eagle.*

Glossary

Many of the terms defined here are illustrated in the general introduction (pp.6 –11). For anatomical terms in particular see pp.6 –7.

• **ADULT** A fully mature bird, able to breed, showing the final plumage pattern that no longer changes with age.

• **BARRED** With marks crossing the body, wing, or tail.

• **BROOD** Young produced from a single clutch of eggs incubated together.

• **CALL** Vocal sound often characteristic of a particular species, communicating a variety of messages.

• **COLONY** A group of nests of a highly social species, especially seabirds but also others such as the Sand Martin and Rook.

• **COVERT** A small feather in a well-defined tract, on the wing or at the base of the tail, covering the base of the larger flight feathers.

• **CRYPTIC** Of plumage pattern and colours that make a bird difficult to see in its habitat.

• **DABBLE** To feed in shallow water, with rapid movements of the bill, sieving water through comb-like teeth to extract food.

• **DECLINING** Populations undergoing a steady decline over a number of years.

• **DIMORPHIC** Having two forms: sexually dimorphic means that the male and female of a species look different; otherwise indicates two colour forms.

• **DRUMMING** Sound made by woodpeckers with rapid beats of the bill against a hard object, or by a snipe, diving through the air with vibrating tail feathers.

• **EAR TUFT** A bunch of feathers on the head of an owl, capable of being raised as a visual signal and perhaps to assist camouflage.

• **ECLIPSE** The plumage of male ducks that is adopted during the summer, when they moult and become flightless for a short time.

• **ENDANGERED** Found in very small numbers, in a very small area or in a very restricted and declining habitat, so the future security of the species is in doubt.

• **ESCAPEE** A bird that has escaped into the wild from a collection of some kind, such as a zoo or wildlife park.

• **EYE PATCH** An area of colour around the eye, often in the form of a "mask", broader than an eye-stripe.

• **EYE-RING** A more or less circular patch of colour, usually narrow and well-defined, around the eye.

• **EYE-STRIPE** A stripe of distinctive colour running in front of and behind the eye.

• **FAMILY** A category in classification, grouping species or genera that are closely related; ranked at a higher level than the genus.

• **FLIGHT FEATHER** Any one of the long feathers on the wing (primaries and secondaries).

• **FOREWING** The front part of a wing, including the outer primaries, primary coverts, and secondary coverts.

• **GAPE** A bird's mouth, or the angle at the base of the bill.

• **GENUS** (*pl.* **GENERA**) A category in classification: a group of closely related species, whose relationship is recognized by the same first name in the scientific terminology, e.g. *Larus* in *Larus fuscus*.

• **HINDWING** The rear part of the wing, including the secondary feathers, especially when it has a distinctive colour or pattern.

• **HYBRID** The result of cross-breeding between two species; usually infertile. A rare occurrence in the wild.

• **IMMATURE** Not yet fully adult or able to breed; there may be several identifiable plumages during immaturity but many small birds are mature by the first spring after they have fledged.

• **INNER WING** The inner part of the wing, comprising the secondaries and rows of coverts (typically marginal, lesser, median, and greater coverts).

• **JUVENILE** A bird in its first plumage, that in which it makes its first flight, before its first moult in the autumn.

• **LEK** A gathering of birds at which males display communally, with mock fighting, while females choose which one to mate with.

• **LOCALIZED** More than 90 per cent of the population occurs at ten sites or less.

• **MOULT** The shedding and renewing of feathers in a systematic way; most birds have a partial moult and a complete moult each year.

• **MIGRANT** A species that spends part of the year in one geographical area and part in another, moving between the two on a regular basis.

• **ORDER** A category in classification: families grouped to indicate their close relationship or common ancestry; usually a more uncertain or speculative grouping than a family.

• **OUTER WING** The outer half of the wing, comprising the primaries, their coverts, and the alula, or bastard wing (the "thumb").

• **ORBITAL RING** A thin, bare, fleshy ring around the eye, sometimes with a distinctive colour.

• **PRIMARY** Any one of the long feathers, or quills, forming the tip and trailing edge of the outer wing, growing from the "hand".

• **RACE** *See* Subspecies.

• **RARE** Found in small numbers or very low densities.

• **SCAPULAR** Any one of a group of feathers on the shoulder, forming an oval patch each side of the back, at the base of the wing.

• **SECONDARY** Any one of the long flight feathers forming the trailing edge of the inner wing, growing from the ulna or "arm".

• **SONG** Vocalization with character particular to the individual species, used to communicate a claim to a breeding territory and attract a mate.

• **SONG-FLIGHT** A special flight, often with a distinctive pattern, combined with a territorial song.

• **SPECIES** A group of living organisms, individuals of which can interbreed to produce fertile young, but do not normally breed, or cannot produce fertile young, with a different species.

• **SPECULUM** A colourful patch on a duck's hindwing, formed by the secondary feathers.

• **STREAKED** With small marks that run lengthwise along the body.

• **SUBSPECIES** A race; a recognizable group within a species, isolated geographically but able to interbreed with others of the same species.

• **SUPERCILIARY STRIPE** A stripe of colour running above the eye, like an eyebrow.

• **TERTIAL** Any one of a small group of feathers, sometimes long and obvious, at the base of the wing adjacent to the inner secondaries.

• **UNDERWING** The underside of a wing, usually visible only in flight or when a bird is preening.

• **UPPERWING** The upperside of the wing, clearly exposed in flight but often mostly hidden when the bird is perched.

• **VAGRANT** An individual bird that has strayed beyond the usual geographic range of its species.

• **VENT** The area of feathers between the legs and the undertail coverts, surrounding the vent or cloaca.

• **VULNERABLE** Potentially at risk due to a dependence on a restricted habitat or range, or to small numbers.

• **WINGPIT** A group of feathers – the axillaries – located at the base of the underwing.

• **WINGBAR** A line of colour produced by a tract of feathers or feather tips, crossing the closed wing and running along the spread wing.

• **YOUNG** An imprecise term to describe immature birds; often meaning juveniles or nestlings.

Index

Acknowledgments

DORLING KINDERSLEY would like to thank Umesh Aggarwal, Balwant Singh, Jessica Subramanian, and Narender Kumar for DTP assistance, and Rimli Borooah for indexing. This edition: Designer Fiona Macdonald, Editor Lizzie Munsey, Jacket Designer Silke Spingies, Jacket Editor Manisha Majithia, and Web Designer Natalie Glenister.

PICTURE CREDITS
Picture librarian : Richard Dabb
Picture research : Anna Bedewell, Carolyn Clerkin, and Ben Hoare
(Abbreviations key: t=top a=above b=bottom c=centre l=left r=right

Anders Paulsrud: 106(tl).

Anthony McGeehan: 176 (tl) (cl).

Aquila Wildlife Images : Mike Wilkes 46 (crb).

Ardea London Ltd: Chris Knights 47 (cr) (tl), John Daniels 128 (cal), Uno Berggren 193 (cla).

Bob Glover: 24 (tl), 29 (crb) 34 (tl), 48 (tl), 62 (tl), 97 (tr), 169 (tr) (crb), 180 (bc), 185 (bl), 187 (cl).

Bruce Coleman Ltd: Werner Layer 196 (br), Paul Van Gaalen 205 (bc).

Carlos Sanchez Alonso: 14 (bcr), 21 (cra), 67 (car).

Chris Gomersall Photography: 1 (c), 7 (ccr), 8 (cb), 10 (ccl), 11 (bl) (tcr), 12 (br), 16 (tl) (clb), 17 (tl), 23 (tr), 26 (clb) (br) (bca), 30 (tr), 35 (cr) (cb), 36 (crb), 37 (tr) (ca), 38 (crb) (br), 39 (tr) (crb), 42 (cl) (crb) (br), 43 (cr) (br) (car), 44 (tl), 46 (tl) (cl) (cr), 50 (tl), 56 (crb), 57 (tr) (cl) (cbr), 59 (cb), 61 (crb), 65 (c), 66 (cra) (clb), 68 (clb) (cb) (br), 70 (cla) (cla), 74 (c) (clb), 77 (br), 79 (crb), 81 (cr), 82 (tr) (ca), 83 (cb) (br), 84 (tl) (c), 85 (tr) (c), 86 (cr), 87 (bcr), 92 (tr), 93 (ca) (cr), 96 (cl), 97 (bc), 98 (tl), 99 (cr), 100 (cl), 101 (bra), 102 (tl) (cb), 103 (crb), 104 (tl), 105 (tr) (c), 107 (cl) (clb) (crb), 108 (br) (bcr), 117 (crb), 118 (tl) (ca), 119 (cra), 119 (tr), 121 (ca) (crb), 122 (cb) (crb) (br), 123 (cr) (bcr) (cbr), 125 (crb), 125 (cra) (crb) (cbr), 126 (br), 127 (tr) (cra) (cbl), 128 (cl) (bl), 130 (tl) (bc), 132 (cl) (br), 134 (tl) (cal), 135 (tr) (cra), 136 (bcl), 137 (ca) (cl), 139 (br), 140 (tl) (clb), 141 (tr) (c), 143 (tr), 146 (tl), 147 (tr) (c), 148 (tl), 149 (tr), 150 (tl) (c) (bcr) (cal) (cbl), 155 (tr), 160 (cl), 162 (tl), 163 (c) (bl) (bcr), 166 (clb), 167 (tr) (c) (cb), 168 (cla) (cr) (br), 171 (crb), 172 (tl) (cr), 176 (tr) (ca), 181 (tr) (cl), 182 (cl), 184 (ca), 186 (br), 190 (tl), 191 (c), 194 (tl) (cr), 195 (cb), 197 (cr) (cl), 198 (ca), 209 (tr) (cl), 211 (cr) (cal), 213 (tr) (bl), 214 (cl) (cbr), 215 (cra).

Chris Knights: 11 (br), 33 (tr), 50 (clb), 79 (tr), 127 (cr) (crb), 135 (c), 156 (cl), 158 (clb), 161 (crb), 192 (bc).

Colin Varndell: 16 (trb), 19 (tr), 21 (crb), 23 (cra), 109 (tr), 137 (cra) (br), 189 (cr), 201 (br).

Corbis: Eric and David Hosking 78 (crb).

David Cottridge: 10 (br), 11 (car), 24 (cb), 25 (cb), 29 (br), 31 (tr) (cra) (car), 34 (crb), 37 (bra), 38 (bcr), 39 (c), 41 (crb) (car), 43 (tr), 45 (tr), 59 (crb), 61 (bc) (bra), 62 (cla) (crb), 63 (tr), 76 (cra), 88 (cl) (br), 90 (br), 91 (br), 92 (c), 104 (crb), 110 (cla), 113 (cla), 115 (crb), 119 (cal), 120 (cla), 126 (ca), 132 (cla), 135 (cl), 161 (cla), 164 (tl) (cra), 168 (ca), 178 (cr), 184 (br), 186 (cl), 206 (cal).

David Tipling: 17(cr), 159 (cbl).

FLPA – Images of nature
15 (cca), 24 (trb), 31 (tl), 45 (bl), 54 (tl), 67 (tr); F Merlet 13 (cb), Fritz Polking 196 (cbl), Fritz Siedel

197 (cla), George McCarthy 15 (bc), 20 (cra), 33 (crb), 64 (crb), 71 (cra) (car), 87 (bcl), 90 (cla), 98 (crb), 101 (clb) (bla), 103 (tr), 119 (cb), 122 (cla), 123 (ca), 125 (ca), 129 (tr) (crb) (br), 130 (cra) (cr), 131 (cla) (cra) (bc), 132 (bc), 148 (cl), 155 (bc), 175 (c), 178 (clb), 185 (tr), 188 (bl), 192 (tl) (cra), 206 (cbl), Hans Dieter Brandl 90 (tlb), Martin B Withers, 96 (br), P Harris/Panda Photo 83 (tr), Richard Brooks 23 (crb), 29 (tr), 34 (ca), 57 (cbl), 76 (br) (bca), Robin Chittenden 45 (cal), 92 (br), 126 (tr), 129 (cbr), 133 (cbl), 138 (bcr), 145 (bl), 152 (tl), 156 (bcr), 175 (bl), 176 (crb) (br) (cbl), 184 (bl), Silvestris 26 (cra), W S Clark 212 (br), Winfried Wisniewski 107 (tr).

George McCarthy: 20 (cra), 33 (crb), 64 (crb), 71 (cra) (car), 87 (bcl), 90 (cla), 98 (crb), 101 (clb) (bla), 103 (tr), 119 (cb), 122 (cla), 123 (ca), 125 (ca), 129 (tr) (crb) (br), 130 (cra) (cr), 131 (cla) (cra) (bc), 132 (bc), 148 (cl), 155 (cra), 175 (c), 178 (clb), 185 (tr), 188 (bl), 192 (tl) (cra), 206 (cbl).

Goran Ekström: 39(cb), 52(cl), 89 (cr).

Gordon Langsbury: 7 (cbr), 41 (bra), 54 (bcr), 83 (ca) (cra), 123 (tr), 131 (tr) (clb), 173 (br), 190 (bc).

Hanne & Jens Eriksen: 47 (cb), 54 (cal), 56 (tl), 62 (clb), 72 (cra), 76 (cla), 98 (bla), 116 (bl), 117 (cal), 142 (bl), 182 (tl), 212 (tl).

Henry Lehto: 45 (bra), 107 (cla).

Huttenmoser: 60 (tl) (ca) (cra).

Jari Peltomaki: 92 (cl), 193 (tr).

Julian V. Bhalerao: 28 (clb).

K. Taylor: 167 (bl).

Laurie Campbell Photography: 35 (tr).

Mark Hamblin: 16 (crb), 17 (br), 18 (trb), 32 (clb) (bc), 36 (tl) (cra), 38 (cla), 41 (cal), 44 (tr), 49 (clb), 50 (cl), 51 (cla) (cra) (clb), 55 (ca) (tcb), 56 (cbl), 64 (cra), 70 (br), 79 (bl), 81 (bl), 85 (bl), 91 (cra) (c) (br), 93 (ca), 94 (cal), 95 (tr) (br), 109 (cbr), 111 (cr), 114 (c), 118 (cla), 126 (bc), 136 (bl), 137 (cr) (cal), 140 (ca), 144 (c), 145 (cb), 151 (bc), 153 (c), 154 (cbl), 160 (tl), 162 (c), 189 (cl), 192 (br), 197 (ca), 195 (cr), 196 (cra), 202 (bl).

Matti Rekila: 85(cr), 193(cr) (cb).

Mike Lane: 149 (bra), 15 (cra), 17 (ca), 22 (tl) (bc), 23 (ca), 25 (tr) (bla), 27 (tr) (ca) (cb) (crb) (bra), 29 (ca), 30 (bcr), 31 (crb) (br), 32 (cra), 33 (cal), 36 (bra) (cal), 37 (crb) (bl), 39(cr), 41 (bcr) 43 (cla), 50 (crb), 54 (bl), 55 (cla), 64 (br), 65 (bla), 66 (ca), 69 (c), 71 (cb), 77 (br), 78 (clb) (cb) (br), 79 (ca) (cra), 86 (b), 99 (cra) (bra), 100 (cla) ,101 (bc) ,102 (cl) (clb), 103 (cb), 109 (bl) (cal) ,110 (tl) (cr), 111 (ca), 116 (cra) (ca), 117 (cbr), 124 (cra) ,125 (cbl), 127 (cal), 128 (cra), 137 (tr) (cbl), 138 (cbr), 139 (cb) (crb) (bcr) (car), 140 (cbl), 142 (cl) ,146 (cb), 150 (cra), 151 (crb), 153 (crb), 158 (cr) (bl), 159 (cr) (crb), 164 (c), 166 (br), 170 (c),172 (tr), 177 (cr) (br), 178 (bl), 181 (br), 183 (bl), 188 (tl), 190 (br), 205 (tr) (bl), 206 (cra).

Mike Read: 80(cl),126 (tl), 161 (bl).

N.H.P.A: 13 (crb), 165 (cl), 173 (crb), Bill Coster 201 (bl).

Nature Picture Library: 171 (cl), Rico & Ruiz 20 (br), 75 (cl), Dietmar Nill 80 (tl), Klaus Nigge 216 (tl).

Oxford Scientific Films: Mike Brown 76 (cb), Paolo Fioratti 93 (tr), Paulo de Oliveira 196 (tl).

Philip Newman: 204 (bl).

R.J Chandler: 11 (clb), 44 (cla), 48 (cb), 100 (cr), 111 (cb), 141 (br), 172 (bl).

Ray Tipper: 25 (crb), 28 (tl), 70 (crb), 98 (cl), 113 (br) ,133 (cla).

Rene Pop: 168 (cbl).

Richard Brooks: 19 (crb), 74 crb, 78 (bra).

Robin Chittenden: 6 (bc), 7 (br), 88 (bla), 157 (clb), 183 (cl).

Roger Tidman: 172 (tl) (cbr), 40 (cb) (crb), 7 (br) (bcr) (bcra), 8 (br), 11 (crb), 12 (c) (bcr), 18 (crb) (cca), 20 (tl) (cla), 21 (br) (bcr), 22 (ca), 23 (bl) (bc), 24 (br), 25 (ca) (cra), 29 (br), 30 (cra), 32 (ca), 33 (br) (car) (cla), 34 (clb) (bcr), 38 (tlb), 39 (cb), 41 (cra), 42 (bcr), 43 (ca) (cl) (tcb), 44 (clb) (bc), 45 (tr) (cla) (car), 46 (clb), 47 (cra), 49 (tr), 50(tr), 51(br)(cbl)(cbr),52(clb), 53 (tr) (cr)(cb), 55 (bcr), 58 (clb) (cb), 59 (cr), 61 (tr) (cra), 66 (tl), 67 (trb), 68 (ccr), 69 (tr), 70 (tl), 71 (bl) (bca), 73 (cr), 74 (cb), 75 (tr) (cb) (crb), 79 (cb), 80 (cra), 81 (ca), 89 (br), 94 (crb), 95 (bc), 96 (cr) (crb), 97 (ca) (cr), 98 (tr), 107 (tr) (cla), 110 (cb) (cbr), 111 (tr) (bl), 112 (tl), 113 (cr) (car), 115 (ca), 116 (cb), 117 (ca) (cl) (clb) (bl), 119 (crb), 120 (clb) (cbr), 121 (cla) (crb), 123 (cra), 124 (cal) (cbr), 125 (cr), 126 (cra) (bl), 127 *(cr), 128 (clb), 129 (tc) (c), 130 (tr), 133 (br), 134 (ca) (br), 135 (c) (br), 136 (bcr), 137 (crb), 138 (br), 140 (cr), 142 (tl) (car), 145 (bcl), 147 (bl), 148 (cla), 149 (c), 152 (c), 154 (tr) (ca), 155 (bc), 156 (ca), 158 (tl) (tr), 160 (cr) (br), 161 (c), 162 (cra) (clb) (br) (cbr), 166 (ca) (bl), 169 (cra) (c), 170 (tl), 173 (tr) (cr) (cb) (cal), 175 (tr), 179 (cca), 181 (ccb), 182 (cr) (cca) (trb), 184 (cl), 187 (br), 190 (cr), 198 (tl) (bl), 199 (br), 203 (cb), 203 (cl), 204 (tl) (cla) (cra), 205 (c) (bl), 208 (cr) (bl), 209 (bl), 210 (cra) (cl) (br), 212 (cl), 214 (tl) (cra), 216 (bl).

Roger Wilmshurst: 24 (bra), 36 (cla), 38 (tr), 40 (cr), 41 (tr), 47 (ca), 48 (cr), 62 (tr), 66 (br), 67 (crb), 78 (cla), 82 (bca) (cbr), 86 (tl), 88 (tl) (cr) (rca), 90 (tl) (tr), 99 (tr), 100 (br), 112 (ca), 115 (cb), 128 (cr), 142 (cb), 143 (c), 144 (cb), 146 (cr), 150 (crb), 168 (tl), 177 (cra), 178 (br), 182 (cra) (bl), 183 (tr) (c), 185 (br), 200 (tl), 201 (cr).

RSPB Images: 126 (cl), 128 (tl), 131 (cr) (crb), 133 (cr), 135 (bl), 138 (clb), 144 (tl) 166 (cr), 171 (tr), 174 (crb); Andy Hay 42 (tl)(tr)(ca), 112 (cl), 121 (tr), Barry Hughes 64 (clb), 109 (cr), Bill Paton 15 (tr) 82 (cl), Bob Glover 2 (c), 15 (crb), 59 (tr), 66 (cb), 74 (tl), 87 (c), 96 (tl),111 (clb), 119 (crb), 122 (clb), 125 (tr), 200 (cl), 202 (tl), Carlos Sanchez Alonso 38 (clb), 71 (crb), 107 (c), 192 (ca), 196 (cl), 200 (cr), 204 (cl), 208 (tl), 209 (cr), 215 (cr), Chris Gomersall 201 (tr), 214 (bc), Chris Knights 30 (br), 53 (ca), 65 (tr), 80 (crb), 97 (cl), 101 (tr), 103 (clb), David Hosking 130 (cl), David Kjaer 18 (cra), 36 (clb), 49 (cr), 58 (tl), 67 (br), 100 (tl), 124 (cr), 194 (bl), 197 (clb), 202 (bcl), Dusan Boucny 72 (tl), E A Janes 108 (c), 116 (tl), George McCarthy 118 (clb), Gerald Downey 56 (cbr), 64 (cla), 206 (cl), Gordon Langsbury 37 (cl), 60 (cl), 123 (cr), 199 (tr), Jan Sevcik (cr), 56 (clb), 94 (cra), 203 (tr), John Lawton Roberts 32 (tl), 92 (tl), 95 (cl), Malcolm Hunt 13 (cra), 24 (cra), 115 (tr), Mark Hamblin 11 (tr), 12 (bl), 18 (clb)(bra), 46 (cbl), 49 (cla), 51 (tr), 70 (clb), 77 (tr), 78 (tl) (ca), 81 (crb), 91 (cr), 202 (cr), 204 (bra), Maurice Walker 16 (ca), Michael Gore 19 (bc), 76 (clb), Mike Lane 30 (trb), 46 (c), 52 (ca), 69 (cbl), 84 (br), 114 (tl), 120 (tl), 133 (cal), 177 (tr), 206 (tl) (br), Mike McKavett 14 (tl), Mike Read 108 (bcl), Mike Richards 93 (tl), 94 (tr), Paul Doherty 207 (c), Philip Newman 24 (clb), 77 (crb), Richard Brooks 14 (br), 48 (cr), 51 (crb), 61 (ca), 83 (cr), 91 (bca), 100 (bl), Robert Horne 17 (tr), Robert Smith 76 (tl), 94 (cl), Roger Wilmshurst 10 (ccr),

101 (cr), Stanley Porter 124 (clb), Steve Austin 102 (crb), 110 (cl) (cbl), Steve Knell 21 (tr), 24 (ca), 32 (tr), 53 (cra), 196 (cal), Tony Hamblin 13 (tr), 105 (crb).

Sampo Laukkanen: 85(br).

Steve Knell: 116 (cl), 166 (tl).

Steve Young: 185 (bc), 7 (tr) (bra), 13 (c) (bcr), 14 (cla) (crb), 28 (ca), 29 (cla), 30 (clb), 31 (trb), 34 (br), 37 (bca), 40 (clb), 54 (cra) (cl) (crb), 55 (tr), 56 (tlb), 58 (c), 62 (bla), 63 (cb), 64 (bcr (tlb), 65 (clb), 68 (tl), 71 (tr), 73 (tr), 82 (cr), 109 (cra), 114 (clb), 121 (ca) (cbr), 122 (ca), 133 (cra), 137 (bcr), 139 (c), 142 (cla) (cbl), 143 (bl), 144 (bc), 146 (cra), 148 (cr), 150 (tr) (cr) (br), 151 (tr) (cra), 152 (crb) (br), 153 (clb), 155 (cr) (crb), 156 (cb) (br), 157 (c), 158 (crb), 163 (bcl), 164 (bl), 165 (tr) (c), 170 (crb) (br), 171 (br), 174 (tl) (cl) (br), 176 (cr), 177 (bl), 179 (cra), 180 (tl) (bl) (cca), 181 (cr) (crb), 182 (bla), 183 (clb) (bla), 184 (tl), 186 (cra), 187 (tr) (bc), 189 (tr) (br).

Tim Loseby: 32 (crb), 36 (br), 43 (clb) (bla), 45 (crb), 47 (crb), 52 (tl) (cb) (crb), 55 (clb) (br), 56 (cla), 63 (cr), 65 (cl), 117 (tr), 122 (tl), 132 (cra), 145 (tr), 154 (tl), 160 (bl) (cbl), 186 (cla).

Tom Ennis: 186 (tl).

Windrush Photos: Alan Petty 98 (cl), 99 (cl) Anon 53(cr), Arnoud B van den Borg 45 (br), B Hughes 109 (cr) Chris Schenck 103 (cl), 9 (tr),David Cottridge 53(br), 17(clb), David Tipling 20 (clb), 21 (cla), 22 (clb), 27 (trb), 15 (bra 37 (cla), 40 (tl), 46 (ca) (crb), 50 (cla) (bra), 54 (car), 61 (cla), 63 (cl) 64 (tl), 67 (cb), 68 (ca), 83 (bl), 90 (cl) (bra), 91 (bc), 94 (clb), 96 (ca), 97 (crb), 111 (cla), 114 (cbr), 118 (cbr), 124 (tl), 132 (tl), 134 (cl), 137 (cra), 139 (tr) (cr), 140 (c) (bl) (bc), 143 (br), 147 (br), 149 (bl), 151 (cr) (br), 153 (tr) (bl) (br), 154 (bc), 157 (tr) (bl), 159 (tr) (bl), 161 (br), 179 (ccb), 182 (clb), 184 (cra) (trb), 185 (ca), 186 (bla) (cbl), 187 (bl) (bra),193 (ca), 195 (tr), 99 (bl), 211 (tr), 113 (cal), 116 (clb) Goran Ekstrom 210 (cl), 72 (cb), 82 (tl) Ian Fisher 188 (br), J Hollis 73 (clb), J Lawton Roberts 89 (tr), Jari Peltomaki 14 (clb), 52(cb), Kevin Carlson 107 (tl), 15 (br),55 (cb), Paul Doherty 207 (tr) (br), 82 (br), 165 (bc), 172 (cra), 173 (c), 180 (br), Pentti Johansson 81 (tr), 92 (bc), Peter Cairns 16 (br), R Chandler 110 (cra), Ray Tipper 28 (cla), Richard Brooks 113 (crb), 38 (tl), Tom Ennis 116 (tr).

Yossi Eshbol: 129 (bc).

All other images © Dorling Kindersley

For further information see: www.dkimages.com